THE ODYSSEY OF SOUTH SUDAN RED ARMY:

THE LOST BOYS AND GIRLS OF SOUTH SUDAN

Series-4

THE RED ARMY OF THE UNACCOMPANIED MINORS ON THE 5TH EXILE EXODUS FROM KENYA TO WESTERN WORLD.

INSIDE: EPICAL STORY OF SOUTH SUDAN LOST BOYS / GIRLS (FORMER RED ARMY / UNACCOMPANIED MINORS REFUGEE FROM KENYA. ON RESETTLEMENT TO USA AND AND AUSTRALIA

Mapwar Mabor Pur

Author's Background

The author is one of the four thousand South Sudanese lost boys and girls resettled in the United States and Australia between 1999- 2005. After my village was burned down in Yirol (Burdit vicinity) district in 1985 -87. I t separated from my family as SPLA soldiers attacked the town of Yirol early in the morning of 1986, and General Marial Chanoug Yol, the commander of the SPLA, led us to flee early as children of ages from 6-25 years in the jungle trek fleeing to Western Ethiopia.

Due to a hostile civil war between SPLA/M revolutionaries and the Sudan military regime, which killed two million people, I the author had no choice as many thousands of other children than to trek barefooted from various villages crossed war troubled South Sudan to Western Ethiopia, where mainstream of the SPLA/M trained it soldiers. Many children were forcibly conscripted into SPLA/M forces and he became a child rebel in the uprising against the Khartoum government from 1987 to 1992. I was among 10,000 child soldiers and refugees in organized refugee camps to stay in Panyido, Sarapam, Itang, Dimma and Bilpam (1987-1991). I trekked with the Red Army of Panyido refugee camp during the downfall of the Ethiopian government in 1991 to Pachalla and crossed to Kenya through the border town of Lokichioggio with 16,000 Red Army's 1992 and with other red armies disarmed by

UNICEF for children and sent to school in Kenya at the same time from Polataka. We were stationed in the Kakuma refugee camp as unaccompanied minors in 17 groups of minors by UNHCR for 10 years before 4000 thousands of unaccompanied minors got resettled to the United States of America and Australia (1999-2005).

I joined the United States Army in 2010 after completion of my bachelor's degree in Computer science (2008). Military trained in Fort Leonardwood, MO, and did Advance Instruction Training in Fort Lee, Virginia (2010). Stationed in South Korea under command 194th Support Bridge in South Korea and brought back to the mainland under command, serving in the US Army 36th Combat Engineers Brigade station in Fort Hood, Texas. Served under command 36th infantry of Texas National Guards at Camp Mabry Austin and Weslaco, Texas, as a commissioned 2nd Lieutenant officer after completion of Reserved Officers Training Courses at the University of Texas at Austin, Texas. The author is a bachelor's degree holder in computer science from Herzing University (2004-2008), an MA in intelligence operations from American Military University (2011-2012), MS in Computer Science at the University of Texas, Austin (2013-2015); MPA at Arizona States University (2015-2017). The author earned many IT certifications in various fields. Born in South Sudan and resettled to the United States (2001) as a resident of Atlanta, Georgia, where he became a US citizen, went to school, and enlisted into US Army forces.

Dedication

This little piece of memories epical writing is dedicated to myself, for I suffered the cause of catastrophic life in the Sudan civil war that had taken away my childhood life, teenager, and entirely of my youth life. I salute myself as a former child soldier who served in guerilla warfare since the age of seven years in the jungle bushes of South Sudan; my wisdom started to flourish then. After I liberated the people of South Sudan with other compatriots as, the youngest country gained full independence in 2011, and here I am now again guarding, protecting, and defending the freedom of the United States of America.

I am serving the country that has saved me and secured freedom for me and the people of South Sudan, South Korea, and to every southern region of the world. Shall freedom flourish with commitment of brave compatriots? I dedicated a piece of this writing to victims of the South Sudan wars (1983-2015) and to everyone who seeks wisdom in the midst of the humanistic turmoil of war, hardship, poverty, conflict, and life bearings. I dedicated these epical memories to my lovely Son, daughter (Riel and Akuol Pur), and their mothers (Fikirite Eshetu Fentaw and Debra Alek Marol Agok).

Contents

Preface

In order to understand what it means to be a child born in a happy family, whether it is a peace or wartime, in a village, town or in the city, and in few years later, before reaching teenager age, you were forcibly conscript, recruit, or kidnap into joining rebel, government or militia forces. You must develop both foundation of learning and an understanding of the key elements critical to child soldiers' lives. I wrote this book to provide a framework for understanding child soldiers' causes and learning this information necessary in a way that emphasizes the uniqueness of each child soldier group affected by the men`s war and know each individual child soldier's epical war story in each country of origin. Understanding each group of child soldiers, depending on regional or country they fought men`s war, starts with strong relationships between child soldiers and their associates. This epical book emphasizes the necessary information, skills and knowledge that can enhance understanding, association and empathy in building and maintaining relationships with current and former child soldiers. This book underscores the critical importance of taking the turmoil of child soldiers into account and considering it in decision-making processes.

A comprehensive assessment is essential when addressing this complex issue. When we look at the dynamics and dilemma of child soldiers, it is easy to see why it can be a challenging experience to deal with as many child soldiers died at an early age during the war, leaving survivors in non-life functioning state of mind. Considering the different experiences of war and survivability in each group of child soldiers, you may wonder how long or yet would it take you to understand what each child soldier went through in each regional or country torn apart by war. Until you understood what each child soldier went through during the war and after that, it would be hard to provide help, assistance, love, support and necessities to child soldiers and associates. Each child soldier needs the provision of new life support and with conceptual foundation and introduction of new skills, training and education necessary for understanding of new life with implementation of a change with success.

The Lost Boys of Sudan1991: Since the late 1980s, Sudan's civil war has displaced a huge number of people, and among them, at least 20,000 children, mostly boys, who watched their parents killed and their villages burnt. Boys as young as six years old walked a thousand miles in search of safety. Hungry, frightened and weakened, they crossed from Sudan to Ethiopia and back, with many dying along the way. Here, 3,500 unaccompanied "Lost Boys" arrive from Itang Refugee Camp in Ethiopia to Nasir in Southern Sudan. --- Photo by Wendy Stone/Corbis Sygma | Location: Nasser, Sudan. (Photo by Wendy Stone/Corbis via Getty Images)

My personal child soldier's experience, as narrated in this book, will help you understand the comprehensiveness buried in tragedy and turmoil faced by child soldiers for the rest of their lives. The following are three main goals in writing this epical book:

Accuracy:

This book is the result of many years of experiencing tragedy of war flashbacks, facing life challenges and hardship during war and after the war. In writing, it is crucial to convey the authentic narrative of what it truly means to be a child soldier within the Red Army of South Sudan and the immense hardships endured after demobilization, as experienced by a 'Lost Boy' of Sudan. This book places emphasis on informing with information based on scale that measures what each Red Army child soldier went through during the war and is currently under the umbrella of Red Army regiments and lost boys of South Sudan. The narrative serves as a vehicle to ensure that these facts are grounded in the rigorous and up-to-date realities of the hardships endured during both wartime and peacetime.

Simulation:

Simulation of the Red Army experience and the lost-boys / girls to describe, narrate and explain child soldiers' epical war, hardship life, rehabilitation, disarmament, education, family reunion and other unseen factorials. The book narrative utilizes realistic facts to help you understand and feel the inside history of what it really means to be a current or former child soldier. Furthermore, to complement the factual content within the narrative, I have included photographs, specific battle locations with their dates, and insights into the integration of the Red Army under different command structures. Chronicle treks, journey, deployment, redeployment, disarmament, displacement, fleeing, and family reunion and many other events involved with the Red Army, or former Red Army (Lost Boys/girls) epical history in the odyssey has been narrated in chronological dates, times of events and places of transition.

A structural approach:

The structured approach highlighted in this epic book has defined child soldiers in terms of major key elements that can easily break down the narrative in sounding and understanding stages. These elements of narrative breakdown- Red army names under different transitions, regiment commands, structured groups, organizations, community activities, education standards, social life, SPLA/SPLM operations, tribes and military batches of sectional trainings. All the structured organization defined book chapters, pages, and sections as it made the narrative transition smoothly for learning and understanding of Red Army epical history.

The Approach:

The title of this book, communicating in group of lost-boys /girls: building relationships for the group of Current Red Armies, Former Red Armies and the lost-boys/girls in general for effectiveness speaks to the fundamental components group of Child Soldiers' interactions: building relationships and child solders group hardship life evaluation and performance. In this book, child soldiers from around the world can explore the unique dynamics of their epic journey and the conversations it sparks, promoting openness. It may offer essential insights that can contribute to success, enhance group roles within the soldiering community, define tasks, and outline the processes of rehabilitation, ultimately supporting meaningful life transformations. By examining each child soldier's epical war lifestyle from the inside view, the red armies of South Sudan will come to one understanding that builds a dynamic capacity of learning, working together and treating each other with love, care and support in a unique. To be competent in battling life after the chaos of the odyssey, as this book emphasizes, a lost boy or lost-girl must learn to identify other former child soldiers' war situations, odyssey hardship and rehabilitation issues. Each Red Army life in the Odyssey is unique as well as each child soldier's life during war and after the war is completely different, but learning how to assess, understand and respect the epical war lifestyle in any situation faced by each group of child soldiers is the key for support and co-existence. In essence, the goal of this book is to provide a toolbox from which all child soldiers can draw in any hardship imagination, group situation and life in Odyssey – whether planning a function with a social club to fit in the society, campus, or in newly united family, former child soldier must learn how to forgive and forget war tragedy. A child of the Red Army must start this process where he or she becomes aware of their own life odyssey during and after the war, and knowing yourself in the odyssey life. One can find means of rebel life and ways to improve living aftermath of child soldering in order to enhance affected child soldier group dynamics in the odyssey. The emphasis here is on understanding the Sudanese child soldier life, news for reflection, life-changing skills assessments and new life mean practices for those who went to war at the youngest age.

The Features:

This book contains numbers of features to enhance your learning, understanding and knowledge about South Sudan's current Red Army situation and, former Red Army (The Lost Boys) and general child soldiers, particularly in Africa. Putting pieces together in a narrative, there are core elements in defining meaning in each Red Army regiment, battalions, batch and sectional group. The elements are group size, the interdependence of the original tribe, means of recruitment, militarization, social life, SPLA support,

NGO involvement and the Red Army's group structure. These elements are introduced, described and narrated in each chapter as a special feature so that you become more aware, familiar and understand each sectional group of the Red Army battalion, regiment and militarized batch. The knowledge grounded in a solid child soldering narrative is based on the witness life experience and advice from those experienced the same lifestyle as a former child soldier and this explains epical life history in the odyssey, where survival life is grounded in the skill of a soldier regardless of a soldier's age.

The skills grounded in this soldering current Red armies and former Red Army's are based on the best advice for communicating epical life for the lost boys of South Sudan and general child soldiers groups across the world. Thus, the narrative skills presented and suggested in the epical book are experience-based. For example, Chapter 1 uses the characteristics of the first groups of village boys and girls who happened to fled the army struggle in the first war across South Sudan between the first infantry of the SPLA Koriom regiment and the Northern Sudan regime troops under Nimeri that eventually caused holocaust to the first fleeing boys. The extensive use of realistic weapons of war in the Sudan Civil War 1983-2005 was first at its largest and imminent and that resulted in the burning down of villages, schools, churches and mosques across the country. In addition to describing what happened in the first exodus of villages' boys and girls fleeing out of South Sudan to the neighboring country of Ethiopia could be explained through the use of extensive examples in each chapter as provided in transcripts of each Red Army stage of service as group under leadership of the SPLA/SPLM and Non-profit organization.

The Insider Organization:

To establish a strong foundation, the first five chapters delve into the remarkable history of South Sudan's Red Army. This narrative begins with the origins of the Lost Boys and their mission, followed by the second exodus, a journey that led them from Ethiopia's challenging conditions to the turmoil of Sudan. It goes on to recount the experiences of the Red Armies during their third ordeal and concludes with a narrative of the fourth peaceful transit of the Red Army into neighboring Kenya in 1992. By exploring the concept of the Red Army exodus and its application to each group of Red Army battalions or teams, the transition and transit stages in the history of South Sudan's child soldiers become clear, forming a captivating odyssey of resilience and determination.

The second set of the epical narratives is organized into chapters from chapter 6 –10, address building relationships, team of boys' decision making, problem-solving at boyish age, tribal conflict management, and child solder leadership—both as interaction opportunities and interaction problems that are a regular and dynamic aspect of red army battalions` interaction. The second set of Red Army Odyssey is narrated in these chapters from 6 – 10, the 4th Fire that Struck no Fear, the Bright Star Campaign {BSC}, SPLA Commando 1 & 2 Red Armies, the world's wildest Child Soldiers, the Red army with red cross - all with red god and narrative of the lost-boys 5th exodus from Kenya to U.S, Australia, East Africa and Canada. Increasing lost boys' and girls' skills in life-making was drawn from this epical narrative of odyssey, and the tragic life experience kept helping them maximize their red armies' group on the experience of epical interaction efforts. Despite the extensive tragic life experience I went through, each lost-boy (former Red Army) is facing the same hurdles and memories, but friendly interaction, togetherness and a peaceful mind led to victory on the blueprint for each current and former Red Army group's success. Each Red Army child soldier in each battalion was Armed with specific principles, trained skills, safety procedures, food hunt techniques, survivability tactics, and military fighting tactics, as well as leadership capability no matter what age they were in during the Sudan civil War and even now.

INTRODUCTION
PART 1

a. Who are south, North, West, and Eastern Sudanese

b. Map of Sudan showing south, west, east and northern

c. The South-north history of the conflicts

d. The south-north struggle and its hardship causes

e. The final solutions to south-north conflicts

Who are South, North, West, and Eastern Sudanese?

The lack of investment in humans living in South Sudan since the creation of Sudan land has resulted in to what international humanitarian organizations call a "lost generation" who lost parents, lost educational opportunities, lost access to basic health care services, and little prospects for productive employment in the small and weak economies of the south Sudan. Sudan has two distinct major cultures—light-skinned black Arab and dark skin Black African--with hundreds of ethnicities and tribal divisions with many language groups, which make up an effective major problem. The northern states cover most of the Sudan and include most of the urban centers.

Recognizing the importance of our cultures to our very existence, we provide detailed information on our diverse and numerous ethnic communities. There are about 597 ethnic groups in Sudan as a whole, speaking over 400 languages and dialects. In a bid to create peace and harmony, we provide information on all aspects of community life, such as history, religion, livelihood and politics, among other aspects. It important that people know about their neighbors so that there is peaceful coexistence among them. Most of the 22 million Sudanese who live in this region are Arabic-speaking Muslims, though the majority also uses a traditional non-Arabic mother tongue (i.e., Nubian, Beja, Fur, Nuban, Ingessana, etc.) Among these are several distinct tribal groups; the Kababish of northern Kordofan, a camel-raising people; the Ja'alin and Shaigiyya groups of settled tribes along the rivers; the semi-nomadic Baggara of Kordofan and Darfur; the Hamitic Beja in the Red Sea area and Nubians of the northern Nile areas, some of whom have been resettled on the Atbara River; and the Negroid Nuba of southern Kordofan and Fur in the western reaches of the country. Sudan's population reached 40.2 million. Southern Sudan was reported to have had a population of just over 8 million people. Southerners consider this to be a gross underestimation of their numbers.

The southern region has a population of around 8 million and a predominantly rural, subsistence economy. This region has been negatively affected by war for all but 10 years of the independence period (1956), resulting in serious neglect, lack of infrastructure development, and major destruction and displacement. More than 2 million people have died, and more than 4 million are internally displaced or become refugees as a result of the civil war and war-related impacts. Here, the Sudanese practice mainly indigenous traditional beliefs, although Christian missionaries have converted some. The South also contains many tribal groups and uses many more languages than in the North. The Dinka (pop. est. more than 1 million) is the largest of the many Black African tribes of the Sudan. Along with the Shilluk and the Nuer, they are among the Nilotic tribes. The Azande, Bor, and Jo Luo are "Sudanic" tribes in the west, and the Acholi and Lotuhu live in the extreme south, extending into Uganda.

Sudan was a collection of small, independent kingdoms and principalities from the beginning of the Christian era until 1820-21, when Egypt conquered and unified the northern portion of the country. Historically, the pestilential swamps of the Sudan discouraged expansion into the deeper south of the country. Although Egypt claimed all of the present Sudan during most of the 19th century, it was unable to establish effective control over southern Sudan, which remained an area of fragmented tribes subject to frequent attacks by slave raiders.

Map of Sudan showing south, west, east and northern

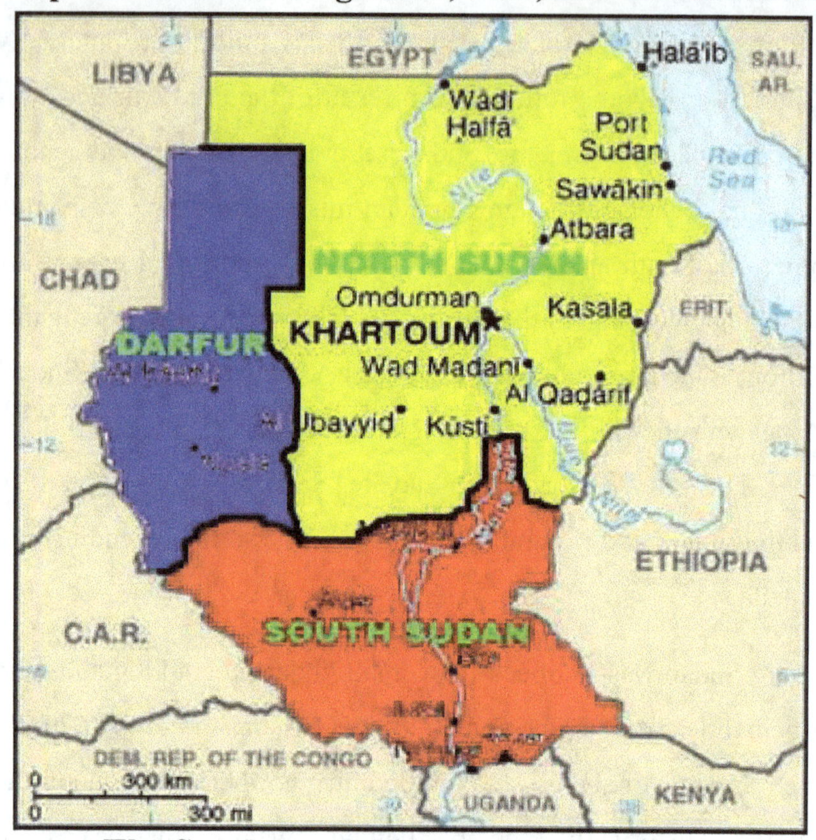

The South-north history of the conflicts

Sudan was the largest country in Africa, with the biggest problem on the soil of Africa. Many Western friends doesn't know Sudan on the map because it is hidden by its numerous problem or known by its bad actions. It is located just south of Egypt on the eastern edge of the Sahara desert. The country is surrounded by nine neighboring countries as of Egypt, Libya, Chad, Central Africa Republic, Dr. Congo, Uganda, Kenya, Ethiopia and Eritrea. The Red

Sea is the main port that created important Port Sudan for the export and import of heavy shipped goods. The main economic resource is oil, cotton and livestock in the south.

As in other developing countries, oil has not yet been discovered or developed for the benefit of entire Sudanese citizens but instead pocketed by a few elites in the government or society. Eighty percent of the oil export revenue is used to fund the military and armed the war wage against South, Darfur and Eastern Rebel. Many American or other parts of the world have heard of Darfur as another part of the world that is not a region within Sudan. Darfur is the western part of Sudan, about the size of Texas State. Darfur, inhabited by Fur and other tribe of western Sudan, is bordered by Libya, Chad and the Central African Republic. Darfur hosts living of six million Sudan citizens and lives among the poorest people of Africa, where basic development and even infrastructure are difficult. Citizens of Darfur depend on subsistence farming or nomadic herding for survival. Even before the war outrages them, the Darfur people used most hardship and difficult life.

The current crises in Darfur began in 2003 as mean and way to end decades of negligence, slavery, and lack of clean water, poverty, underdevelopment, oppression, and conflict in Darfur caused by two rebel groups – the Sudanese Liberation Army/Movement SLA and Justice and Equality Movement JEM.

The two tough rebel wings posted a challenge to Sudan President Omar Al-Bashir and the president response in the same brutal way as he did brutal responded to the South Sudanese. It is important to understand that all Darfuris are Muslim and black Africans, the distinction is that black Arab is primarily of descriptive of lifestyle and commonly local herds and nomadic, representing 35 % of the Darfur population. African Darfur is 65% of the sedentary farming lifestyle. These two groups of Darfur African have been coexisting and live together, sharing their grazing land and farming on the same lands as Muslim brothers and Sudanese. Their villages' disputes were resolved by chief and traditional mechanisms, but when the Sudan government jumped, by divided this peaceful Muslim Darfur by supporting and encouraging light-skinned black African Muslims, whom they consider the Arab black type to launch an attack against the dark skin Muslim Darfur.

In 2003, following the government's launch of a genocidal campaign, underlying tensions over land, water sources, and the distinction between light-skinned African Muslims, who are often considered Arab, and dark-skinned Darfur Muslims were further exacerbated. The government actively armed and encouraged certain groups to attack and seize the land and water sources belonging to the dark-skinned Darfur Muslim population. Most of the rebels come from Agrarian farmers, mainly non-Arab Black African Muslims from a number of tribes. Sudan's government quickly armed up and launched an offensive attack against the rebels by arming and powering local tribal's warriors and militiamen known as Janjaweed (devil on horseback), which is different for the case of South Sudanese as they know them as Muralyin. Janjaweed is an evil group armed by the government and got recruited from Black Arab African Muslims who herd cattle, camels and other livestock. Janjaweed were armed with AK-47s, machetes, horses and many small arms to wipe out, destroy food and water supplies and loots attack the village. Jan Jaweed murdered, tortured, raped women and took slaves from captives as the target a village. Every village attack launched by Janjaweed armed militiamen was supported and proposed by the Sudan Government and many accusations were filed against the Sudan Government, but they have not responded, as government denial is always a key to evil defense. Sudan Air Force attacking gunships and Antonovs are painted white just like UN assistance aircraft and that confused local displaced Darfur what to expect from any arrival airplane. When a plane approaches, villagers don't know whether its mission is to help or bomb them. This scorched earth campaign by the Sudanese government against Darfur's sedentary farming population has resulted in many negative impacts, direct violence, disease, and starvation and it claimed up to 400,000 lives of the locals displaced Darfur population. About 2.3 million Darfuris have fled their home villages and been displaced into internal camps (IDP) within Darfur.

More than 200,000 camped in Chad as this population is depending on the UN and other Humanitarian organizations, which also faces hard times from the Sudan government, which expels and restricts NGO operations in Darfur. Displaced refugees and IDPs depend on UN and humanitarian livelihood, food, water, shelters and basic healthcare daily supports.

The original copy of today's "Southern Sudan policy" held in hand by Khartoum government was enunciated in 1931 as an indirect policy rule between Northern and Southern Sudan. The Southern Sudan policy highlights one country, which is broadly divided into northern Muslim Arabs and the southern Sudanese, who associate themselves with Christians, pagans and black Africans. In 1946, Egyptians forced their sovereignty over Sudan and that left Sudan a struggle for two self-determinations: northerners were seeking their self-determination from Egyptian occupancy and southerners were seeking self-determination from Northern Sudanese power occupancy. The Mount chaotic of Sudan problem elevated high in 1946 when many educated southerners protested against disparities in grade pay level, justice, or issues of second class citizen status. It was this date of 1946 before 1947 when educated Southern Sudanese aided the idea of J.W Robertson, civil secretary, who circulated a small piece of memo among officials of southern Sudanese. The memo was running around a circle of southerners with an outline change in policy that instructed sounding off and a declared opinionated voice of the southern Sudanese to remain as part of northern Sudan, be joined to Uganda or Kenya, campaign for total separation of independence.

The origins of the civil war in the South date back to the 1950s. On August 18, 1955, the Equatoria Corps, a military unit composed of southerners, mutinied at Torit. Rather than surrender to Sudanese government authorities, many mutineers disappeared into hiding with their weapons, marking the beginning of the first war in southern Sudan. By the late 1960s, the war had resulted in the deaths of about 500,000 people. Several hundred thousand more Southerners hid in the forests or escaped to refugee camps in neighboring countries.

By 1969, the rebels had developed foreign contacts to obtain weapons and supplies. Israel, for example, trained Anya Nya recruits and shipped weapons via Ethiopia and Uganda to the rebels. Anya Nya also purchased arms from Congolese rebels and international arms dealers with monies collected in the south and from among southern Sudanese exile communities in the Middle East, Western Europe, and North America. The rebels also captured arms, equipment, and supplies from government troops.

Militarily, Anya Nya controlled much of the southern countryside while government forces occupied the region's major towns. The guerrillas operated at will from remote camps. However, rebel units were too small and scattered to be highly effective in any single area. Estimates of Anya Nya's personnel strength ranged from 5,000 to 10,000.

Government operations against the rebels declined after the 1969 coup. However, when negotiations failed to result in a settlement, Khartoum increased troop strength in the south to about 12,000 in 1969 and intensified military activity throughout the region. Although the Soviet Union had concluded a US$100 million to US$150 million arms agreement with Sudan in August 1968, which included T-55 tanks, armored personnel carriers, and aircraft, the nation failed to deliver any equipment to Khartoum by May 1969. During this period, Sudan obtained some Soviet-manufactured weapons from Egypt, most of which went to the Sudanese air force. By the end of 1969, however, the Soviet Union had shipped unknown quantities of 85mm antiaircraft guns, sixteen MiG-21s, and five Antonov-24 transport aircraft. Over the next two years, the Soviet Union delivered an impressive array of equipment to Sudan, including T-54, T-55, T56, and T-59 tanks and BTR-40 and BTR-152 light armored vehicles.

In 1971, Joseph Lagu, who had become the leader of southern forces opposed to Khartoum, proclaimed the creation of the Southern Sudan Liberation Movement (SSLM). Anya Nya leaders united behind him, and nearly all exiled southern politicians supported the SSLM. Although the SSLM created a governing infrastructure throughout many areas of southern Sudan, real power remained with Anya Nya, with Lagu at its head.

Despite his political problems, Nimeiri remained committed to ending the southern insurgency. He believed he could stop the fighting and stabilize the region by granting regional self-government and undertaking economic development in the south. By October 1971, Khartoum had established contact with the SSLM. After considerable consultation, a conference between SSLM and Sudanese government delegations convened at Addis Ababa, Ethiopia, in February 1972. Initially, the two sides were far apart, the southerners demanding a federal state with a separate southern government and an army that would come under the federal president's command only in response to an external threat to Sudan. Eventually, however, the two sides, with the help of Ethiopia's Emperor Haile Selassie, reached an agreement.

The Addis Ababa accords guaranteed autonomy for a southern region--composed of the three provinces of Equatoria (present-day Al Istiwai), Bahr al Ghazal, and Upper Nile (present-day Aali an Nil)--under a regional president appointed by the national president on the recommendation of an elected Southern Regional Assembly. The High Executive Council or cabinet named by the regional president would be responsible for all aspects of government in the region except such areas as defense, foreign affairs, currency and finance, economic and social planning, and interregional concerns, authority over which would be retained by the national government in which southerners would be represented. Southerners, including qualified Anya Nya veterans, would be incorporated into a 12,000-man southern command of the Sudanese army under equal numbers of northern and southern officers. The accords also recognized Arabic as Sudan's official language and English as the south's principal language, which would be used in administration and would be taught in the schools.

Although many SSLM leaders opposed the settlement, Lagu approved its terms and both sides agreed to a cease-fire. The national government issued a decree legalizing the agreement and creating an international armistice commission to ensure the well-being of returning southern refugees. Khartoum also announced an amnesty retroactive to 1955. The two sides signed the Addis Ababa accords on March 27, 1972, which was thereafter celebrated as National Unity Day.

The remembrance of 1947 comes in after southerners failed to produce a united future solution for southern Sudan, and this is the same issues of unity affecting southerners in finding a united solution for southern Sudan. Many educated civil services southerners disagreed as some were supporting unity of the South with the North, some demanded separation and an independent South and some were lost in the memo agenda. The 1947 conference was a test failed by southerners and misjudged of the northern nationalists who were the chief political actors in the minds of southern Sudanese. The failed conference of 1947 served as an eye opener to Southerners, which led to the 1954 Mind Speaking Conference, where Southerners evaluated their powers, knowledge and capabilities to stand up for the separated South or accepted being weak and join the North as they chose to be part of the north. Southerners had never forgotten to spell out two options and clearly to Northerners as to either autonomy south or autonomy north all under one federation, which now New Sudan agenda and a divided Sudan in self-ruling independent south and North. It is not and never be easy striking that mainly Muslim of northern Sudan would never accept to unite with black pagans or Christian southerners.

Millions of lost lives in twenty-five years of conflict between south and north since from 1983 to 2005 would have been saved if only the 1954 Juba conference had been taken seriously by Northerners or southern Sudanese. In 1954, Southerners held a weeklong conference as the reinforced conference to a failed 1947 or to brief what Southerners called a failed Northern promised to fully file agendas forwarded by the southern in a case box of united Sudan for justice and equality for all Sudanese regardless of gender, race, color, religion or regions. In the 1954 conference, chiefs, civil service and educated southerners discussed tough agendas of whether there was a united Sudan, federation or sort of separation, as northerners weren't seem to be the source of the Sudan problem. The same agendas brought forward by every next generation of southern Sudanese from 1931, 1947, 1954, 9172, 1983, and 2005 CPA and it goes on until south Sudanese would stick to a complete federation, separation or United Sudan, but southerners can never do it without a game player government of Khartoum. Since the government of Khartoum took power in 1955 or early than that date, the northern government had never cleared out any positive agenda about the future of Sudan as a united, federated or separated country, but the northern government has been broiling Sudan's problem with a cover top microwave public opinion.

There is no date that is ever fresh in the Southern Sudanese mind from lost boys' generation to lost men generation, the date of 1947 which is the first self-image mirror for southern Sudanese. It was the first conference dated where southern Sudanese educated civil service were given and had chance to discuss and determine the future of Southern Sudan and this generation of 1947 failed us. The second Sudanese Civil War (1983-2003) pitted the north and south of Sudan against each other was triggered by Muhammad Jaafar Numeiri's dissolving of the country's assembly, his attempt to prevent the country's oil revenue from reaching the south, and his imposition of Islamic law, or Sharia law, which alienated large segments of the population. A rebellion exploded. Numeiri was overthrown in 1985. But the conflict escalated. After ten years of relative relaxation in the peace agreement signed in Addis Ababa in 1972, south Sudanese still walked back into their used jungle struggle, proposing war as a final solution to end Northern Sudan's deception of peace and unfulfilled promised agendas of the 1972 incomprehensive peace Agreement {IPA}. South Sudanese routed back to war in 1983 with former Anya 1 captain John Garang as the chief actor who formed SPLA/SPLM after defection and launched offensive fight against the Sudan government. The lost men generation of 1972 didn't also fail us.

Captian Garang De Mabior was the only college graduate in Any-Any forces, as the peace agreement was in negotiation, Garang wrote a letter to SSLM leader Joseph Lagu and rebel command forces and his letter was to advise the rebel high command that there should be no peace deal unless rebel of Any-Any 1 reached or captured government stronghold position. The rebel of Any-Any 1 was receiving rebel hardware only from Israel and it was a chaotic time when Israel encountered with it six-day war with Egypt and that southern rebel with fewer hardware supplies. Garang hoped that peace negotiation would take place after the Anya-Anya 1 rebel had occupied large part of Southern Sudan. In any case, the peace agreement was signed on 27, 1972, recognized on Feb 27th, 1972 and agendas were implemented on April 4th, which had gave South

Sudan self-determination status. After the signed agreement of 1972, Captain John Garang and many other comrades in rebel arms under commanding of Colonel Emmanuel Abuur Nhial, Major Stephen Madut Baak, Major Albino Akol Akol, Lt Colonel Afred Deng Aluk, Lt Colonel Joseph Kuol Amuom, Lt Colonel Gai Tut and William Abullah Chuol were trying to disrupt peace agreement of 1972 and were in favor in the continuity of war. Colonel Abuur and his opposing commanding forces discovered late that the whole of Southern Sudan was in favor of peace, so the conspirators decided to join the peace process and they pledged that if the government of Sudan should dishonor any agreed agendas in signed peace, that would warned return to war.

The Any-Any 1 forces and high commanding officers were absorbed into the Sudan army. However, commissioning officers in the Sudanese army and former rebels officers organized the underground revolution movement while discretely avoiding Sudan security detection. During absorption and training, Captain Garang and Lt Colonel Stephen Baak were identified by the Sudan security sector as conspirators who would have the potential to resume south war. The ring leader of Any-Any 1, Colonel Emmanuel Abuur Nhial, the most respected and honored former rebel army, was promoted to Brigadier and appointed second in a commanding force of Sudan and sent to Wau away from Bussere. The other top former rebel leaders were sent for training abroad and after they got back, they were posted to North Sudan. John Garang was also sent to USA military training at Fort Benning commandership course (1974-1981).

After Garang de Mabior got back from the United States with his Ph.D., he was promoted to the rank of Colonel and posted to the army general headquarters in Khartoum as the deputy director of the research unit. This move was made to enable the authorities to check his work and keep an eye on him as well as his activities before it became too dangerous and late in risking the signed Peace of 1972. Fortunately far, that colonel found it harder to connect and reactivate the underground movement as many of his former southern rebels were promoted and scattered into to northern part of Sudan. Colonel Garang still set up his underground cell movement over all southern Sudan, concentrated mainly in areas where battalions got stationed and entirely manned by former officered by promoted southerners in the Sudan army. These battalions were 103 (wau), Battalion 104 (Malakal), Battalion 105 (Bor), Battalion 110 (Aweil), Battalion 111 (Rumbek), Battalion 116(Juba) and Battalion 117 (Torit and Kapoeta). Garang made his house in Hajj Yousif in Khartoum East, where his commanding and post Colonel activities affected the political environment of the City. Sudan's situation got worse as the discovery of oil in 1978 caused commercial quantities in the south. The Sudan situation was worsened further by aggravated government attempts to redraw boundaries between the

South and North, and in addition to digging Jonglei Canal. The Sudan problem was inflammable when the government was forced to set up the oil refinery in the north instead of the South, where oil was drilled. Southerners demanded the building of the first refinery in the South and had government. Too many demonstrations broke out in Khartoum, where students protested against government plans. Adding worse to flame fire, president Nimeri decided in 1982 to divide the south into three regions, but they plan could take place Nimeri government decided to transfer the ordered of former rebels of Any-Any 1 forces to the Northern section. Between 1981-and 1983, governments started moving transferring former rebels from the South to the North, where they would not posted any threat to the signed peace agreement of 1972. The transfer soldiers from the South were recruits from villages' warriors and were making big deals and some refused with motive of not transferring to North.

In brief, enough attempts were recorded by Southerners as from the cited refinery in the north without Southerners approval, attempt to redraw boundaries between South and North, attempt to divide the South into regions and in addition to the imposition of Islamic law in September 1983. Southerners put all these factors together and the conclusion was to set a blaze of fire in May 1983. In May 1983, orders were fully commanded by an underground cell movement voice to attack the headquarters of Battalion 105 stationed in Bor, adjoining Battalion 104 at Ayod and Waat and

Fasholla. Colonel Garang led the mutineers across the borders to Ethiopia, where in August 1983, the Sudan People Liberation Army and Sudan People Movement were formed and recognized as political organizations.

The SPLA was formed in 1983 when Lieutenant Colonel John Garang of the SPAF was sent to quell a mutiny in Bor of 500 southern troops who were resisting orders to be rotated to the north. Instead of ending the mutiny, Garang encouraged mutinies in other garrisons and set himself at the head of the rebellion against the Khartoum government. Garang, a Dinka born into a Christian family, had studied at Grinnell College, Iowa, and later returned to the United States to take a company commanders' course at Fort Benning, Georgia, and again to earn advanced economics degrees at Iowa State University.

By 1986, the SPLA was estimated to have 12,500 adherents organized into twelve battalions and equipped with small arms and a few mortars. By 1989, the SPLA's strength had reached 20,000 to 30,000; by 1991, it was estimated at 50,000 to 60,000. Many members of the SPLA continued their civilian occupations, serving in individual campaigns when called upon. At least forty battalions had been formed, bearing such names as Tiger, Crocodile, Fire, Nile, Kalashnikovs, Bee, Eagle, and Hippo. These forces of SPLA brought down President Nimeri Jafaari, Sura Adaap, and Sadi

Almahdi and weakened Omar Al Bashir's forces since the 1980s. The CPA generation of 1983 did succeed us in to separation and creation of the South Sudan from Sudan. The South Sudan future is counted on the lost men generation of 1987.

The south-north struggle and it hardship causes

The history of what is so-called present Sudan or, formerly the land of Cush, is long and it has been a long epical conflict struggle for decades and it contains various episodes of revolutionary civil war to all current conflicts in the country of Sudan. The leader of the SPLA/M movement Late John Garang, was asked in Jimmy Carter in Georgia Atlanta in his visit time by one white woman who simply asked a question of why are those who called themselves Arab in Sudan controlled power and where were the African South Sudanese at the time when minority Arab control the power of the country. To answer the Georgian white female question, it is not a matter of getting the present scope of the conflict and interpreting it in your own words. The root causes of the conflict in Sudan need a long understanding of the old developed historical causes and the knowledge link of the current conflicts complexities.

Until Sudan was invaded in 1820 by a family of Mohammed Ali, who was heading a Turco-Egyptian expedition, and at that very present time little was known about Sudan, except that there was a little description of the so-called Arab travelers who called Sudan " bilad el Sudan" or land of the black people. The extension of the so-called present Sudan modern records started from that period, although Northern Sudanese found another way around to distort the true history of the country for their narrow-minded reason. It was non-Arab, non-Muslim, non-Middle Eastern, and Black people nationalities were the ones controlling the entirety of Sudan, known as Western, Northern, Central, Eastern and present Southern Sudan. Even the present capital of Khartoum itself got its name driven out of a meaningful Nilotic word that means Karatum, which literately means joint, meeting place or junction, suggesting the joining of the Blue and white Nile rivers. The indigenous black people of Sudan from Nubia Mountain stretch out to western Sudan, control by Fur and to Southern Sudan, controlled by all its current African tribes were in control of the whole of Sudan, and Arab immigrants invaded Sudan as travelers, traders, and sellers who immigrating across Nile rivers from East to west seeking permission from indigenous Africa to settle and received guidance from indigenous people just like Arab tribe in Northern Sudan still doing right now.

The Turco-Egyptian invasion and the establishment of the an Islamic Turco-Egyptian regime in the Northern Sudan by 1821 until Mahdiyia rebelled in 1881, and this phenomena has changed the balance of lives and forces in the favorite of Northern settled Arabs tribes who had collaborated with Turks and Egyptian government. Enslavement of the Southern Sudan areas, Nuba

Mountains and Funj had added to the worsening relationship of Northern and Southern Sudan. Slavery and exploitation trade was still fresh in the memory of the South Sudanese in relation to their compatriots in the west and central Sudan and this was a factor in shaping the relationship between two parts of the same Sudan. Mahdist`s States ruler in the North was overthrown by the Turco-Egyptian force so that the slavery trafficking trade in slaves would boost up the financial resources of the Turco-Egyptian rule in Sudan. The nationalities in Southern Sudan were overwhelmed by the Khalifa army forces that ransacked southern Sudan in search of slaves and trade resources of gold, diamonds, ostrich feathers, ivory, ete. The Khalifa army forces were later composed of the South and Western Sudan indigenous black African captured and converted into Islamic and then used to terrorize their own people in the South and West.

The conquered of the Sudan by the Anglo-Egyptian forces had brought inherent factors and huge contradictions between the national unity of the Sudan and the national interest of the condominium parties in reflection of itself and the rule of policies adopted by the national colonial administration in it social and economic development of the Sudan. Southern Sudan pacified and affirmed control of the new colonial power authorities and that was the establishment of the hostility to the so-called Northern Sudan. The hostility of the Southerners was also engineered by other factors like social and political changes, religious forced issues, cultural differences, economic development and racial harassment of the so-called Arab tribes in the South. This difference has caused the creation of a gap between the North and South and this made the colonial authorities to adopt different policies of rule to govern and administer Southern Sudan in a unique way.

Cutting off South from the rest of Sudan by being govern and got ruled out separately and led the rebellion of 1924 called White Flag League against the British rule under Ali Abdel Latif and eventually, South, Nuba Mountains and Ingessina Hills were sealed off in isolation from the rest of Sudan, under what was called the "the closed Districts Ordinance". The colonial ruler continued with a separated dimension rule of the South and further decided policies of creating the Southern provinces in order to consolidate and completed separate socio-social, administration, socio-economic and political evolution of the South and that had triggering two parts of Sudan under Anglo-Egyptian administration.

Until the same separated administered two Sudan: South and North got geared reversed in the policy of 1947 where south and North Sudan were declared two separated administered entities with one formal travel consular in Sudan. The most significant factor in the development of the two separated South and North Sudan is the impact of the relationship between citizens of the same country. This dynamic has resulted in an unequal distribution of resources, power, and economic development, primarily because the colonial government focused its attention on North Sudan, neglecting the development of South Sudan, as well as the regions of West, Central, and Eastern Sudan. This situation has resulted in North Sudan's economic prosperity and development, often to the detriment of South, West, and Eastern Sudan. Consequently, North Sudan has enjoyed advantages in advanced education, social development, and overall civilization due to the colonial government's uneven development policies, which isolated and administered South Sudan separately from the rest of the country. North Sudan gained advantage over Southern Sudan not because Northern Sudanese are more intelligent than Southerners but because of the North proximity to Egypt and the rest of the Arab world, to which the Northern Sudanese have access to and allies with. Many Northern Sudanese found easy access to educational facilities in Egypt and other Arab worlds because of the linkage in the Arab cultures, social life, Islamic heritage and calling themselves black Arabs. These acts of the black light-skinned Africans denounced themselves as Arab and part of the Middle Eastern in brotherhood under Islamic is what is killing Eastern Africans in Sudan, Eritrean, Somalia, Ethiopia and other part of Africa where the poison of Islamic infested. This religious and political identity awareness in Sudan and other part of Africa play a great role in shaping citizens awareness of their origin as people of north Sudan associated themselves a lot with Egyptians as Egypt too further interest in Sudan through north Sudanese and that is why Egypt handed them the power of Sudan because Egypt old empire rulers knew that black African who were not converted to Islamic couldn't be trusted to preside power in Sudan because Egyptian living depend on Nile waters.

Absolute exclusion of South Sudan from the north has left south without accessible education facilities since the 930s and since south didn't it own government to deal with its development issues, south remains helpless and remained the poorest part of the world up to now. South Sudan only access educational facilities from fewer Christian Missionaries school in the south and also in the neighboring countries like Kenya and Uganda. The education issues didn't only increase the gap between South and North but also produced political and docile servants of the local colonial administration. Christian education, which stresses out the separation of the Church from the State, couldn't be incentive to engage in political activity in Sudan, which could lead to challenging the authority of the colonial administration, which is now still challenging the present Khartoum government. As South Sudanese engaged in missionary Christian education, which was the last mandatory choice access to education in the south, was eventually another obstacle that caused South Sudanese to get discouraged from participating in Sudan politics, political debate, or even can`t get high positions or job in Khartoum or else not seen practicing political dissent which was punished and dismissed by from the school or at job.

The northern Sudanese politicians' proximity allied with Egypt and the Middle East, as far geographically, cultures, religiously and social life are concerned, has given them opportunity to earn leadership experiences and acquire political skills in organization, agitation and action of political survivability. In contrast, south Sudan remained trapped in the same political backwardness. The history of Sudan taught in primary schools in the north was different from the one taught as inclusive in to the syllabus of the Southern Sudan schools. It got worse when the northern political elite excluded the south from the political process as the means of marginalizing the south to prevent the south from sharing power in the government of Sudan. The absolute marginalization of South Sudan from Sudan's political administration and economic life of the country has led to the mutiny in the south by August 1955, just after the eve of independence, leading to the civil war that lasted for seventeen years. The weak economic base of the South Sudanese wouldn't permit them to keep the opposition in politics for a long time and the South Sudanese elites had just woken up from long-sleep years of political inactiveness. The Sudanese State power is a northern institution handed over to them by the British colonial authority prior to the Sudanese gaining independence in 1956. Since the very independent day after the British handed the power of Sudan in North Sudan hand up today, Sudan as a country in African land has been serving and representing the economic, social, cultural interests, and religious proxy of the Muslim and Arab countries in allies with the Middle East just other African countries which act like Middle Easterners born on African soils.

The final solutions to south-north conflicts

There is no final solution to South-North Sudan conflict, even after hosting two countries on the same land of Sudd. It's essential to briefly consider the lack of commitment among a significant portion of the political elite in both the South and North. This situation bears some similarity to the approach taken by British policies during the final years of colonization in South Sudan. The British policy aimed to let South Sudanese decide whether the political future of South Sudan and the fate of its southern citizens should be closely aligned with their East African kin or whether they should be associated with Arabs and Middle Eastern people, as was the case for other black Africans who had already lost the battle for change and had integrated themselves into the category of black African-Middle Easterners. The seventeen-year war of Anya-Nya one between north and south was ended in Addis Ababa in March 1972 after a signed agreement between the regime of Gaafar Nimeri and the Southern Sudan Liberation Movement led by Joseph Lagu. Just like SPLA-CPA, the Addis Ababa agreement had guaranteed South Sudan regional autonomy within the United Sudan, SSLM-IPA, and there was a set up of the High Executive Council exercising executive powers with independent public services commission in the south.

The southern people regional assembly with executive power was established and run in Juba and it brought relative sustainable and stable peace in the south temporarily. One of the key factors that contributed to the failure of the Addis Ababa Agreement accords was the way politics in the southern autonomy region, from 1972 to 1983, became heavily centered on the personalities of Abel Alier and Joseph Lagu. This was perceived by many Southerners as a power struggle between these two individuals, which ultimately provided President Nimeiri Gaafar with the upper hand. He successfully exploited this internal division to undermine the agreement and manipulate the situation to his advantage, ultimately playing divisive and detrimental political games against the southern factions themselves. The failure of the regional government in Juba to address the political issues related to the failed implementation of the Addis Ababa agreement accord had resulted in to several armed uprisings between 1972-1983. But these armed insurrections remained isolated with military incidents and that eventually didn't change any political dimension in Juba.

The leadership method of the SPLM/A had generated wrong operational measures approached to the entire movement and this was illustrated by the many examples of serious internal contradictions within the movement's leadership ranks. Failure of the SPLM/A system of leadership recognized that the uprising nature of the contradiction was a result of leaders personalities clash out and could not be solved or get resolved by other rank in the movement, like the removal of Dr. Lam Akol from the office of foreign relations of the movement in 1990 and his redeployment at the war zone where he failed miserable and that was what probably fit him against Dr. Garang, as it was mentioned by Adwok Nyaba. The same personal leaders contradiction occurred between Arok Thon Arok and Korubino Kuanyin as well as William Nyuon and Kuol Manyang Juuk, but SPLM/A failed to come up with a systematic solution to deal with high ranks conflict of personalities. There was a lack of an established investigation team to thoroughly examine the events and to research potential solutions for addressing the troubling incidents within the movement. One significant example is the horrific episode in May 1984 when around three thousand recruits, predominantly composed of young men, women, girls, and thousands of boys trekking from Northern Bhar el Ghazel, were ambushed and tragically massacred by the forces under William Abdalla Chuol in the desert near Akobo, close to Fangak. The absence of a dedicated investigative body hindered the effort to fully understand and address such grave occurrences. Very few out woods reached the SPLM/A training centers and this action kept repeated itself in many cycles of occurrence, as it happened in the Lou area in 1986 when over two thousand recruits, mainly police and prison officers from Rumbek, were also massacred by Anya-Nya 2. As the resulted, massacre of Dinka recruits by Anya-Nya 2had led to the SPLA troops on the way back to Sudan with fully armed, passing the Nuer land of Lou and Jikany, which SPLA launched devastation by running down villages to the ground, grains destroyed, livestock looted, men, women and children discriminately killed.

There was no accountability in the movement as the whole affairs became a network of close, confident leaders where no responsibility for the most serious problem went un-investigated and allowed flaws to flow inside the movement leadership in the administered camps and liberated areas. For example, the officer in charge of the Bilpam training camp was not held accountable for the death of starvation and diseases that killed more than three thousand Nuba Mountain Red Army under training in Bilpam in 1988, which later discovered that their food was sold on Gambella market and the same mistake proceeds to what happened similarly to the death of the hunger and starvation of the hundreds recruits from Dimma refugee camp that went uninvestigated. The death from thirst and starvation of more than five hundred SPLA combatants and recruits from Eastern Equatoria in early 1985 had never been investigated as Arok Thon Arok was in charge of the commanding force expedition. Victims were easily forgotten and never remembered, while the SPLA characteristic of rushing to forget, erase and forge victory way ahead had reflected a bad image of the society SPLA claim to lead in vain of devastating consequences.

There are many merits to conclude from succession of the south and both halves of the Sudan. The fact that southern succession would bring peace is a topmost advantage. What the Sudanese need most is not unity but peace so that citizens in both the north and south can rebuild lives in peace and harmony. The true wheel behind people's struggles and history can never be reverse as Sudan will never return to its original shape following fifty years from now after awareness of its citizens has taken place and is still low. In Sudan, where national identity holds significant importance and wields a strong influence, various ethnic groups such as the Southern Sudanese, Nuba, Ingessina, Fur, and Beja are not exempt from the struggle to retain their love for their humanity, languages, cultures, faith, and self-dignity. The main obstacle NIF party is not a static or sleeping force as it quickly moves, reverses gear and responds with a quick reaction at any event, national uprising, regional, or international and it quickly makes its own political calculation for survivability. The South Sudan self-determination has been and is now being accepted as the only focal point that will bring a final peaceful resolution of conflict in Sudan as it is a means recognized and supported regionally and internationally. The fact Darfur, Nuba, Ingessina, Beja and Fur put up an uprising against the regime of NIF is the fact that growing awareness of self-identity is partly encourage by the same continual oppressive policies of the NIF regime whose ascension to power in the coup 1989 still represent unchangeable characteristic of radical section Jelaba and that has exposed the true color of the NIF predatory class A. The referendum of 2011 will bring every lasting solution to Sudan's problem by South Sudan succession to its independence or else return to war will be the last option on the list, which may later lead to a final peace through power defeat at the barrel of the weapon. SPLM, as a primary South Sudan party, got too much open options to dismantle South Sudan's national issues and this includes peaceful resolution of the tribal conflicts and freedom exercises on the right of self-determination and accord implementation of the referendum that will require a lot of work in the high level of national organization. The awareness of the people is a primary succession so that South Sudanese will exercise freedom of right to vote for South independence from the North. The SPLM and its leadership, the entire people of Southern Sudan and other marginalized areas must be readily prepared for real phases of struggle if the NIF regime alters the referendum and the entire of CPA to the point that what was signed to be held ceased fired has been violated. After

South Sudan's independent war of liberation continued in Darfur, Abyei, Kordofan and Nuba Mountains by SPLA-North and, it seems like the New Sudan Vision will live forever to unite the entire Sudan back into one largest country of Africa.

INTRODUCTION: PART 2

a. Innocent lives forces to flee out

b. World child soldiers

c. Historical causes of Sudan red army uprising

d. Tribal conflicts over child soldiers in S. Sudan

e. Who are lost-boys of South Sudan?

Innocent lives forces to flee out

It was thought to be a good year in peaceful villages around the Southern part of the country before rebellion cycle of war sparked up again in May 1983. Rural towns, villages, cattle and everything for life was destroyed as SPLA Koriom, Mourmour and Kazuk battalions hit southern Sudan regimes in tough row attacks of multiple towns and garrisons. Thousands of children were forced to escape persecution, displaced and driven across the border to Ethiopia for safety with, escorted or without SPLA troop protection. Many of these children, including the author, were part of a larger group of displaced individuals, which comprised thousands of women, girls, old men, youths, disabled individuals, and others. They traversed the jungle daily for three or four months alongside SPLA troops, making their way to western Ethiopia, where the SPLM/A had stationed its operations. Thousand of these children were driven by a lack of school vision as schools closed down at the entirety of southern Sudan. Thousand more children were forced by their regional commanders of the SPLA, like Bor regional SPLA commanders who forced children out of their parents and moved them to Ethiopia for whatever reason called seed battalion to grow and got breed in the juggle to replaced SPLA long vision.

As soon as these thousands of children reached western Ethiopia SPLA camps in 1984-1990s, SPLM camp organizers officers would mobilized the treks and sorted out male children from female children, women from men, youth from elders and disabled from trainee soldiers. Children aged six to fifteen were escorted to join the existing battalions of the Red Army stationed in Itang, Bilpam, Sarpam, Dimma, and Pinyudo camps. These hundreds of Red Army battalions in five SPLA military training camps lived within a well-organized battalion system, undergoing comprehensive military training for durations ranging from three months to a year. Some were armed to safeguard the homes of commanders and SPLA officers. The SPLM's strategic objective was to utilize these thousands of children stationed in the five camps to draw attention from the UN, NGOs, and children's organizations. The assistances which were offered by UN and NGOs were received in assistance of food, clothes, money, and non-food items used by the SPLA commanders and officers. The SPLA did continuously military trained, armed and developed many red army battalions in the Itang, Sarpam, Bilpam, and Dimma camps and one last selective service in the Pinyudo camp. The case of Pinyudo Red Army Terap (seed) regiment was treated very differently from any other Red Army battalions in the other four camps.

The optimal strategy for the Red Army was to target the Pinyudo camp, and other valuable resources and services for refugees were directed towards enhancing the facilities at the Pinyudo camp. Terap battalions in the Pinyudo camp were the best of the most SPLA protected, secured and peaceful, equipped to fit peace of mind in education. Although Terap Red Army were very little children forced out of their villages and parental hands by the barrel of Kalashnikov, these battalions of Red Army suffered fade of the SPLA military torturing trained and SPLM teachers abuse as well how the entire Pinyudo camp was depending on the red army to build SPLM officers, commanders and officials huts, fenced and works for them like little slaves. Another radical SPLM/SPLA mistake plan was placing the Non-Pinyudo Red Army on fire like every trained red army of Nuer, Shilluk, Nuba, Ngok, Bhar el ghazall, Bor and Equatoria in either Dimma, Itang, Bilpam, Sarpam and Bongo was armed, deployed and did engagethe regime enemy at war zones. Accept the Pinyudi Red Army and Adikdik battalions in Dimma were they only out-wood Red Army battalions which didn't get prepared by the SPLA for immediate regime engagement at the frontlines.

The advantage of the Red Army, minors, and Lost-boys has never ended up to today as most cases, SPLM/A always depended on the lost-boys until they grew lost-men of Southern Sudan. Advantages uses of Red Army for SPLM/A accept Pinyudo Red Army is a havoc effect that left hundreds of Lost-boys living in the United States or Australia mentally retarded and will live entire live in crisis centers or on mainstreets of downtowns. Hardship life cycle from fled, escapes, refuge and asylum has traumatized lost-boys as many lives on alcohol, drugs, homeless and jobless.

The best place for lost-boys to live right now is coming back to South Sudan and lives in the same village left twenty five years ago, since living America or Australia is a lawful mistake that is burying lost-boys alive. Lost-boys are target of abuses, discrimination, prejudice, mistreatment, harassment, law institutional racism and hate crime setup in the western world and this has made lost-boys education and living very difficulty. Lost-boys are target because of their unique dark skin color identity, anti-racial sociality, cultural different, way of conducts and quite manners. Accented English, dressing style and way of life differentiate lost-boys and make them vulnerable to American institutional hate, racism, discrimination and law.

SPLM/A offered fake services for children red army camped to go school, live refugees, demilitarized, disarmed or not deployed, but still red army remained a soldier property of the SPLA until tough war called to ordered red army battalions for battlefield. Fake children services were offered to red army to pool donors, UN, NGOs and other children organization where offered assistances end up in hands of teachers, officers, commanders and little hardly reached red armies. The internal contention and contradiction within the SPLA during the 1980s revolved around allegations that the SPLA high command leadership was engaged in practices of high tribalism, nepotism, and corruption. This involved favoritism towards certain Red Army battalions while neglecting others. Most children who came to western Ethiopia camps from marginalized Southern Sudan didn't lastly made it to America or Australia accept Bor regions lost-boys and where it male children forcibly recruited and conscirpted by SPLA regional commander Kuol Juuk, currently minister of defense of south Sudan. Those conscripted male children were protected by the SPLA troop when fleeing to Ethiopia, back to south sudan and to kenya until they made their way to America, Australia, and Canada. It was unfair for the SPLM/A to secure, protect and kept one regional children red battalions in Pinyudo camp rather than doing the same to all Red army battalions in the movement as far as all regions of southern Sudan must have children from Itang, Bilpam, Sarpam and Dimma training camps. Red army SPLA abuses of red army non-Terap red army

As mentioned by Adowk Nyaba in his book, SPLM/SPLA

was not just having power centered around greedy leaders, tribalistic leaders, corrupt and ignorance, but leadership was shorted signed to overseen future unbalance leadership and disadvantage of bring up one sub-tribe children as future seed for the continual leadership and neglected other tribes or regions to have the same children future plan. What is rotten in the SPLM leadership system is a tribal greediness and favors of selfishness where each leader in high power position would love masquerading of public fund, donation and aids relief to bring up individual tribes future. Tribal bad leadership in the SPLM influenced lost-boys in a political way of tribal thought rather than South Sudan national thought; now many lost-boys think inbox supporting their tribal thought ideas in political tribe SPLM leadership. The question to either educated lost-boys would make different by providing cohesive national politics than is different from their tribe SPLM leadership or lost-boys may follow footstep of their tribalistic SPLM leaders. Certain tribal-oriented SPLM leaders with questionable motives have been accused of hindering the crucial political careers of the Lost Boys in South Sudan. Many Lost Boys find themselves entangled in the complexities of tribal conflicts within SPLM leadership, potentially limiting their chances of success in South Sudan's political arena.

Tribal political division has already started where lost-boys from Bor region would leaved US, or Australia to joint their own SPLM team leaders in Juba, or encourage development only in their region they come from and the same ideology mindset is done by lost-boys from Bhar El ghazel, Shilluk and Nuer. Some key element lost-boys are criticism of Salva Kiir administration and yet their tribal political mindset is a tribal own leadership havoc. SPLM tribal conflict commission is to resolves the pass on tribal leadership of corruption, tribalism, nepotism and destruction of tribal youth mindset in new emerging young youth generation. The worse leadership havoc system in South Sudan can only be fixing by Lost-boys who would come up out of their tribal tied family hood as well as avoiding their elders' tribal advice in order to achieve different political measure against the old system of the SPLM/A failed leadership.

Lost boys in general are paying tributes, gifts, price and thankfulness to the SPLM leadership, UN, NGOs, Ethiopian government, Kenyan people, Ugandan, South Africa, Australians people and to Americans for their well cares, love, sheltering, protection, feeding, security, clothing, education and provision of full humanity assistance to South Sudan. Lost-boys in the run of twenty five years in the epical odyssey attribute thankfulness to all helping hands within the odyssey. Lost-boys are now giving back a must gratitude to the SPLA/M teachers, caretakers, community elders, SPLA Black army escorts, South Sudanese communities and all tribes bypass in the odyssey. Lost-boys give thanks to the SPLM/SPLA leadership of late Dr. John Garang, Kuol Manyang,

Pieng Deng Majok, Jurkuc Barach, Late Poring and to all SPLA combatants who had shaped and provided needed security for the red armies in the Pinyudo camp and all paths of the odyssey. Lost-boys had bypassed all peaceful tribes villages and appreciation is the great words to honors all tribes which accommodated lost-boys by providing shelters, food, security, directions and even companionship while in the lost juggle odyssey. Thanks you great tribe of Anyuak both in Sudan and in Ethiopia, Murle, Toposa, Didinka, Turkana and Amish. Lost-boys would loves to appreciated all the education providence NGOs like Radda Barner, LWF, FACE foundation, Arap foundation, UNICEF, UNHCR, JRS, Catholic Saint Bhakita and to all American and Australians education financial Aids. Lost-boys loves would goes out to all resettlement agencies, foundations, Americans lost-boys volunteers, Australians lost-boys volunteers, Americans friends and families who had encourage lost-boys and help them cope with western lifestyle from the welcoming day up to now. The Lost Boys express their heartfelt gratitude to the mothers of resettlement from various organizations, including all churches, Catholic Charities, World Vision, IRC, JVA, INS, IOM, Lutheran Church, and the Church of Baltimore in Maryland.

World child soldiers

Around the world of conflicts, there are questions still not being answers about who the child soldier is? What causes them to join the men`s war or make them become child soldier or children of war?, what do child soldier do? Where do they live? And what is the future for the child soldier. Who is a child soldier? A child soldier has been defined as a person under the age of eighteen who directly or indirectly participates in an armed conflict as part of government armed force, militiamen, rebels' paramilitary or any rebel group. While some children wield assault rifles, machetes, Pangas, knives, spears or rocket propelled grenades on the front lines, others are being used in combat support roles as messengers, spies, cooks, mine clearers, bullets carriers, suicides bombers, porters and sexual slaves. It is not uncommon for them to participate in killing, raping, looting, robbery, and drug trafficking. Today in most of the armed conflicts raging in the world, an estimated three hundred thousand children are active participants in combat according to UN report 2009.

Life on the frontlines at any war zone is offensive and ravaging as to brings children face to face with the horrors of war. Too many children have personally experienced or witnessed extremism or hostility of physical violence, including direct executions, death of squad killings, disappearances, torture, arrest or detention, sexual abuse, bombings, forced displacement, destruction of home or property and massacres. They have been robbed of their childhood and held slaves of future futility. They have been brutally maimed in cool blood as well as mental retarded for life by their foes. Because of their emotional, physical immaturity and poverty of their parents children are easy to manipulate and can be drawn into violence against their will. With an acceptance of their innocent will and that they are too young to resist or understand, children remain as vast recruiting source of the world rebels and irresponsible governments. Both boys and girls may be sent to the frontline of combat or into minefields ahead of older troops to cause blew off the planted mines. Some have been used for suicide missions or forced to commit atrocities against their own families and neighbors. Others serve as porters, cooks, guards, servants, messengers, or spies. Many child soldiers, mostly girls, are also sexually abused including being kept as concubine, wife and a sexual object for the squad or by rebel commanders.

At the frontline of any combat zone, Children are killed and wounded at far higher rates than their adult comrades, because their underdeveloped mind lack fighting's tactics. Those child soldiers who survive frontlines assaults often suffer fade of trauma, injury, abuse, and psychological scarring from the violence and brutality they had experience. Even if some of them find way out war zone; some are rejected by their families and communities and remained isolated. Many child soldiers are option less as they loss an opportunity to acquire an education, job skills, or any hope for the future even after being demobilized and disarmed. The use of children to fight adults' wars is not limited to a single country or continent, but has become a worldwide problem. The problem is most critical in Africa and Asia, although children are also being used as soldiers by governments and armed groups in many countries like Americas, Europe and the Middle East. However, the problem is not limited to developing countries. Industrialized countries are also facing personnel shortfalls and have also increased efforts to attract young recruits in any way that can be defend. According to the Coalition to Stop the Use of Child Soldiers, the report believes that more than one hundred twenty thousand children under eighteen years of age are currently participating in armed conflicts across Africa. Evidently some of these children are not more than seven or eight years of age. African countries mostly affected by this problem are Algeria, Angola, Burundi, Congo-Brazzaville, the Democratic Republic of Congo, Liberia, Rwanda, Sierra Leone, Sudan and Uganda, Somalia, and Central Africa Republic. Furthermore, Ethiopian forces engaged in an armed conflict against Eritrea, and the clans in Somalia, have both included an unknown figure of child soldiers as Minnesota Somalis children got killed in Mogadishu as suicide bombers.

In addition to the obvious risks taken by both children and adult comrades' participating in the same armed conflict, children are often at an added disadvantage as combatants compare to adult comrade. Their immaturity leads them to take excessive risks according to one rebel commander in the Democratic Republic of Congo. Soldiers tend to receive little, not remember any training or not trained at all before being thrust into the frontline combat.

Reports from Burundi and Congo-Brazzaville added that child soldiers are often massacred in combat as a result. When they are not actively engaged in combat, child soldiers are develop at the manning checkpoints, patrol or guarding town or bodyguard for commanders or any rank officer. Adult soldiers can normally be seen standing a further 15 meters behind the barrier so that if bullets start flying, it is the children who are the first victims. Girls too are used as soldiers, though generally in much smaller numbers than boys. many males, females joined one of the factions for their own protection and safety. Girl child soldiers became the girlfriends or wives of rebel leaders or members: 'wartime women' is the term they commonly use for themselves.

Majority of African States set eighteen as the minimum age for recruitment, whether voluntary or through conscription, but this law has been violated beyond it State`s constituency. Africa is in the process of increasing its minimum age for voluntary recruitment to eighteen and Mauritania may also be rising its minimum age from fifteen to eighteen. In Angola, a country severely affected by the phenomenon of child soldiers, the government recently reduced the age of conscription to seventeen years. Another factor is the lack of systematic birth registration; even younger children are inevitably recruited even if the will or law to prevent underage recruitment existed. Likely reducing the minimum age of conscription to seventeen is currently lawful since international law sets fifteen as the international minimum age.

Burundi and Rwanda have the lowest legal recruitment ages on the African continent, seemingly at the age of fourteen or sixteen years for volunteers, although Uganda has formerly claimed to accept children apparent age of thirteen to be enrolled with parental consent. In Chad, parental would consent to allow the minimum age of seventeen to be effectively reduced. Concerns also exist as to legislation in Botswana, Kenya, and Zambia where children of age of eighteen can lawfully be recruited. Libya accepts volunteers at seventeen years, if not younger. In South Africa, in a state of emergency, children of fifteen years of age or above can be used directly in armed conflict as amended by the Constitution. In Sudan, recruitment into the Popular Defense Forces can start lawfully at fifteen years.

If only domestic legislation were always respected in practice, the problem of child soldiers in Africa would be significantly reduced or eradicate. Many African States like Benin, Cameroon, Mali and Tunisia to name but a few are following appropriate recruitment procedures that prevent underage troops being recruited into the army. Whereas countries like Somalia, Sudan, Angola, Burundi, Congo-Brazzaville, Democratic Republic of Congo, Rwanda, Sierra Leone and Uganda have children recruited not more than seven or eight years of age. Children do volunteer to join the armed forces but it depends on how one interprets the word volunteer. In DRC, between four to five thousands children responded to a radio broadcast calling for twelve to twenty year olds to recruits to defend their country but most were street children and suburb country side poor parented children. Yet tens of thousands of children are forced to join up, sometimes at gunpoint.

In Angola, forced recruitment of youth continues in some of the suburbs around the capital and throughout the country rural areas. It has been claimed that military commanders have paid police officers to find new recruits and Namibia has collaborated with Angola in catching Angolans who have fled to Namibia to avoid conscription. In Eritrea newspaper reports, a seventeen year-old Ethiopian prisoner of war, Dowit Admas, interviewed by a British journalist claimed that he was playing football in Gondar High School when Ethiopian government soldiers rounded up 60 boys and sent them to a military training camp. In Uganda, there have been persistent reports that street children in Kampala have been approached by soldiers and forced to join the army in order to be sent to the Democratic Republic of Congo. Sierra Leone nine years ago a reports by AFRONET have clearly detailed the fact that rebel forces recruit children below seventeen years of age and demonstrate that children as young as five were to enrolled. In Uganda, the Lords Resistance Army (LRA) systematically abducts children from their schools, communities and homes. Children who attempt to escape, resist, cannot keep up, or become ill are killed.

Historical causes of Sudan red army uprising

Some 2 million people were killed; tens of thousands of children were orphaned. Lost boys group are remnants group among the 27,000 red army group entering Kenya in early 1992. Thirty thousand could be the estimated number of former Red Army {lost-boys} in the wartime, while now in the USA; the lost-boys total could be four thousands. In 1980s of wartime, the system of red army squad by squad headcount can dispute whatever previous red army's outnumbered or from apartment to apartment bed can be an easy way lost-boys headcount themselves.

The south Sudan red army uprising, which sound like USSR or Russian red army in Sudan, was of different meaning to the South Sudanese struggle used of the name red army. Although South Sudan was an ally of Ethiopia, Zimbabwe or, Cuba, even Russian at, it started off, still the names red army could tune ears to cold war or sound so communistic.

A cycle of civil war blew up in the third round in the south in 1983 and thousands of young south Sudanese men jumped into bushes and trek thousands of miles to western Ethiopia. By late 1985, SPLA had already stationed thousands and thousands of south strong men trained and armed as black soldiers. As every region or part of south Sudan became a battlefield, children, women and elders had nowhere to refuge. The uprising of the red army came as the result SPLA's high command order out thousands of children from villagers in all southern Sudan regions to trek thousands of miles to western Ethiopia camps. The civil war caused South Sudanese to act out of their Fear, villages' massacres and tied persecution posted by the northern regime and militia paved the way for thousands of families, including children, to voluntarily trek, escaping to western Ethiopia where SPLA could guarantee protection. Thousands of children joined the war for security and retaliation against the regime and thousands were trained, armed and stationed by the SPLA in camps or liberated jungle camps controlled by the SPLA army.

Literally, this idea of snatching out only boys children away from their parents and got trek way miles to Ethiopia was engineered in Bor area by those whose among them were murdered by the same SPLA. It was a thought by Bor leaders of the SPLA ranks to have male children of Bor be saved as future seed in case the war would finished and diminished the youths and women per undermined period war would taking it raging struggleThe implementation of the children's idea in Bor was spearheaded by high-ranking SPLA officers, guided by Late Majier Gai and Joseph Kuol, and enforced by Kuol Manyang. The effectiveness of the idea was largely attributed to Kuol Manyang's enforcement policy, which instilled fear in parents by threatening them with a firing squad if they resisted allowing their male children to embark on the journey to Ethiopia.

Thousands and thousands of male children all over Bor regions, villages, cattle camps, rural cities and families started daily trekways to Ethiopia in 1986-1990s with full support from the SPLA Bor leaders and SPLA troop protection. Bor SPLA high ranks knew the idea plan of these little kids would work for Bor town and generally for the whole of Sudan if the idea succeeded and yes, the idea worked, but the question couldn't be determined if majority of these young Bor lost boys will present actually side of the Bor leaders dreamed vision or it is going to be a dream submerge by error. The same ordinary Kuol Manyang who was hated by the entirety of Bor in 1980s because of the forcible idea of taking kids away from their love parents to trek to Ethiopia in 1980s, Governor Kuol is now being praised highly by lost boys' parents in Bor and Lost-boys who are now educated youths. Lost boys from Bor in the USA gathered one evening in their central States apartment, contributed money and decided to honor Kuol Manyang for his leadership as well plannedned and successful ideas of the late 1980s;

eventually, Kuol was granted his award certificate of achievement by lost-boys. Bor children forced out of their villages were destiny and settled in Panyudo camp, grouped into thirteen groups, school opened for them, military trained and peacefully settled there far away from active SPLA war activities. Forcibly driven out of parents, The idea was copied by other SPLA high ranks from different southern regions and children mission to Ethiopia refugee camp has become every region mission lately. There were children from Bhar elghazel, Nuerland, Nuba, Ngokland, Equatoria and Shilluk children. Differently, male children who came to western Ethiopia from other region than Bor came voluntarily and the movement of these children was not as more organized, planned and guided, just like Bor children who were more organized by the SPLA Bor supported leaders as well as the plan was also protected by the SPLA high ranks from Bor.

Another question was where did the collective and majority of these children forced out from parents, war, and school vision drive children from southern Sudan to Ethiopia got settled by the SPLA high ranks who were responsible for refugee camps settlement of the displaced and children. Thousands of Bor forced out children were mainly settled in Panyudo refugee camps far away from military training and SPLA deployment activities. Terap Red Army Battalion was one of the Red Army Children battalionss that survived frontline deployment for a good reason, known by the

SPLA leader, Dr. John Garang. Three thousands of Nuba and Maban children placed in the Bilpam training camp died away of hunger and diseases, as it was mentioned by Adwok Nyaba, under poor SPLA training on leadership. Thousands and thousands of Nuer, Shilluk, Ngok and Nuba were directed and settled in Itang, Zinc, Sarpam, Bilpam and Langwei as SPLA used these groups of Children for direct military training in Bonga and Bilpam training fields. Red army battalions in Itang were Katiba Grenade, Mutpa and other thousands of red army battalions stationed in Sarpam camp awaited military training in the field of Bonga and Bilpam military training fields. More than 11,000 of Nuers and Shilluk children which redouble12 000 Bor children stationed Panyudo camp, were military trained, armed and deployed by the SPLA,for instance, SPLA huge Intifada regiment was composed of thousands of Nuer and Bhar el ghazel child soldiers as included with red army 1, 2, 3, 4 and Jebel battalion deployed. Dimma camp primarily consisted of children from Bhar el Ghazel and Equatoria, with a significant number undergoing military training, being armed, and subsequently deployed by the SPLA. This deployment encompassed units such as Nganyin, Gerdale, and Zelzel 2 battalions.

Even in the liberated SPLA areas, villages and regions rather than Bor areas like in Bhar el ghazel, Equatoria, Nuer land and Ngok, more children were conscripted by the SPLA, trained and deployed at frontline like the red army of Bol Madut, Malou trained red army, current SPLA red army battalion mainly come from Bhar el ghazel. The majority of red army Bright Star Campaigns Commando 1, 2, 3, and 4 were mainly Nuer and Bhar el ghazel underage children armed with AK-47, hand grenades and small armies forced to capture western equatoria towns from Sudan army forces in 1993-96. The question remained tough to answers of why Terap battalion mainly Bor red armies survived deployment by the SPLA until majority of Terap red armies made their way to USA and Australia?. Terap red army battalion was the only one out-wood and most immune red army battalion to survived SPLA armed deployed, scattered back to villages, enemy death from fire, survived multiple hostile tribal attacked, hostage kidnaps, survived deathly diseases and made it safe way across the borders from Sudan to Kenya and to US as well as Australia.

Tribal conflicts over child soldiers in S. Sudan

It is now getting worse quarrelsome as it was a more quarrelsome case in 1980-90s, as John Garang, late leader of the SPLA/M, was blame on the issue of too many red army of Terap battalion from his own tribe Bor region being stationed away from other red army in Pinyudo refugee camp. Pinyudo red armies were stationed away from various SPLA active deployment training fields. Pinyudo camp had a huge twenty some thousands of red army reserved and stationed for the future SPLA vision as they were refers to as Seed battalion, whereas Itang, Bilpam, Sarapam and Dimma camp had more than fifty thousand of Red Army's stationed for the SPLA recruitment, training and army deployment purpose. Pinyudo was eighty percent Bor red army's, while Itang camp was ninety percent Nuer red army's as well as Dimma was eighty percent Bhar al Ghazel Red Armies.

Not only Garang was fighting back the blame on how SPLA was using child soldiers to fight men war, Garang was at the same time hitting back on what his high commands called tribalistic movement where Garang only reserved huge number of Terap red armies' battalion as a future seed battalion from his own Sub-Dinka tribe of Bor region. In the midday Garang parade meeting with Seed battalion in Pinyudo, one of the Red Army's teachers from Bhar el Ghazel raise a question on why SPLA didn`t regarded bringing equal number of Red Army's children from all over South Sudan tribes or regions. The teacher's question hadn`t got answered by Garang; instead, some SPLA Garang army guards took the handled away from the teacher and the teacher got disappeared in front of the set down red army public field parade. The respond answer was torment if any SPLA officer, soldier, or anyone from Nuer, Bhar el ghazel or Equatoria asked Garang a question on Red Army's plan within the movement of the SPLM/A. It was common sense and dodgeable question on how and why SPLM reserved stations thousands of Dinka or sub-tribal Bor children in many Ethiopia camps. Or why Dinka called movement collected, protected, guided and stationed a huge number of red armies while there was no or less number of Equatorian, Nuer, or any other tribe or region in Southern Sudan served and protected most by the SPLA as future seed of Southern Sudan.

The answer seem to be simple, but it may mean another indirect meaning because Dinka is the major tribe in South Sudan and there were thousands of Dinkas SPLA army men as the uprising revolution started in Dinkaland. All major SPLA battalions that defeated and destroyed the northern regime were ninety percent Dinka, Nuer, Shilluk and Nuba, but that doesn't mean there should not have equality and justice to have other tribes children encouraged by the SPLM/A to bring share of their children as future seed for southern Sudan. Dinkaland was hit hard by the ravaged war and many Dinka children, women and youths had nowhere to escape for life except going to Ethiopia in 1980-90s and that brought a number of Dinka Red Army's to the huge protected camps as SPLA mobilized these children and trained, armed and deployed them. What about Nuer, who had the second largest SPLA black army battalions as well as huge number of red army battalions compares to Dinka? Where are Nuer Lost-Boys in US or Australia?. Adwok Nyaba would asked this question it might have been address it his book by referring to the unquestioned death of three thousand Nubian red armies in Bilpam, same to thousands of Nuer children who capsized with dug-out canoes and ferry steam in the Nile and Akoba river while on the way to Ethiopia camps.

The biggest SPLM South Sudanese camp in western Ethiopia from 1980-90s was Itang and it was followed by Pinyudo camp. Itang camp was the most Nuer families, Nuer red armies, Shilluk, Nuba, Bhar el ghazel populated and disorganized camp. Pinyudo camp mainly inhabited by ninety percent families and red army from Bor region was very organized and UN supplied with very enough food, clothing and non-food item and other extra assistance more than any other refugee camp in western Ethiopia. Dimma near Equatoria exit gate to Ethiopia was mainly resettled by Equatorians, Dinka and less number of Nuer, and Dimma was also less UN food supplies compares to Panyudo camp. Red army battalions in Dimma were at the most critical hardship lifestyle. Nuer, Nuba, Shilluk and Equatorians in the Kakuma refugee camp went on long strike and demanding Minors head of lost boys resettlement program to explained in detailed why their children were neglected opportunity to be resettled to US, or Australia, the explaining went back to what Adwok Nyaba called a one hand man power centered movement which answers would get traced and dug out from huge backward mess of what should have been done better by people right citizens.

The war on lost boys' mission has never end and it is a bitter caused of ethnic line between Dinka and Equatoria-Nuer-Shilluk who still demand the right answer from the movement SPLM/A leaders of 1980-90s. Nuer leaders are so bitter against Dinkas Red Army mission and on how Non-Dinkas Red Army battalions were deployed and exposed to hardship and frontlines lives fires while Dinka underage Red Army battalions were reserved for school and refugee protected living facility in Panyudo.

Other southern Sudan tribes complained out the same about Dinka planning to have anarchy or kind of kingdom ruling power in Southern Sudan by missioning Lost-boys for the same purpose. Lost boys mission has not causes problem between Dinkas and Non-Dinka ethnic tribes of Southern Sudan, it also causes fundamental inter-tribal issues between Dinka Bhar el ghazel, Ngok and Bor on how mission of the male children was planed and handled by single one regions SPLM/A high rank from Bor region and not fully included other region equally to contributed seed children to make future equality of South leadership. Still even right now Lost-boys are unknown to many Sudanese or world around, lost-boys history, background and who they were or are right now is still hidden.

Who are lost-boys of South Sudan?

Many Sudanese fellows are lost fellows just like lost-boys by guess naming who lost-boys are? And this is exactly anonymous not appreciated by Lost-boys. The world often perceives lost-boys as parentless, homeless, and among the most impoverished individuals resulting from the historical wartime strife in Sudan. These boys, sometimes labeled as uncivilized or village boys, were exploited by the Sudan People's Liberation Army (SPLA) for war purposes or embarked on arduous journeys from their villages to distant lands such as America or Australia in search of education and the promise of a better life. Who are Lost-boys of Sudan? And what are their suffering and ambitions? Well, lost-boy is a group of Boys like Peter Pan known in America for his lost odyssey. It started in 1985 where teenagers boys under age of fifteens were forced to leave and got separated with their families, parents, siblings, relatives by civil war started in 1983-2005. as well as got forced into displaced refugee, SPLA recruitments, army training camps in western Ethiopia and school vision drive and in search of life across neighboring countries.

Extracted by war and SPLA forces from villages, rural town and liberated areas; as eventually gathered in to secure the hands of the SPLM/A in protection and movement security provident. 45,000 Villages boys' names changes in to refugees' boys after refuge diseases of hunger, cholera, jiggers, homesickness and eye blindness triggered suffering in homeless under tress camps. SPLM/A organized this huge number of villages boys into five main military training camps in western Ethiopia from 1985-90s: Pinyudo, Dimma, Itang, Bilpam and Sarpam. Refuges boys were suffered rebels military trained by the SPLA for three or up to one year in militarization fields, and later, after field discharged their names changed again to Red Army referring to large teenagers SPLA regiments in the movement struggle. Hundreds of the SPLA Red Army battalions got trained, armed and deployed to liberated majority part of Southern Sudan from Sudan regime in 1986 to 1990s. Accept one Red Army Terap regiment composed of twelve battalions was named as seed regiment mainly from one ethnic sub-tribe of Dinka was marked as out-wood without deployment and now they are here as lost-boys. Lost-boys originated as village boys, transitioning into the roles of refugee boys and members of the Red armies before ultimately becoming minors who embarked on an epic journey, solidifying their status as Lost-boys.

The name Red army slide change after eighteen thousands Red armies entered Kenya in 1992 to escaped Sudan regime persecution after captured of Kapoeta; eventually, Red armies were resettled in Kakuma camp and Kenyan administrators changed names to Minors. Minors were separated from the chains of their SPLA military lifestyles as they entered in to civilian lives in the refugees' camp of Kakuma. Again, Minors fled Kakuma camp to USA, Canada and to Australia and their names changes from accompany minors to Lost-boys. The irony behind boys naming are those who named them, the meaning of the names and the life situation associated with fleeing epical history. Boys' names and naming is always associated with a country of asylum, or refuge, associated NGOs in services, tragic faced lives, environmental situation and services being offered by assistants. While most of the Red armies were schooling in Ethiopia camps, they were refers as school boys as it was also happening in Kakuma camp when minors were also school boys. Lost-boys names were given to changes minors' names and to baptized boys to become American as they entered into another lost assistance provided by new Americans assistants as they were leaving Kenyan assistants with minors' names.

Lost-boys naming is getting endless as boys are now lost-men and acquired other names called Arrival Lost-Men after reaching long time lost villages in searches of their long lost parents. The generation of lost-boys is coherent and still the same as it was from genesis lost epical war historic. Lost-men fleeing journey is endless and it will continues forever's until reaching heaven where God will settled them down for rest, but still it is unknown in heaven if lost-boys would still be fleeing in heaven dodging hell and other unknown diseases over there in heaven.

Lost-Boys are generation of refuges, child soldiers, orphans, school-less age, war time victims, exile group, with educated lost-Mind, community leaders, God children, future leaders, SPLA leadership seeds, determined will, workaholic hands and with natural homeless heart. Lost-boys who emerged up from unknown villages' lifestyle, rural country side of South Sudan villages and in to cities are now known by the SPLA forces and it leadership as successful combatants when it come to the war SPLA fought for twenty some years; Red army battle always ranked successful and victories over Black army and as black army accused Red army of not worry at frontline by leaving any family, wife or kids behind and that why Red army fought to death victoriously at any frontlines.

Considered orphans due to their communal living arrangements, Lost-boys resided in groups comprised of companies, comrades, friends, roommates, relatives, or a collection of colleagues. The Red army isolated living conditions were akin to orphanages, resembling a gathering of minors within the camp. This generation, shaped by the hardships of life, learned the values of hard work, determination, and a focus on both present and future education. The Lost-boys, having grown up on the frontlines of war zones, developed an ambitious and humanistic mindset. Remarkably, many Lost-boys pursued higher education upon reaching destinations such as the United States, Australia, or East Africa, resulting in a significant number of them attaining degrees in various fields. Notably, this generation stands out as Africa's young men who, despite their challenging upbringing, strive to work with communities and various humanitarian organizations. The future of the SPLM/A ruling party has been centered around the Red

Army, Minors and now around Lost-boys and many lost-boys grew up with ambition to rule next after Salva Kiir Mayardit, the President of Southern Sudan. Closing along with mighty God, Lost-boys praise, adore and worship God of Christianity a lot, many lost-boys believes that God has a great plan for them and that their future depend on God, who drove them around the world, just like children of Israel. Lost-boys are the best tool of leadership when it comes to united and leaders southern Sudanese community in the Australia, US and even in East Africa; it is very easy recognize Lost-boys in western world because of their unique epical history it is remarkable that lost-boys community get support from white, black, or even Asian communities in the west.

The historical narrative of the Lost-boys has garnered widespread recognition worldwide, distinguishing them as refugees who receive unparalleled support compared to other refugee groups, such as those from Somalia, Liberia, or the Democratic Republic of the Congo, within the United States. Although everyone in the world describe and know lost-boys in very positive ways, there are still those who negatively describes or know lost-boys in very negative ways. Lost-boys are positive and optimistic about life.

As Sudanese or other world fellows who misunderstood Lost-boys and describes them as a group of survivors, criminals, backward, homeless, unusual guys, singles, gays, innocent, uncivilized and war mentally retarded, as well as drug additives boys who are lacking fatherhood images. There is no lost without missing and there is no missing without death, or else trauma will still kill a lost and found child. Thousands of lost-boys died away in the long lost epical struggle, thousands more became criminals, thousands more are traumatized, mental retarded in crises centers, thousands more became homeless and jobless as well as thousands more became parents, and thousands more are soldiers in the US army, SPLA army or rebels in East Africa and thousands more are degrees holders with or without professional jobs in USA and Australia. Being traumatized by long chronic diseases of hardship, endless suffering and traumatic loneliness; eventually, many lost consider used of alcohol, drug abuse, prostitution, jobless, and crimes of stealing, fighting, robbing and cheating as a means to remedy deal with a fuck-up life since from the beginning of the odyssey 1985-2005.

Eventually, lost-boys who chose this path to conclude terrific life end up residing in jails, on main streets, in graveyard side, in crises center, hospitalized and even back to their place of birth in South Sudan village as life in the Western world has no mercy on who was a damn child soldier with war wounds in his heart. Negative perception is traumatizing many lost-boys in America, Canada and Australia, where job searches, job retention, or keeping jobs become a problem. Relatively, there is a problematic attitude where lost-boys complain about their Western friends, co-workers, and battle buddies and relate to being overlooked, treated low, single out as innocent target and even discriminated against in an institutionalize way in American society. You got pay on how you look and got treated on how you sound in American society. Most lost grew anti-social because people run away from them or causes them problem when intermingle into large diversity of American and Australian societies, since naming calling such as lost-boys are too dark, tall, bony physical structure, rude look, mean and with negative attitude by responding to people negatively. Lost-boys are racialized negatively and perceived as being with negative attitudes by Americans, Spanish, Black African-Americans, or even Asian teammates, classmates, co-workers, friends, battle buddies, colleagues, as well as they are backward and uncivilized with rude, antisocial, retarded with an accused act of name calling as gay boys due to their male Africans` closeness or living together in brotherhoods in one single bedroom apartment, sharing one single bed.

Lost-boys are the center heart of the Sudanese community, church members, political mind buddies, tribesmen in local villages, and assume tomorrow leaders who love motherland, South Sudan. Traveling to Juba, the capital of South Sudan and visiting government officials of South Sudan on agendas related to how officials misuse and utilize public internal revenues on development in a hope that make lost-boys think about the future of South Sudan as hopefully leaders of South Sudan, or even dream of peace for the entirety of the Sudan. Lost-boys seem to be more tribalistic when southern Sudan tribalism affairs crop up in a community and lost-boys would be seen as a solution to dissolves tribalism factor, but lost boys are most of the time seem justified themselves with the cost causes of their lost-history. Lost-boys are very sensitive and easily influence and converted to support either tribalistic side where they belong when it comes to southern Sudan tribalism, which is national catastrophic factor. This prompts a critical question about whether educated Lost-boys possess charismatic leadership abilities that extend beyond the shadows of figures like John Garang in Southern Sudan. It raises inquiries into whether these educated Lost-boys would contribute to the strengthening of Southern Sudan's national fabric, potentially challenging issues such as tribalism, nepotism, corruption, and deficient leadership that have persisted.

Lost-boys are known for being selfish by favoring only Dinka side in development as well as they failed to united themselves or even united the Sudanese communities in the united States. Lost-boys are known for quarreling, arguing, disagreeing and debating small issues of their inter-sub-tribal problems rather than the national level of South Sudan, boys failed to strengthen American hopes to fully believe in lost-boys as they only next generation which will bring up the war ravaged backward South Sudan. Hundred of White and black Americans who were very closed allies, honored in respect of lost-boys, and offers themselves as donors, funders, assistants, volunteers, friends and colleagues are now victims of broken hearts as Americans grew mistrust, hated, hopeless and got no faith in Lost-boys as they used to in the first time.

Few Americans who still have interest in lost-boys have open their eyes to see which sides of lost-boys to offers assistance either Bor, Nuer or Bhar el Ghazel lost-boys side. Lost-boys tribal arguments had open Americans eyes wide to see the horizon of boys hatred among themselves on bilateral issues on the borderline of tribal conflicts in Southern Sudan; eventually, that negative act alone has created and erode away American hope that lost-boys group must be supported in education because they are they last good generation to defeats both Southern Sudan and western enemies in Africa.

American Investment in Lost-boys generation has failed due to failure of lost-boys to demonstrate capability of leadership to uplift South Sudan and this big mistake by lost-boys is a great failure for the South Sudan's future supports from United States of America. Lost-boys grew up supporting, cares, educated and raise themselves with support of the UN, NGOs and the SPLM. This epical hardship of survivability is a center piece cause of the lost-boys mental retardation, crook living life as hopeless couldn't overcome courage of no life achievement in futility. For the country which they suffered so much, lost-boys still hope to bring change to the country of South Sudan, whether to build it modernity huts in respective villages or work for the government of South Sudan to deliver services.

The Lost Boys Foundation of Nashville was created in the fall of 2004 by photographer Jack Spencer and a small group of volunteers after witnessing firsthand the tragic circumstances many of the young men still face in the Nashville community. One such circumstance was the death of Pel Gai, a much beloved young man, who was the victim of a murder in a Nashville nightclub. Since there was no money to bury Pel, a group of the Lost Boys, along with Spencer and a few others, raised the $5,700 that was needed to bury him. It was this event that inspired Spencer to make a difference in the future of the Lost Boys of Nashville. "The irony of Pel's death confounds me, Spencer says." "They have seen such terror, grief, loss, sadness and horror only to come to our land of opportunity and then senselessly murdered." Four of the boys sent to Nashville have been killed in the few years they have been here.

The epical tragic story of Lost boys death by killing in the USA doesn't end in Nashville, Tennessee, but lost-boys deaths spread across the country and spill over the world. Hundred of lost-boys are killed in various States, jailed, wounded and law crippled across the US. Many lost boys lost their lives while visiting back to South Sudan, were these young lost men went back to search for their lost parents, relatives and families, fell into conflict zones and never made it back to the USA or Australia.

CHAPTER 1

The LOST-BOYS 5TH EXODUS FROM KENYA TO USA AND AUSTRALIA

1. THE HISTORICAL PROCESS OF UNACCOMPANIED MINORS TO U.S AND AUSTRALIA FROM KAKUMA REFUGEE CAMP IN KENYA

2. THE 5th FLED TO HEAVEN PARADISO: U.S.A AND AUSTRALIA (1999-2005)

3. ON BAREFOOT IN TO VEHICLE AND IN TO FLIGHT FLED FROM NOWHERE TO NOWHERE

4. WELCOME TO AMERICA! THE FOUND HOME IT IS A NEVER FOUNDLAND

5. UNACCOMPANIED MINORS BECAME LOSTBOYS IN WESTERN COUNTRIES

6. THE LOSTBOYS IN THE 3rd PROMISED LAND {USA} AND AUSTRALIA

7. LOSTBOYS GREW LOSTMEN: EDUCATION IS A KEY MSSION

1. The Historical Process of Unaccompanied Minors to U.S and Australia (1999-2005)

A miracle happens with a blink of the eyebrow; and every hardship life posted to the person who is not a caused is rewarded at anytime. The emergency booming of minors faiths that encouraged many churches in the camp to open and worship has had impact many churches in the world to pay visitation to Kakuma refugees' camp. Booming faiths of minors had shot news in to the airs world of the servicing assistance as it had persuaded Norwegians churches, Presbyterian churches of England, Kenyan churches and church of Baltimore to visit the camp. In early 1995, the church of Baltimore volunteers happened to visit the camp under Refugees Children Care of African churches. Representatives of the Baltimore churches explored the camp until they reached minor groups of zone four Episcopal churches. These Baltimore church missionaries had entered in to another mission than what they exactly went there for by inquiring the camp of where about minors came from as well as visited minors' schools and social places as well as their living in makuti huts in the camp. These Baltimore church members' enquired minors' history from minors' center of caretakers' administration as well as members did interacted with minors and conversed with them in their groups. Since minors didn't hid their epic history from foreigners enquiry viewpoint, church members got narrative epical life history from the few minors in some groups out of nineteen minors groups. Minors who grew up in the cycles of war, fled, escapes, and in hardship refugees lives, looked skinny in long tallest height that was a surprised to interviewers members of the Baltimore church and to other children NGOS visiting minors in the camp were all surprises.

Every single minor out of ten thousands in the camp resided in nineteen groups answered the same question asked by the members of church or NGOs. Where are your parents, relatives, and siblings? I don`t know. Do you know either they died or alive? I don`t know? , since when last did you see them? Since 1987, or 1986, where did you go after escaping persecution? I went to Ethiopia and lived refugees camp from 1987-1991. How long you lived Kakuma camp? , nine years. What do you want to be in future? A doctor, a professor, a president or education is only key in life. Since minors lived in a company of five, three and two boys in the group, church members asked each boy at a time as well as got the same answers from each minor in all nineteen groups of ten thousand minors. Baltimore church members took pictures, videos and written notice as well as interviewed boys` names with them. After Baltimore church members visited the camp several times to proven their project enquiry and evident of their minors' epical history which was presented to US Refugees Immigration Services.

History of the minors' process started as Baltimore church members brought news back home to US after their visitation and exploration of the minors in Kakuma refugees' camp. In additions to Dr. Julia of Joint Volunteers Agency {JVA} proven evident of the minors` sufferings in the camp for nine years and it seemed to be a ready time for another fifth fled to unknown from unknown destination. Baltimore and JVA looked in to minors` struggling lives in the camp and it hadn`t no different from USA struggling for life out of less parental assistance.US Immigration Refugees Services had affirm strength of the minors in how they could managed to successfully lived hard living of America and through minors hardship faced in rebel, jungle and in refugees lives that automatically qualified them for approval of welcoming them to America as US IRS urgent resettlement agencies process to started in the camp.

Resettlement agencies in the camp which were dealing with communities' resettlement were switch on to minors' resettlement. Refugees' resettlement agencies supported minors' resettlement as well as agencies added approvable to it and recommended minors for resettlement. Minors were self-reliance and had lived independently from no parental or relatives supports since at infantry age; many minors in the camp own small kiosk business and some minors are working in the camp as well as some were schooling and that qualified minors for a quick resettlements proposal. Some of the minors were doing job-study or work eight hours a day and school at the same time. Some minors were schooling and do business after school including the author of this book. Some minors trade in the evening and school in morning.

A resettlement teams hit the camp on Monday with cameras, videos camera and some other heavy baggage staged on UNHCR Toyotas heading to minors` groups in each zone. Minors were interviewed in front of the cameras as well as their pictures were taken in fronts of their cage *makuti huts*. The resettlement team toured minors in their respective groups as well as meeting with caretaker teachers in the camp on behave of the minors' socio-social program. Resettlement agencies included Joint Voluntarily Agency, Australia resettlement, Oslo refugees resettlement agency and many others resettlements agencies. Minors were jumping up and down when the camp protection officer halt a quick stop in zone one minors groups and spontaneously called minors out of their huts and he had a quick meeting telling minors linkage about resettlement process. It was the time and the time was a ready time when traumatized minors knew it was the right time for 5th fled to unknown destination; since many minors knew Kakuma camp wasn`t their destination and even where the last fled takes halt wouldn`t be the last destination. The confirmed number of minors presently at the Socio-Social program compared to the number of minors at the started of the camp 1992 was 7,000 against 16,000 of

1992.

Socio-social program was formed by the Joint minors' resettlement agencies in the camp to define minors' pre-resettlement process. The announcement of the news for the minors' socio-social program started with minors` teachers and group caretakers meeting in the UNHCR compound with the Camp protection Officer to explain the socio-social program and the process of the minors scale. After several meetings with minors, socio-social Kenyan officers pulled out the names lists of minors {former Red Army} when they were in Ethiopia and ticket marked names against ration card names found in Kakuma ration card with correct names in the UNHCR database. The socio-social program started with scheduled calls of zone 1, 2, 3 and 4 minors to Nursery school 2 in zone 3 for application filing. The filing document application and name confirmation started with fostering care minors in community groups and lastly finished up with minors groups in four zones. In every morning and Sun down evening time, minors would lined up in Nursery school 2, as socio-social workers were busy calling names, taking photo sizes, signing a completed application and filing documents in cabinets. Minors were very happy as they chatted with their Sudanese teacher, socio-social workers, and some Kenyan about a skeptical program called socio-social, which wasn`t mention the resettlement process. Multitudes of minors walked in companies to the nursery school 2 as minor boys happily played, joke, chat and horse play on the stony road to nursery school for their filing application. Minors weren`t sure of what program meant as it didn`t mean or associated anything with resettlement process to USA.

Since Socio-Social program workers explained the program to be the started of the minors' resettlement process, Sudanese refugees hadn`t believed it to be a minors resettlement program; eventually, Sudanese elders in the camp mistrusted the program as well as minors doubt the program too. Rumors ran every corners of the camp and speculation angered Sudanese minors' teachers and elders who questioned Socio-Social worker head officers to described socio-social program and how it linked minors' resettlement process. Rumors were generated around in the camp that Socio-Social program was a plan drawn by the diplomacy of president of Sudan, Omar Hassan Bashir and Kenya president Daniel Arap Moi to process minors by this special program that would uplift minors to Khartoum as surrenders of the SPLA children to radical regime government of Khartoum. Socio-Social program was interpreted to be a John Garang`s plan, SPLA leader who organized this Socio-Social program with American government for the purpose of getting minors to USA in order to be recruited and military trained as marines to supported the SPLA army in Southern Sudan. Some rumors speculated Socio-Social program to be another way of minors' headcount or another project carried out by UNHCR on behaves of minors' project of aids or assistance. The motive behind rumors was believed to be propaganda of bad Sudanese refugees who were jealous about minors program of resettlement, bad politics and tribal jealousy contribute to a misleading speculations and bad rumors about minors' resettlement program. Communities' women refused minors resettlement because of the two claims that their own minors` boys  wouldn`t go for resettlement, and another claims was that after all minors left to USA, who could marriage their left behind daughters since civil war has claimed lives of men accept hid minors.

Speculations and different rumors got minors confused as some minors refused photos taking and denied form filing application for the reason of rumors concept. Some minors mistrusted the program and decided to sold their names to others minors whose names hadn`t appeared in the lists. Majority of minors didn`t believed Socio-Social program to be a starting resettlement process due to the concept of false believed and concept that such a huge population of minors wouldn`t be resettled in USA at once time, since resettlement to USA took individual refugees three to five years to process and granted resettlement status in America. Minors who came to back to the camp for the falsified resettlement process got confused and went back to their Kenyan high schools as they didn`t trusted Socio-Social to be of the minors resettlement type. Some minors would confronted socio-social workers and got angered as they abusively talked to Socio-social Kenyan workers. Some minors went back to Sudan where they were doing their business as they didn`t trusted minors resettlement which started with socio-social program.

JVA had categorized minors' process in to three priorities: priority one {P1}, Priority two {P2} and priority three {P3}. P1 was basically underage fosters care minors considered ages range from 12-17 and P2 was the basically overage minors in group cares with age ranged from 18-35. The third priority {P3} was the last process in resettlement for marriage minors and their families, complainants, failed interview minors, and new cases of minors for resettlement. Third priority included resettlement process for caretakers' teachers, accompanied women and accompanied minor girls in community group. The Socio-social program launched interviews in bypassing UNHCR protection units' office by doing units files Bio data sheet application, check card, correspondence names, ages, photo size taking and the process passed to JVA interviews. Bio data application contained the birth place and year which minors entered Kenya as well as full names recorded. JVA started interviewing underage of Foster cares in three parts; personal interview which included confirmation of personal identity on Bio data filed. The secondly interview was pertaining minor`s parents, siblings or relatives questionnaires. The final interview confirmed life history in minors' handwritten paper.

After Socio-Social Bio data filings, JVA interviews, than come final interview with international Naturalization Service {INS}. INS could dropped the case in to the trash if interviewee minor failed INS interview where interviewers were U.S citizens working in Kenya U.S embassy side. Juliana was a director of the Socio-Social program as well as head officer in JVA office, she did met with minors on weekly basis to explains how the new step system work and what should minors do in any step of the resettlement process. Minors zonal meeting was weekly held by Juliana to described and explained key tips to successful interviewed so that no single minor would failed any stage of the interview. Set down quietly and very listenable zonal minors hadn`t no questions to asked after Juliana discussed and elaborated important key points boys should remembered when in interview room with either JVA or INS interviewer. As multitudes zonal minors set down on the rough ground, others stood up and caretaker teachers with Socio-Social Kenya officers set on the few benches under the shaded trees, Juliana spoke to the minors on some questions and responses answers which might lead to successful interview or failed. She spoke to the minors on how to remember their handwritten life history and matching fled history from Sudan to Ethiopia and from Ethiopia back to Sudan and from Sudan to Kenya and than ready to flee to US. Juliana meeting was interpreted by Sudanese interpreters of Arabic, Dinka and even Kiswahili to minors who wouldn`t understood accent of the Kenyan English.

Juliana`s awareness of JVA interview questions such as why do you flee Sudan? What was happening and what caused problem in Sudan? Were the few questions Juliana discussed answers with minors so that they would passed their interview with JVA and INS. Juliana with Sudanese caretakers, interpreters and Kenyan Socio-Social workers had oriented minors for weeks before JVA, INS and IOM process started in the camp. Meetings held from minors zones to groups as Juliana and her Socio-Social program team advocated successful process with minors who definitely ought for US resettlement as their 5th fled called in. All minors in twenty groups had to gather for meetings held in zone 3 several times with Socio Social program teams headed by Juliana and Maker Kur head of the Sudanese minors` teachers. Dr. Livingstone met minors in zone 3 several times to explained how America would looked like and what boys would expect of it as well as assuring minors of their exactly process of their resettlement. In front of the cameras, minors' cries in front of Livingstone and his teams as minors explained described their life history to him. Minors' boys stood in surrounding circles as some set on the rough floor while Livingstone spoke to them in zone 3 minor group 3, each boys asked question and Livingstone answered their questions relating to how long would the process took, and opportunities for schools in America. Livingstone was the heavy figured man who couldn`t stood for two minutes, so he answered one question being asked by meeting minors and set down for a rest of two minutes. He was set on wooden benches as his teams stood up with bags and cameras in use. In my country lives is hard and if you don`t work harder, you wouldn`t survived, he said.

Every morning at eight o'clock, minors went to schools and in the afternoon the went for the process of photo taking and application filing for their Socio Social resettlement process in zone 3 nursery school buildings. Each group had a turn in photo taking as far filling ended in the light dawn where Kenyan photo takers would leave for UNHCR compound closing their work. A big question arises after the Socio Social teams completed minors photo taken and application filed where the numbers of minors estimated for resettlement process was under seven thousand compared to 16, 000 children number arrived Kakuma camp in 1992. The minors' resettlement teams questioned UNHCR office on where did they children went in all these nine years? Where were ten thousand minors resettled in Kakuma camp on arrived date of 1992? UNHCR office hadn`t provided answer than forwarded the question to the head of the minors` teachers, Maker Kur and Maker Thiong, minors` school director. Maker Kur answered the question by taking the team in to minors` group and showed them what amount of ration food they eat, clothes they wears, huts minors sleep in, and living style of no parents. Missing ten thousand minors had fled the camp to join the Southern rebel SPLA; some minors were conscript or mobilized by the SPLA to join SPLA arms. Some went to Kenya for schools and others fled to Uganda, Ethiopia and others refugees camp in east Africa. The minors' lives shown by Maker Kur had convinced minors' resettlement teams' as well proof evidence of minors numbers in answering questions.

Minors resettlement process had delayed after rebel leader John Garang denied minors resettlement in the first time as that aroused tension which wasn't easy between minors resettlement agency as well as minors' rebel leaders of the SPLA. SPLA leaders had refused minors resettlement for the sake of claiming that if minors got resettled in US, there wouldn't be no youth to fought the long civil war. Resettlement agencies wanted to resettle minors for the sake of minors' better life changes and future education. Sudanese elders in refugees camp didn't wanted minors resettlement as they had a believed concept that minors would get lost in the far land country of no culture; furthermore the expected America to be a land of opportunities as well as high crimes. Elders predicted minors to be lost in to America and hardly return to Sudan to bring benefits home after completion of their high education. Delayed of minors resettlement process posted anger in minors as they accused Kenyan socio social workers of delaying process because of Kenyan jealousy thought that largely Sudanese minors will benefits from resettlement to USA. Minors lost trust in Kenyan socio social workers who sold some minors files applications to others youth in the group community who were seeking resettlement. Some of the minors who had taken photos and had their photo sizes attached to their filed applications had experienced headache time as JVA couldn`t find sold applications to unknown Sudanese refugees youths. Missing files and applications was a big issue of quarrels as hundred of minors who lost their files had to filed complains against Kenyan socio social workers, but JVA took in the account minors complains by retaking photos and refilling applications again.

Underage minors started interview with JVA in the main UNHCR compound by mid year of 1999. UNHCR protection office open Field Post offices in each zone and these offices were used by the Ration department officials to deals with refugees lost ration cards and others social issues, but these Field Post offices were used by the JVA to posted minors interview schedules in the camp. Underage minors started looking up their names scheduled for interview on the boards from Field Post 1, 2, 3 and even on Red Cross letters boards. As the JVA interview of the underage minors began in main UNHCR compound; overage minors proceeded in the Home Craft compound in Kakuma town; eventually, many minors started coming back to the camp from their long distance schools or place of residence outside the camp. Minors began hope in resettlement process as JVA started interviewing and the camp began hoping for minors' resettlement as it started to become true at the beginning of the underage minors` interviews.

Under administration of Juliana head of the underage minors' interview and process program in UNHCR compound, underage minors began fresh resettlement interview with JVA scheduled follow up in UNHCR compound. Underage minors checked the posted names board in every hour of the day, although names were posted once in a day as well as in advance of one week before interview day. As the post man stapled scheduled names sheets on the boards, minors would rush to the board as they crumbled over names look up. Minors would used lighted torch to light names board while checking their names at night time. Little boys were stamped down by the tallest and strong minors in pushily names checking on the board. Up to ten to fourteen names of the minors appeared on the board once in one week. Minors who saw their names on the board would jump up and down with full joy as they ran in to their group to inform all friends about scheduled interview. The interview was schedule in one session for the whole day as interview minors had to spend their day in the interview compound. Every morning dawn, scheduled minors would walk to the interview compound by 6:00am as the interview started at 7:30am in UNHCR compound or in Home Craft. Awaited at the gate, minors would look anxious and ambitious as they gazed at the gatekeeper to open the gate for them to entered interview waiting room. Under the waiting shade minors would sited quietly and waited for their names to be called by attendance check-in and interview interpreters for JVA. In the hot burning Sun, interviewed minors would either carried their water and food or force to drink little water in the compound as well as there wasn`t food for them for the whole day of interview. In the lunch break of their interpreters and interviewers, minors' interviewee would remain sited in the interview waited shades without lunch until interviewers came back from Lunch and resume work. Some minors who got some money would also go lunch in to nearby restaurants and they had to hurry back before interview work started or resume. Majority interviewees` minor who got no money for lunch would set there in the sheltered interview shades for the whole day without food, before they would went back to their group after interview and had evening meal.

JVA interview was basically a confirmation of the minors filed resettlement application done by socio social program and questioned were asked by JVA interviewers depending on minors filed application and handwritten life history done by socio social program. There wasn`t a failing interview result for JVA and minors were very happy and felt joys with JVA interview. Sudanese interpreters helped minors understood questions asked by the Kenyan interviewers on how many brothers and sisters do you have? When last and where did you see your parents? When were you born? This was the tough question where few minors provided answer to JVA interviewers, but, Juliana had provided new birth day date to all minors who didn`t know when they were born; every JVA interviewers gave each minors birth day of 01-01 plus image year or the year of birth on the ration card. Right photo size was taken in right position as minors went JVA interview as well as minors went through different JVA interviewers in the same day. It took a whole day for interview of fourteen to twenty minors to complete as the number of the interviewers and interpreters was limited and that limited number of interviewees minors call in at a time. Underage minors went in to the interview room in group as they were considered group of little kids living together without mommy and daddy. Each underage was asked in turn as well as all should pass questions of relationship or friendship links or otherwise failed interview where they would go back to UNHCR to file for complains and got reprocess again for interview with JVA again. Interviewee minors had to passed through three to four interviewers same day.

Some of the underage minors were fostered care in community groups who had forge sisters or joint resettlement process with little girls of their hosted families or felt sympathy to included minors girls who lives with families in to their resettlement process for the sake of resettlement.

In the JVA interview, minors who lost their file applications, names not matched, photos missing, and multiples photos or files for the same person. It was a big headache of frustration as minors fought UNHCR socio social program workers. JVA interview minors who had their files application with photos presents and the ones missing or included some other difficulties like names, photos changed were forwarded back to the UNHCR resettlement department to investigate or adjusted changes or missing filed applications. Some files applications weren`t responded after scheduled and call-in for interview due to many minors took photos and files applications and left for Sudan, went to school or went distance places as resettlement process wasn`t a trusted one in the first time. Unresponded minors files application were decided for photos and names changes as friends of the missing process minors either gave or sold the files application to someone else who would proceed with resettlement process instead of the missing one. Quarrels over names and files application changes has erupted among minors at the stage interview of JVA, minors who had their files, names and resettlement application changed by someone else had to proposed another changes of the application to original owner. All files application were changes by UNHCR resettlement units who allowed changes only after minors head boys authorized and witness changes. Minors' caretakers would witness and signed files application changes before UNHCR retake and refilled application under new minors for resettlement process. So many minors cheated on used of names that would match ration cards, age, names of their own or bought absentees minors` names to process their own resettlement. Some minors sold their own names and used their absentees' friends' names, as well as some minors files more application on their very same names with a thought in mind that any filed application that came first would let them processed to America than the other filed which could delayed process.

Minors sold their absentees friend names and the price in shillings per a name for the resettlement process was rising from Shillings 1500 to 6000 which was from twenty to two hundred Dollars. Minors fought over sold names and whose names were sold as demands for resettlement process was seen as a chance of coming to America by non-minors youths who were running in shopping for minors names on the market for sell in the camp of resettlement.

Group care Minors were fighting resettlement staff about why they put foster care first and in front of them, group care minors went in fight with fostered care minors of being considered special by the staff who chose them for interview first, then the main minors in the group care.

Question of fear and doubt was posted as minors were to confirm acceptation of US selective Services agreement signed in the JVA form, where minors recalled the time first rumor when gossipers talked about SPLA leaders' agreement of uplifting minors to USA for Marine army training. Many minors signed Selective Service form with a brave face of readiness to joint US marine army training program. Michael Alexander, American official and head of INS, told overage minors in crowned morning meeting, "You are not getting process for US marine army training program, this is a false rumor and if you belief it personally, then you conceal your resettlement process". In the hot Sun, Michael would stand in the open heat calling out listed names of the boys for interview. Minors set in the temporary shaded shelters awaited their names to be called for different interviews in the same day.

Every morning, companies of minors scheduled for interviews would walk to Home Craft or UNHCR compound for a day interview. Minors would carry water or food to eat, while the long day interview would require more power to resist hot Sun heat in the burning soil. At the gate, a huge twenty to thirty minors awaited to be check-in as the gatekeepers called their names in, and minors took set in under shaded shelters. There were many Kenyans employed by JVA as interviewers for minors, and minors had to pass several interviews in a day or sometimes three-day interviews separately in order to complete JVA interviews. Michael would write off "no show" signs on those files whose minors hadn`t responded to when calling names out for interview. Minors were very keen not to miss call out names. Eventually, minors wouldn't even go for the water tap outside the gate until lunchtime after workers went lunch.

The Immigration Naturalization Service interview started right after JVA finished up the boys question and answers. Although the INS interview was the hardest and scare one, minors were oriented several times by Juliana, interpreters and teachers on how to pass the interview of INS. INS interview was one of the failed or passed final interviews where America citizens interviewed minors one by one. Each scheduled name posted on the board composed of forty five and more minors scheduled for one-day interviews in the UNHCR compound. INS interview started with overage fostered care minors in the camp, and that has caused conflict between overage group care and overage fostered care minors. Fostered-care minors were considered by resettlement agency as community base characterized in social manners than group minors, so fostered-care minors were process first for INS interviews. Scheduled minors for the INS interview were asked to bring food, water and the right answers to Interview Avenue for a day successful interview. Under trees, minors awaited on benches as they narrated old stories of Pachalla hunger. Each interpreter called a selected minor's name into an interview room where interviewer awaited with a heap of files for interview auditing. Although few minors understood America English, still Sudanese translators were there to facilitate communication between interviewer and interviewee. Kenyan accent sounds crony, and many American interviewers wouldn't clearly understand it.

INS interviewers questioned minor interviewees on questions related to information accumulated on personal filed applications and the problem of prosecution in Sudan. Why do you want to be resettled in the USA? What would you do in the USA? And since few Minors didn`t know why the wanted to come to US and hadn`t the idea of what to do rather than school. Comparison between the minor Bio data files, life history and family background, as well as questioned answers from the JVA interview, where used by the INS interviewer to determine whether either interviewee minor was on the track of knowledge in what he filed in the resettlement application process. Minors who had recited information told by interpreters to minors that the caused of the war in Sudan was related to the religion problems between animist Southern Christians and northern Muslims. Political issues like unbalance power, resources, and racial problems have contributed movement of struggle in Sudan. Minors creamed all information sipped to them by interpreters as answers to INS questioned interviews. Some interpreters helped minors in the interview room to translate wrong-said answers into right-said answers in the ear of the interviewer American, and finally, the minors passed the interview. Many minors failed the INS interview because the fear, scare and being set in a shacking state where nothing would come out of their mouth to answer interviewer questions, or some minors bubbled with uneasiness to elaborate on interviewer questions; eventually, the interviewer quoted them for a failed interview. Minors cried when explaining their life history to the INS interviewer.

Minors were hit by culture shock when American interviewers girls behaved American in the UNHCR compound where minors set waited for an interview. How interviewer American girls dressed was out of the minor's daily view as well, and American girls smoke a lot outside the shrub compound fences, which minors considered out of women's orders to smoke. Interviewers of the American type had minors` minds confused on how they hold pen and write in the opposite ways. Talking was awesome, and difficult to understand the American English accent as well, and many girls dressed in high heel shoes and tied jeans that were out of minors` mind of, similar signs of culture. Minors set under trees on awaited benches as they saw interviewers' American girls walking in and out of the interview office. Minors began murmuring and gossiping words. They discussed how American girls dressed up and the hurting effect that could be caused when reached the land of such women dressing in tied jeans with body part pointed outside for strangers view.

Inside the compound, minors hadn`t to used full latrine and an untidy smell of craps. Few minors would urinate outside, hidden in Peggu, the short shrubs that made fences under the tallest trees. Since the water tap wouldn`t work, minors drank their carried water or stayed without drinking water for some hours on the interview day. Individual minors who came out of the interview room rushed to and were surrounded by other minors who wanted to enquire sipped information on the questions asked by the interviewer so that they readily interviewed minors would prepared and creamed asked questions with answers in order to pass interview.

Minors were told lastly by the interviewer when to expect result letter of failing or passing interview from Nairobi INS main office. Minors stopped taking their Kenya Certification of Secondary Education or Kenya Certification Primary Education for the seek INS interviews as many American interviewers told minors to tackle their interview for passed resettlement process than their national examinations for there are more examinations to take in the USA. Some minors wouldn`t want to go for JVA or INS interview as national examination day collided with resettlement interview, which was the hardest choice to have minors choose from missing one and getting one. American INS officials told minors, "you have thousands of examinations waiting for you to take in America, so don`t worry about those national examinations." Some minors weren`t convinced enough as they chose to miss interviews and set for national examines guarded by Kenyan policemen. Those minors who had missed resettlement interviews had their files sent back to the UNHCR office or files signed off NO Show and kept for the last complain day in the UNHCR office.

After every three weeks, minors received their approved or disapproved letters from INS Nairobi headquarters. Minors check their names on the Field Post boards, and scheduled names listed for letter collection should be stapled up on the boards. In the evening, minors would crowd Field Post 4 in awaiting UNHCR officials to bring letters out of the compound to Field Post 4; minors set on the stones, benches or on the floor as they chatted, laughed, feared faces, and some just quieted as well as most anxious to see the result of failed or passed resettlement interview. As UNHCR officials were seen coming, minors rushed to the door of the small iron sheet roof building, and they roughly lined up in order to receive their letters. Letters got called out by names as each called minor rushed and went in to through a narrowed way in multitudes to receive a letter in crowded door space. Unsealed open letters received by each minor as minors crowded to see what he got failed or passed. Minors turned away when they saw no picture on right front of the open letter that, mean they failed without reading the whole letter, and when spotted a picture on the letter that meant pass, and majority of minors laughs as they smiled away. Minor lookers turned away, grooming and murmuring when they saw failed letter in the hand of their colleague. Boys who received the failed letter were mock and made felt, shamed and got embarrassed for failing simple interview with INS. Failures wouldn't be shocked and wouldn't even seem not to be talking to anybody as they were ashamed, uneasy, sad and felt sick for failing interviews where failures must go back to UNHCR to restart resettlement process over again.

Many underage minors failed interviews because when they join themselves from one family and later when each individual is interviewed separately, the information gathered would be different, and eventually, they failed the interviews. Failed underage got their files sent back to the UNHCR office to restart the resettlement process again. Minors who had received passing letters from INS would celebrate their victory by drinking too much local liquor as they passed by Ethiopian restaurants to eat Ijera and drink little Taij and *chang*'a liquor. Minors who passed INS interviews with approved letters were congratulated by their colleagues, friends, relatives and caretakers in their respective groups. Minors celebrate day of the INS approval letter by drinking too much liquor until they sleep outside their huts for the sake of happy madness. Some minors' join their community group to participate in traditional dance as well as weekend called in.

It was a pleasure for American citizens who were working with resettlement agencies in the camp to watch camp traditional dances on weekends as the entire camp of Sudanese refugees danced with many custom dance shows in the camp dancing fields. Minors who had passed the INS interview and received their passing envelopes were then looking forwards to facing another screening part of the resettlement process, which was the passing medical test and check-up.

In the evening Sun rest, American workers would get into UNHCR cars and hit the camp to watch traditional dances; they came with their cameras, camcorders and sound recorders to take information from the dancing field. American workers enjoy daily Sunrise and Sunset as they walked on foot around the compound to see and have fun meeting refugees minors who they chat with in their groups. American interviewers always gasp the fresh evening air by visiting minors in their evening groups, visitors took pictures of minors cooked food, inside their huts and how they set together dining on one dish of ugali and bean soup. Watching dancers of the community traditional drama was fascinating to American workers who frequently visited the camp on weekends to watched traditional dancers who they took videos and photos. Nuer young men jumped up and down with traditional made shields and spears, Dinka Agar jumped high and down, as well as Gogrial Dinka ran in dancing circles with beating drum African rhythms, which African-American workers got closer to take closer pictures as they loved to watch men dancers in halved way naked, but underpants was on in the refugee camp fun weekends.

Another hardest passing or failing examination on the way of the resettlement process was minors passed the INS interview with the joy of receiving approval letters from the Nairobi INS regional office. The fears and anxiety of the medical examination weren`t felt by those minors who hadn`t slept with no women, but the fears and frustration were in the face of those minors who might have slept with women one or more times. Minors made jokes among themselves about who got aids and syphilis to surrender himself before the detective test of IOM. International Organization for Immigration {IOM} was servicing the fourth position in minors' resettlement process. IOM was responsible for minors' medical tests, check-ups, medical examinations, minors' culture orientation, treatments, patient counseling, vaccination, and medicine provision to minors during the resettlement process. IOM hadn`t ended its work in the camp but served as a guardian or pathfinder to minors in multiple airports where minors connected their flights to their destination, USA home. In the first time history of the camp to build and set up resettlement medical check clinics, IOM did build one clinic in the camp used for minors' resettlement medical examinations only as far Goal Medical Check clinic in Nairobi used by the camp refugees resettlement agency was put off by IOM for minors special process of medical check and examinations. IOM medical clinic was built and equipped with all medical test and examination labs in no time as the minors process was speeding in less time by early 2000.

Temporary wooden constructed clinic buildings with many rooms divided by curtains and long halves of cut clothes. The X-ray compartment was powered by a generator in the backyard of Ethiopia refugees' community. Barbed wired fence was rounded to the clinic with a wooden gate. In the same fenced IRC clinic of zone five where, refugee patients gathered in the morning as they made lined up in waiting for medical prescriptions. IOM clinic doctors, nurses, workers, and assistants were all hired by Kenyans and a few Somalis refugee women who were helping minors in all medical examinations. Blood tests, stool, and urine examination equipments were brought in by evening big truck and loaded into a temporary wooden clinic. The only cemented floor was the concrete where the wooden trailers were set, and apart from that, everywhere else was a dust of red soil where refugees stamped on and walked into wooden floors stained with black dusts.

Minor application files just kept flowing from Socio-Social program Bio-data files to JVA interviews to INS interviews and to the IOM medical process. IOM officials received approval files ready for medical checks and examinations from the INS office in the UNHCR compound. IOM medical check names scheduled were stapled up on the board in all Field Posts as well as in minors' accessible areas to spot their scheduled names for medical examinations. Like a JVA or INS interview that took three to four days to process, an IOM medical check took four days before minors under testing got the result positive or negative for AIDS, syphilis, STDs, or other major examination diseases. On day 1, scheduled minors would hit the clinic on a cool morning around 6:45 am. The head of the nurses would started to work at 7:45 am in evening morning and evening. Small stones on the stony road pained minors barefoot as they walked chili cool road to zone five IOM medical clinics. As the hostile Sun showed out its red teeth, minors were already awaited as they set on stones, a few benches, on the floor as well as some were standing in quiet conversation and chili voices. Doctors, nurses, and medical workers got down on the UNHCR vehicle, minors rushed into the main clinic door to form unorganized lines. Each minor name on the schedule list was called and checked in as nurses started work as each minor was called in for sample tests as well as examination.

Minors were shivering in the cool conditioning rooms as they passed different rooms in cool air conditioning minors had never felt before. Blood was drawn, check-ups and sample tests taken, but many minors were found with less blood in the veins as well as with low or high blood pressure. Many minors were found with anemia and, diabetes and other unknown diseases. Minors had their urines taken, stool taken and saliva taken for AIDS, STDs and other disease tests. Some minors returned to their group with very weak moves since one string of the blood sample taken was enough to sicken them.

On the second day, minors had overheard rumors that IOM nurses undressed minors naked so that they could check their physical bodies very well. Some minors believed rumors that Kenyan women nurses undressed minors for physical body check-ups. As minors hit the clinic again for the second time, as each minor got called in by the nurse, some just entered the room and started undressing by removing pants, underpants, and other clothes. Knowledgeable nurse would advise the undressed minor to put on his clothes again as instructed on the second-day clinic visitation, which was a weight scale, vision test, height measure, hearing test, and X-ray examination of the heart, lung, and other parts components of the chess. The heavyweight minor was from 51 kilos, which was 135-162 pounds, and the tallest one was from 6:00 to 7:50 height. Eyesight was tested by written letters on the far wall in different appearances, and the vision candidate minor was asked to tell what number or letter the nurse pointed at. Many minors didn`t pass vision or eyesight tests because they messed up the arranged Key letters shown by the nurse. The nurse filed all medical information as the testing and physical examination took place in the clinic. Some minors had to repeat X-ray tests because the X-ray machine wasn`t that powerful to show the minor heart and lungs in good health as the X-ray didn`t clear ribs and other test chess inside contents.

On the third day, minors returned as the fears and frustration overshadowed minors who had sex before. Test for sexually transmitted diseases was a frustration over the failure of the resettlement process. The third day was the result collection day, and minors set there in an anxious and uneasy mood, waiting for the given result paper on the diseases tested. Looking into the resulting paper, a few minors found syphilis, gonorrhea, and herpes infections, as well as many minors affected by low eyesight caused by low-diet food and some other conjunctivitis. Many minors had big scars on their knees, legs, and forehead; these scars were caused by a jungle-lived lifestyle where minors struggled with crocodiles, lions, hyenas, and thorny. Kenyan nurses surprisingly asked the minors why their bodies were full of many scares. Since minors knew that Kenyans didn't know their epic life history, minors wouldn't explain that a lot more than in three words; crocodiles, thorny, and cultural attacks. Minors` legs were curves of dried wounds full of multiple scares, and these scares were caused by the long bushes that lived the struggle. Some minors found the result to be repeated or had a repeated X-ray test since a healthy heart wasn't shown in the X-ray printout carbon paper. Minors' scared cool room where X-ray machine sheltered from the hot Sun. Minors removed their t-shirt so that their chess was placed on the cool machine, and body relaxed so that the machine could take an X-ray of the heart and its side contents.

As minors collect their results on the third day of the IOM medical screening, many boys weren't found surprised in their printout result slip that they were negative for STDs, AIDs, and Asthma, but few minors got either syphilis, gonorrhea, herpes, TBs, Typhoid and heart diseases. Some minors' results indicated medical attention to the lungs or liver serious damage because of too much hot liquor to drink and smoking too much of unpurified big tobacco. Many minors have lost eyesight as a result of lacking vitamins, which eventually causes poor vision. Positive-tested minors were sent to the Kakuma mission or refugee hospital for STD treatment, typhoid medicine, or chronic hunger or trauma was also treated there. The abroad resettlement was meant for the group minors, so resettlement agencies chose not to leave any minor behind in the camp, so minors' chronic diseases weren't a big deal that could block any minor from being resettled to the USA, except those minors with AIDs were the one who completely failed resettlement under the medication rejection. AIDS-diagnosed minors were isolated for treatment in refugee AIDs centers as their resettlement cases were suspended. Minors whose names appeared on the medication rejection list were shamed and felt sorry for, and these minors felt self-hatred and trauma stress caused to nearly or committed suicide.

The fourth IOM appointment day was servicing minors for Medical Orientation day, where minors went both morning and evening attending medical orientation. One hundred and fifty minors who spotted their names on the Field Post board took a barefoot walk to the IOM medical center. As minors gathered outside at the front of the clinic building, they talked about how America`s dream and their dreams, but medical orientation was just about telling minors how sexually transmitted diseases, including AIDS, enter human blood. One hundred and fifty minors would fit three classrooms within the clinic or Home Craft center, where sited minor boys quietly listened to Kenya nurses who lectured in orienting minors` minds away from sexual activities. Minors watched video taps of the AIDS-affected patients and STDs-affected patients, as well as how STDs got transmitted to healthy people just like minors.

Minors felt shy as they had never got exposed to such STD porn where affected private parts of the patients were revealed on the disease control of the video taps porn for STDs awareness and control of sexual refrains. Some minors didn`t want to eat after they returned home from medical orientation class, claiming that what they saw was nasty and out of Dinka culture. It was another culture shock for minors who never saw STDS-affected vagina pictures or videos of penis surrounded by red wounds. Some minors called the IOM medical orientation video a "bad video tap" because of private parts being exposed. Fostering care minors would stay away from women after watching video in the IOM medical center. Facilitators and counselors Kenyan women explained and used interpretive lectures to orient minors as video tap was meant for PowerPoint presentation.

Minor girls acted very shy or looked away more than minor boys do, special when trying to physically putting on practicing condoms, as well as girls got embarrassed by handling a condom or worded of carrying a condom. Minors' girls got to watch the STDs infections video tap in their own medical classroom. Many minor girls didn't want to watch video, as some girls would leave the classroom and go outside to escape what they called pornography sexual orientation classroom. Some girls would remain sat on the wooden bench with their heads bent down or covered their eyes with ten transparent fingers while the video tap played affected the private parts of the patients. Girls spatter a mouthful of saliva several times as well as said some sorry words to show strike against the video tap.

Minors were taught by Kenyan nurses women on how to properly wear and use condoms in times of tough sex. Medical orientation hours ended with condom distribution to minors in orientation classrooms. Each boy had to carry a bundle of condoms home, just like another day of ration distribution that turned into a condom distribution day. Although minors didn`t have girlfriends or whom to have sex with, condoms were left in *makuti* huts as they finally got flown to the U.S. Minors returned from medical orientation day was full of stories where minors waited for medical orientation would attentively listen to instructors as well as some minors prepared to watched HIV/AIDS affected videotapes ahead of the scheduled day.

The fifth day of the IOM appointment was scheduled as minors browsed their names again on the Field Post board and got ready for another orientation. After Medical Orientation, minors had to attend three consecutive days of Culture Orientation, where minors didn`t rest from every morning and an evening course in hot Sunrise to Sunset until the end of the three days of Cultural Orientation. Every batch of the culture orientation was composed of ninety to hundred and some minors ready for culture orientation for three days before they hit their flight date and flew to America. Culture Orientation was the only process stage where minors tasted soda or water given by IOM while taking a thirty-minute break or lunchtime. Every classroom for Orientation was filled with up to 50-96 minors, congested, where boys sat closely next to each other on the congested wooden benches laid in the trailer clinic with classrooms. The first day of culture orientation started fresh in the early morning as the gathered minors walked in lines into the wooden trailer classrooms. They stated minors had one by one received written handbooks with U.S. flag color back covers and the handbook names mentioned "Welcome to America." each minor got his handbook, IOM orientation package of written papers, as well as many other junks for the first-day orientation. The classroom was equipped with a small marker blackboard with lecturer space of lecturing. The classroom was provided with one video tap player to show video in aiding lectures. Lecturers were Kenyan, Sudanese, Ethiopian, or Somali refugees who were employed by IOM, and although we had American facilitators employed by INS.

Daniel Lek, with other former minors, went into the camp through an employment contract with INS to help minors in a culture orientation course. Daniel Lek left Kakuma refugee camp, where he lived as one of the minors. He did succeed in resettlement proceeds and came to the U.S. in 1995, and he came back to Kakuma in 2000 to help his comrade minors in their resettlement. Daniel's empathy with minors in his facilitating class that: "I came back to help you because I belong to our minors red army group, not because of contracted job or money." Daniel cautioned his fellow minors that living in America was very hard, and if you didn't work hard, life would be in your neck, and you would hit the street. Quietly and attentively, the minors were listening to Daniel as he narrated stories of former minors' lives in the U.S. Sudanese who were homeless. Daniel kept informing minors about how he gave his living room to homeless Sudanese boys who are homeless in N. Dakota State because they were jobless.

Each minor in the class listened to Daniel as well, and minors beat their chess and swore that none of them would be homeless in the land of opportunities. Daniel proudly showed his three-year degree in computer to his class minors, and minors gazed at it as Daniel told them that he got better job after his graduation. After three hours of culture lectures, a class of minors would take a thirty-minute break, and after another three hours, they took a lunch of soda. Minors grabbed one small bottle of soda for a lunch, but some minors just began a taste of sparking soda drink for lunch. Some minors who got little money would go to Ethiopian restaurants in order to eat Ijera for lunch as facilitators went for lunch in the UNHCR compound. Minors who got no food or money would drink water for the whole day.

The first day started with a big question of what AMERICA is. Who is living in America? Such big questions were broken down into a short history of America's political scale, American cultures of diversity, and why I keenly love to go to America. Answers provided by minors when the facilitator asked the class what America is were varied. Minors raised their right hand up, "America is the land situated in North America lived by Red Indians." "America is the land of opportunities offered by American to refugees like us." "America is a country of States situated in the continent of Northern America." "America is a country of white and black people who rule the world with their richness," so many answers were provided by minors in answering what America is. Minors were culturally oriented not to be shock in America when they saw half-naked dressing of American women`s styles or when they saw lovers kissing in the public places. Minors were told that it was normal to see girls in tied jeans or exposing parts of their bodies in short dressing. Approaching women for relationship and dating issues in cultural America as well as neighbor's related issues. Facilitators interpreted and explained what the USA is to minors who got little knowledge of America through studies at school, movies watched, and rumors news about America and how minors imagine America to be on their inside minds.

On the second day, minors come back to the culture orientation clinic to dig deep into life in America, school, medical, jobs, and a newfound home in America. Minors were amazed by the explanation of wages and spending as some minors raised so many hands-on questions about wage payments as well as school issues related to tuition questions as they affected free education as they did in Kenya under NGOs and LWF. Minors were oriented not to shock themselves when they lost job after job or at the gaps months of job searches as well as disaster of broke loom in when no money to pay bills they shouldn`t live on cookies. But, some minors have thrown questions on the refuges concept of the Green Card, which refugees believed to be a card carried and used by jobless individuals as an identity to receive free food and assistance at every end of every month. It was cleared to minors when American facilitators described Green Card as the permanent card that identified immigrants with permanent residency status before they become citizens of America. Minors clarified issues like everything in America is free as well as America is free things land where you get everything in abundance as well as full of needs at cheaper cost.

On the third day, minors returned with tired faces and hungry mode of when to finish orientation so as to see their names for flight dates. The third day was all about security and law enforcement in America, as well as safety was concerns. Minors were laughing as they touched and exchanged balls of ice bar in their hands while on their physical weather change culture orientation day. Dialing 911 was cleared out for fire, ambulance, and police rescues. Minors cleared their voices in confirming high rates of gangsters and armed crimes in America as the concept of U.S crime actions movies watched in the camp raises big questions in the culture orientation class. Still, even after facilitators explained questions to doubtful minors, some minors left the graduated culture orientation class with concept that medical and prescription are free in America. One could just call 911, and an ambulance could get the patient to the hospital, get treated, and get home well and pay nothing in the end. Driving was a big area of orientation empathized when minors

Sudanese Americans were taken as examples to minors on how two people would drive the same car, one a driver who pushed his foot on the accelerator and brake as well as one driver looking and watching out the direction where the car drive to. Many accidents were caused by Sudanese Americans drunk and driving, bad driving, or sleeping.

Since three full days was a hell of a daily walk to the clinic for culture orientation, eventually than came the final evening day as the group graduated on the evening of the third day of culture orientation. Outside the orientation by the wooden trailer clinic, English filmmaker Arthur from England was interviewing number of minors as they dialogued their life history in the description as well as filmmaker video and camera their speeches of word and sound. All classes of the orientation in a batch were gathered in the main big hall building inside the trailer clinic, where video taps were shown to underage minors or Sudanese Americans who were orientors to minors. The tap video was played about minors already in the USA as they talked about their first experiences in the U.S. as their assistance and lives were concerns. The head of the U.S INS, Mr. Sasha, all facilitators, and JVA officials stood at the front as they talked about issues related to minors' immigration. The graduating batch of culture orientation minors set on a few benches as some stood up in the mid of the last meeting with their facilitators in the IOM clinic. Each minor was called to the front to respectfully receive a certificate of training completion on IOM culture Orientation. Minors clapped their hands as they called names and walked forward to receive his certificate of training achievement as they shook hands with the INS head officer. Minors were shown books on the GED, SAT, GRE, and other books, which they loved to see ahead in preparation for the school where they wished to enroll as soon as they stepped down on American soil. Education was the key point of minors' number one hope of coming to America.

Minors were called one by one into the next room, where IOM officials handed out flight scheduled dates and some other flight packages. Minors smile and laugh inside their heart as their lips and mouths remain closed. When smiling, Kenyan IOM officials handed each of them a flight date and the final State of residence. Minors were very happy at the end of the culture orientation day, which was accompanied by the handed-out scheduled flight date and address of the final resident, but even though it seemed that minors weren't smiling or showing signs of happiness at all, as the fifth fled began it moment in minors next fled. Minors took pictures with their facilitators as the orientation class ended. American facilitators had each of them join with minors who appeared to bear his home State address; the facilitator would give boys money, converse with them, or escort them on the way to their group. Minors came to their respective groups as the hot Sun ran down on the north side. The minors were excited but with no smiles or laughs as they narrated final-day stories to their friends, families, and relatives. Minors wouldn`t read State names, addresses of final residents, or State agency telephone numbers to their close friends or to fostered family members. Some minors wouldn`t want to talk as they felt heavy hearts and liked to sleep after they heard of their next fled to flight date. Some minors reached out to their group and spread good news to their friends and fostered families, as the flight date was exciting.

The International Organization for Migration (IOM) didn`t just end its work in Kakuma camp but prepared Minors in the camp and guided them all the way to their destinations in the U.S. IOM as Minor's pathfinders in cities of their flight connections to the U.S, and city hit minors on their connected ways. IOM cleared out the stony airport of Kakuma town, preparing to uplift minors from the camp as their process completed to flight. Stony airport of Kakuma was fenced and expanded, controllers set, and big stones rolled to the edge of the airstrip. Minors who passed the INS interview, got approved, passed the medical test as well, and underwent culture orientation was set ready ahead of their flight to the U.S. Underage minors were prepared and ready to go as their process was completed.

Kakuma Stony airport was ready with a connection of a

small flight from Kakuma camp to Nairobi Kenya local airport. On the 5th of Nine months of 2000, the first underage minors' flight hit the stony airstrip of Kakuma, as the first group of fifteen underage minors was scheduled to hit the dusty sky of Kakuma in flying to Nairobi as their first-way city on the way to the U.S. The first group of underage spotted their names on the Field Post board, and they were shocked by the news of the flight date. The news spread to the camp as the minors' resettlement process was closed to recall for reality, but not until some Sudanese refugees promised to leave underage minors to call home after they landed down or when on the soil of the United States of America so that Sudanese would believe minors' resettlement was for real.

The graduated classes of underage minors from their Culture Orientation course of three days were set ready for the flight date and their destination's new home address in their hands. The next job of IOM was to lead the way and get Cultural Orientated minors on the flight aboard to their U.S final destinations. The first group of underage minors was blessed by their community elders, had their party for departure celebration elders' advice, and had prepared for a long journey. There was a lot of party music heard everywhere in the camp; huge nightly loud Congo music hit the camp in every group who got one minor flight scheduled, there was a bye ceremony of food and drink for the leaving minor. Underage minors whose names appeared on the flight scheduled board of Field Post would be rushed to their group after spotting names and started dancing to inform their friends, colleagues, and relatives of the departure date and time.

Underage and Fostered care minors in the community group care were set down by the community elders for advice that America is not a room to go for drinking, fighting, stealing, idleness, or a bar for a luxurious life of planning nothing, but America is a land to grow mature as you be welcome to make us grow. The departing Minors' friends or relatives contributed some shillings to purchase goats, onions, flour, oil, lentils, and other edible food for the party as friends and relatives gathered in small huts or outside to enjoy eating Kasira in soup, Sudanese food styles for occasional celebration for minors' departure. In the evening meeting, where community group elders gathered and sat outside in a circle, sheltered from the red Sundown heat, departure minor (s) would be called at the front for introduction and asked to sit while elders took turned in advising departing minors. Departing minors were advised on four very important areas as strong advice comments by the meeting community elders. Minors were advised on how to fight and defeat war against living hardship life in America. Do not forget your lost parents, siblings, and relatives whom you have never seen for a decade of loss, elders cautioned minors not to forget their motherland by not coming back after finishing their education. Finally, elders seriously cautioned minors not to give up on education.

Sudanese elders were very concerned about minors long lost. Minors were advised by elders to never drink liquor, never sleep with prostitutes, and never stop working harder, as well as to never get lost in America without coming back to their motherland. Church elders, members, and pastors prayed for leaving minors as well as advised them to never forget their God, who brought them out of the darkness and wildness of loss into to land of America. In the night, there came a big party on the moonless or lightless night. A few girls and many boys gathered or sited on long school benches for the party. Some minors would drink themselves to death as soon as they spotted their names for flight dates. Some minors claimed to say bye to hot, unpurified local liquor by drinking themselves to death before the next day of the flight. Underage girls were cautioned in tough advice by elderly women for the whole night before the morning of the next day's flight. Underage girls minors were advised and cautioned on their women's position of living life in a foreign country of exotic culture.

Few minor girls were advised not to have sex before marriage, to control themselves, stay in touch with family, study hard for higher education, not to Americanize away their own mother culture as well, and not to make any babies before marriage. Sudanese elders were very concerned about minors getting in to long lost that they wouldn`t come back to Sudan. Minors` teachers' have advised minors not to forget to come back and find their lost families in the primitives' villages where they left them in the 1980s. Minors` teachers were very concerned about minors` future of education, teachers strongly advised minors to carry out an education as the only tool that could liberate southern Sudan from current backwardness.

Minors were advised that America is the land of opportunities, inclusive of education, food, liquor, crimes, racism, jobs, and many temptations for failure. In the ceremony advice meeting, minors recorded full taps for elders' soundtrack advice and took camera pictures of their elders as well as their friends and relatives. Community performed a traditional dance in the evening to mark the happy departure day of minors. Nightly parties would disco until morning, as few communities' girls shared dancing with boys. On a cold night with the very dim light of the Tilley lamp borrowed by minors from school used for reading in the night, the dominated Congolese Ndombolo music cracked the ears of camp night sleepers. Tap player machine was rented from a few individuals who owned musical tap players.

Group care minors would go into community groups in order to ask girls` parents for their daughters' permission for marriage or so that girls would join them in the nightly disco party. Some mothers would allow their daughters to be elderly minors whom they trusted to take responsibilities for their parting daughters. Some mother wouldn`t permit their daughters to go to minors' parties for fear that their daughters would be spoiled by boys at the nightly party. The nightly party started at 9:00 pm or 10:00 pm, and it would party till morning time. Disco parties were overcrowded and congested as there were not enough space avenues for the accommodation of the huge number of minors and their refugee youths who joined the party. Minors stood up in the backyard of the circle benches where a few minors and elderly youths sat. Very few community group girls would dance with minors in turn of each music soundtrack tap. Sometimes, minors or youth fought over girls in the case of girls who didn`t want to share dancing with each boys for the sake of fair dance sharing.

In the case of the minors in the group care who hadn`t money to do party or hadn`t elders to advise them leaving minors just it happened likely to be underage and Fostered care minors. Within group care minors, there were elders minors who set down with leaving minors for advice, or else group care minors advice themselves as they set in the circle of taking turns giving advice to the quiet, listenable departing minor (s). Some of the group care minors would contribute money for the party but found no girls to party with them. Some minors would gather and party in their group care without worrying about partying with girls. Sitting in one hut for advice, a team of elderly minors acts as the union of minors in advising departing minors on important life issues of living in America as well as education is concerned. After the advice meeting and party celebration night, departing minors would chat and happily laugh and joke, leaving behind friends, colleagues, or relatives where they joke about sending us America`s dollar.

The party went on until the departing minors pulled their handbags out and hit the way to the UNHCR compound, where the last check-in process would be done before the flight to the Stony airport of Kakuma. Drunk to death, minors wouldn`t wake up as they slept in the disco avenue.

Departing minors wouldn`t sleep the night before their morning departure. Minors would get busy at the last minute before the following departure day by settling their debts, distributing properties, and giving away some other belongings, including their hut, bed, clothes, food, or other things being given away to the group of friends, colleagues or relatives who gathered around their lovely minor(s). Distributing belongings to a gathering of friends, colleagues, or relatives was a face fight as many underaged or fostered cared minors faced tough arguments on whom to give each piece of second-hand property. Minors who owned small businesses would take the money and put it in their pocket, give it away, or buy a lot of expensive belongings like hand cameras, few clothes, or shoes. Since refugees believed that going to the U.S. meant going into richness, so you did not need even a clothes or little money to carry with them. So minors used their small business money to help some of their close friends, relatives, or colleagues as some other small minor businesses like kiosk shops, restaurants, rental bicycles, or chicken centre were given away by owners' minors to their partners, friends, or relatives in the camp. Minors who got money before their departure used the money to conduct a big party for themselves or give away money to a girl family whom they love. Some minors invest their small business money into a new love relationship with a girl`s parents and the girl who they love.

2.   **5th Fled to Heaven of Paradiso: To Usa, Uk and Australia Lost Boys Resettlement.**

It was a right time when minors looked up and saw a change in the atmosphere, and the cause made minors to predict how close the next fled was. Kakuma refugees' camp was full of toxins of poisons after nine years of minors' toughest hardship life struggle. It's started raining with dust and bombed by dried stone particles from dark, cloudy, and a dusty sky as the tornado of Turkana district hit high in the year of Sudanese refugees' punishment. The Sun rays intensity hit the ground extremely hot at one hundred fifty degree centigrade. As that extreme weather would have left thousands of Americans dead if it would have to happen here. It was at the right time when minors predicted their 5th fled away from Kakuma refugees' camp after hard-life struggle had hammered minors since the camp resettlement timeline in 1992-2005. Minors yawned for a change through the next 5th fled from somewhere to nowhere. Minors yawned in hardened or black days of no ration as food was hardly reaching the end of the next ration day. Little survived on one meal or no meal a day as finished food ration had cut meals between the end and the next distribution food days. Their stomachs roar like a hungry lioness, and hunger tears fall inside their heart. Food was diminished to two bowls of wheat flour, one bowl of corn, one cup of lentils, half a cup of oil, a spoonful of salt and a spoonful of sugar per individual minor for two weeks. Minors joined this little amount of ration to dintogether, but still, they ran out of food before the next ration distribution. Weaken minors were ready for the next predicted fled for relief since the camp was very harsh in supporting minors' long-trauma lives. Minors were waiting with their small handbags and their luggage packed to hit the road for the 5th fled to unknown destination.

It was a right time for minors to predict the next 5th fled after the camp life was evaluated and diagnosed with limitation points of rations food and drinking water that ran limit from 40 liters to 20 liters and from 20 liters to less than 10 liters per individual day used. Camp water tanks and pipes got old unclean, as well as water taps were limited in use since camp refugees' population increased to ninety thousand. Minors were thirsty and dying of thirst as UNHCR compound shut its ears to too many refugee complaints. Each minor was given a mandatory question of choice to either drink or take a bath. If a minor chose to drink, he wouldn't take a shower, or if he drank, he wouldn't take a bath. Drinking, cooking, washing, and bathing water was limited to the optional use of choice where minors thought about a mandatory next flee in the choice reason for water use limitation as well as food problems in the refugees' camp.

Minors were ready for the 5th fled as the camp weather was getting hot, hot and hot. The natural Sun of the universe was even angrier on Minors as it got extremely hot and began to be a sign of significant assigned punishment to punished homeless refugees in the camp. Rain just rained on refugees` minors since their huts were ruined top opened with a very old structure that collapsed and fell as. Many Minors got killed by the collapsing huts. If in case a very slight wind in the windiest camp of Kakuma, minors` huts collapse, and minor residents die and are taken to zone nine for burials. Minors were no longer protected by their shelters or huts since old huts were just a hill of ants that could fall easily at any time, minors were cold at the night and got fried up on the hot day. Minors got rained on rainy days as well as got wind dusted on the windy day of dusts tornado Kakuma refugees' camp. Schools were closed and classes cancelled on the rainy, windy, or hot days, but Kakuma remained intense in terms of weather changes, or it's extreme climatic effect. Minors were ready for the 5th fled since the weather was a killing matter to be dodged by fleeing to an unknown destination. Bad weather was traumatizing minors in Kakuma camp as minors awaited their next fled after nine years of torment in camp residency.

It was the best time to fled the ragging camp situation since the minors number reduced from 16,000 in the 1992 food census delimited to 7,000 minors by the 2001 resettlement census due to struggling issues of hardened ration days, water of two choices, bad weather, and never less, cutting off minors from SPLA, children organizations, and getting no assistance from any source under any refugees` minors assistance, all these factors reduce minors camp population to less than seven thousands. Minors weren`t getting any help from any source of children assistance as they used to, and since they were cut off from SPLM assistance, Radda Barner weaned them, and UNICEF wasn`t even closed to them, but UNCHR was for refugees in general regardless of minors, women or old men all were equalized on the same cup of ration to shared for just survival, minors faced tragically life in the camp. Minors used to be fed and clothes by the SPLA with material things captured at the war zones of southern Sudan frontlines, as well as secured by the strong SPLA soldiers and armed teachers before they got to Kakuma refugee camp. It was time for minors to seek 5th fled country of asylum besides Kenya since the struggle for nine years hadn`t limited edge or reset time down to end hardship refugee life. Out of 16,000, minors had already fled Kakuma camp to unknown destination places of refuge beside Kakuma camp. Some minors fled back to SPLA-liberated areas, to South Africa, and many to various towns in Kenya. The 7,000 minors were patiently awaited unknown dates next 5th fled with their handbag packed and ready to leave on fleeing at any time of the day or night.

Issue of insecurity in non-secured refugees camp of Kakuma has paved the road for minors long thought of fleeing the camp for the 5th time in their history of fleeing. Armed Turkana militiamen shot dead refugee minors in the day or at night, looted minors` shops, snatched cooking food, beaten up minors in the stream as well as Turkana young men stole minors` belongings while minors went to school. Tribal fighting in the camp has disrupted minors' peace of learning and security of safety, as many minors were jailed by Kenyan policemen after many cycles of Sudanese tribal clashes between tribal communities. Fighting between Dinka Bor vs. Bhar el ghazel, Nuer and Jur, as well as fighting between Sudanese with Somalia, Ethiopian refugees or Turkana young men who shut death nightly refugees, was a gravy problem that added depression in minors' peaceful life. The camp was a poisonous place resided by wrong refugees from across troubled parts of Africa as refugees were gathered in the camp. It was a time for hundreds of minors in the Kenyan jails to be released and hit the fleeing way to somewhere for the safety of a peaceful learning environment for harmony and a better little, easier life.

Issue of outgrown jobs and independent business for minors was unfitting issue in the camp. Majority of minors completed primary school with Kenya Certificate of Primary Education (KCPE) in hand, as well as majority of minors, completed their Kenya Certificate of Secondary Education (KCSE) with a handful of Technical training Certificates from Trade schools in the camp. There wasn`t a university or college in Kakuma refugees camp except one corresponding long-distance learning facility built in the camp, and it was named as University of South Africa. Graduates` minors from Kakuma Refugee, Napata and Bor Town secondary schools were looking forward somewhere to flee to where they could find universities and colleges so that they could pursue their further education in high learning country of asylum. Minors in less paid jobs were predicting somewhere to flee to find jobs that could equalize their experience, as well as minors in business were hoping for the next 5th fled to where they could make a lot of money rather than little earn profit on small struggling businesses. Minors, who were jobless since when they were born, were hoping for the next journey, fleeing the camp to somewhere where they could find their first-lifetime job. Walletless minors looking ahead, fleeing somewhere where they could turn UNHCR ration card ID into town-registered resident ID.

Issue of God's mission for minors had caused minors` 5<sup>th</sup> fled to the U.S. since refugee camp was full of satanic works, high traffic of temptation, minors` degrading faith in God, minors` idolatry work of dating, adultery, thievery and many others sinful things done by minors who slipped away from their loving God; has eventually unpleased God who caused minors to move next 5<sup>th</sup> fled to U.S for another trial of believe. Minors` faith in God increases, gaining strong momentum when minors are on fleeing, and inversely, minors faith decreases as minors longing settled down in their refuge residing places. Minors God wasn`t happy with minors in the camp because majority of minors had quit praying to God and joined sides of rival tribe communities in fighting each other with stones. God wasn`t happy with majority of who had stopped going to school as they allowed themselves to a defeated victims of traumatized life of refugees that turned them into thievery, robbers, rebels and manyatta prostitutes of the Chaga`a hot liquor drunkards. God caused minors to flee for a change of faith through punishment of suffering fleeing.

Issue of outreach of universities and colleges for minors has opened minors' vision to see a new great land for the next 5th fled for a better education where final Ph.D. would be earned by only willing minors. Minors were stressed out outside the front office of Sister. Louis, JRS, Arap Foundation and other sponsorship organizations were offering further education in Nairobi or in Kakuma camp. Minors trek to South African cities in search of education after completing secondary and no way out for college or university admission, which couldn`t be afforded for walletless minors. Minors dreamt of the great land where student loans and other scholarships would be found after 5th fled to unknown refuge land. Graduate of KCSE minors were jobless, stressed out in SPLA-liberated areas, working for a paid Food for Work to fund their double high tuition in Kenyan colleges. Many minors who completed held KCSE were working in the camp as teachers, businessmen, social workers, constructors, nurses, as well as peace educators for refugees just to save little paid shillings for tuition payment for college education in Kenya. It was a time when minors demanded 5th fled in their hearts to find a promised land of last education achievement.

Issue of improving life and the taste of half a better life for minors was another cause of minors accepting resettlement from resettlement agencies, which finally processed minors for the 5th fled into to soil of U.S.A refuge cities. From the bottomless hell of a life, minors were dreaming of the next flee into a great land where food wouldn't be measured by bowls, cups, spoons or by days measured by individual wallets. A better life and a taste of city life was a dream of hope for minors who stood by as they welcome and accepted the 5th fled resettlement process for the USA or Australia. Fleeing into a refuge city where water wouldn't be an option for either to drink or bath, freedom of water use in your own apartment was a dream for the minors 5th fled to U.S soil of promises. Minors 5th fled was a miracle of all other fled because it was a "resettlement impossible" in the minds of minors and other refugees who hadn't believed it even now minors in the U.S. All the factors of spoonful measured food, optional water, insecurity, abundance of minors, the sake of education, sake for better life taste, bad weather and God mission contributed minors' proposed resettlement into the U.S as minors 5th fled led resettlement into 3rd minors' promised land. It was at the right time when minors packed their handbags and hit the flight journey to flee.

Starting of overage minors flight uplifted from Kakuma stony airstrip to Nairobi, Turkana gunmen missed hearing that Sudanese were leaving the Kakuma refugee camp; eventually, Turkana gunmen launched every nightly dawn gunpoint robbery on minors. Turkana gunmen shot dead minors in their shop and looted items and other belongings in minor groups. Gunmen looted clothes, food and other little minors` belongings in robbery attack, leaving minors without food for two weeks before next rations distribution day. Kenyan police stationed far away from the camp had done little about shot-death refugee minors.

Majority of lost-boys believed 5th fled to USA OR Australia was God's doing and since the 5th fled happened unexpectedly and in an extraordinary way, it was believed to be God's plan even by those Lost-boys who had never gone to church before since the history lost-boys creation. Pagan lost-boys believed that there was God who was the master of their odyssey journey and yet still didn't want to go to church for prayers. At the beginning of the Odyssey, many lost-boys believe that God is the one driving them into all these bypassed wildness as they don't look at the adversaries factors that cause flee but assume flee is caused by the cause curse of their escaping fled directly come from God, but a cause of God to shape them. Lost-boys who are believers associated their lost Odyssey history with those of Israel's children. God sent them into wildness and gave them a land that is now Israel. As the minor's process of resettlement was taking place in the camp, minor's faith in God went up, and every morning and evening, Sunday and every other day, minors could be seen attending under trees churches and got involved in frequently church activities and services in both Catholic and Episcopal church.

As the minors' flight began taking off from the stone airstrip of Kakuma town, Sudanese church elderly mothers, youths, and pastors who were carrying Bibles and surrounding airstrip barbed-fenced wiped and cries out lord alleluias, guide them as you have been doing lord, as prayers continued. Minors prayed before they stepped onto the plane and group elders had already prayed for the leaving boys. It was a blessing mentioning God's name in the Odyssey and having minors thank God for unexpectedly fled to the USA and Australia. It was observed that lost-boys faith and love of God worshipping increases when they are faced with many percussion troubles in the Odyssey, moreover lost-boys faith in calling God's name happens when lost-boys are on the next movement fleeing stage or after they shortly arrive at their newly temporary destination. Lost-boys have never got themselves away from the church, even after they have arrived in America or Australia.

cxxviii

There was no time wasted by lost-boys as soon as they entered and stepped their foot down on American soil and did not go to church in the first week of the first Sunday just to go and say THANK YOU, LORD. Underage minors who arrived in America first were taken to church by their foster parent's family, and they had enjoyed the opportunity to worship either in the black or white-dominant church. They were happy without complaining that it wasn`t a Dinka church, but God church of the living God. The newly arrived overage minors were taken to churches by their already-arrived arrived lost-boys as well as volunteers, American friends, or by the sympathetic resettlement agencies or case workers. All lost-boys would empty their apartment going to church in the first week of arrival as God's faith increases in pagan lost-boys, too. Greeting multiple American congregations or being called upon on the altar of the church for introduction, lost-boys said few words of introduction, as well as few lost-boys felt strange and not saying anything at all. Many lost-boys opted to attend few Sudanese churches on their USA arrival as many lost-boys favored Sudanese churches more than American churches.

Not longer since lost-boys didn`t feel comfortable attending American churches or other African churches in the United States, they opted to attend Sudanese churches and later felt that Sudanese didn`t really motivate their faith, so lost-boys decided to get their own church worshiping and praying space in any county they are resettled as majority. Lost-boys started to pray in community halls, schools, or even meeting spaces in any county as their Sunday services were full of all lost-boys congregations. Lost-boys who were catholic were helped by catholic churches to get praying and worship space in the main church so that they could pray, worship and adore the lord in their own mother tongue, or traditional way of Dinka worshiping. Then lost-boys own their praying space as well as getting their preaching pastors from within themselves or from the main church that helped out or offered them worshipping space. Churches in the USA had offered lost-boys much assistance at the first arrival time. Lost-boys received space in the many churches of their own for any activities, worshipping, funerals, weddings, meetings or any anniversary conducted by lost-boys is hosted in their given church space.

Many Sudanese in Sudanese communities around the States had started to attend lost-boys churches, and even those Sudanese who attended Sudanese church before lost-boys arrival had switched to lost-boys churches because lost-boys churches were more linked with American or worshiped in the most traditional Sudanese or East African way which was different from any other Sudanese church worshipping system. The Sudanese community in the USA tends to like lost-boys churches as many services were offered, and the Sudanese community was drawn to lost-boys as it did in the Kakuma refugee camp when the minors church was used as the centre services for the entire camp of the Sudanese communities. Every Sunday, lost-boys church was full of children, girls, women and elders from Sudanese community as they opted to attend lost-boys churches across the United States. Lost-boys are welcomed as they love the Sudanese community, and in addition, lost-boys offered services to Sudanese community as the community offered services to lost-boys too. It was a company as lost-boys felt at home whenever they could see mothers and sisters as well as elderly fathers in their churches. Mingling with the community was source of happiness to many lost-boys as they saw church and community as combined power for the growing people.

Lost-boys churches welcome many preachers and pastors in American churches or from Sudan, as well as Some pastors and preachers who came from Sudan or any part of Africa visiting lost-boys in the United States and started preaching in lost-boys churches, as lost boys churches got filled up on any visited from foreign preaching pastors on visited mission.

As time went by, living in America got toughest on lost-boys, and it wasn`t unusual to see the drawback of many lost-boys who used to attend the church on their first month's arrival and then sort to sit on top of the eight package bottles of beer on Sunday. Many lost-boys got Americanized in the first three months of arrival. They went to church for a few Sundays just to say thank you,

God, for bringing us to America, and then after a few weeks, they immediately started drinking empty twelve bottles of can beer liquor and dating American girls as well. As some went way to nightclubs in a search of dirty happiness or started Americanized themselves in American dirty ways. Halves of lost-boys churches started to disappear, and then after two to five years in America, some lost-boys churches started to cease and got closed out due to very poor attendants' issues. Lost-boys got jobs that kept them working on Sundays, and that resulted in poor attendance as well as many lost-boys got stuck in the middle of busy America with school work and a job to earn living, so they dropped going to church. Other half of lost-boys church congregations were drawn back by the devils who have been working in their lives since from the creation of the lost-boys Lost Odyssey. Their own group of lost-boys still keeping up with the church were married, and families lost-boys as they tried to get their families known to God or ease some of their families problems with the word of the lord. Lost-boys offerings in their church were one of the poorest in the world, as each lost-boy in congregations offers a dollar or less, and that results in less than fifty dollars offering per lost-boys small church. There was nowhere to donate or get money to rent small spaces for worshipping or get free space for lost-boys church.

Although many lost-boys don`t attend the churches, they still want to use church services on their wedding day, funeral or any other services offered by the same church which they had quitted a long time ago. The old church would still welcome lost-boys back to practice their services activities at little pay cost or no pay at all. As lost-boys drew back from their church, women and elders who used to attend lost-boys church started disappearing, too. Since lost-boys appetite for the church died down, many small lost-boys worshipping halls closed and out and any lost-boys who were sons of living God and believed that God was the father of the lost Odyssey, they only worshiped or prayed with American churches or some lost-boys joint some other African churches around the States where they come from. Few lost-boys churches still operating and do Sunday services in their small hall or in the main church banquet, but not as many as congregations as they used to be from the beginning. Strong will believers lost-boys still practicing faith as they were doing in Kakuma or way backtrack down on the way of lost odyssey, these particular lost-boys go to church every Sunday and got involves with church activities regardless of how tied their work or school schedule may get complicated. These will faith lost-boys have majority may come from Episcopal Church and few go to Catholic Church.

American Churches offered assistance to lost-boys in many different ways, and one way was giving away free good news holy Bibles both in English and Dinka versions. Lost-boys received free donated things like furniture, food and other material things. Few

American churches help lost boys get their GED or pay for their tuition, as many ESL classes were offered by the churches. Coming of lost-boys to America was an eye opener to many American churches and to know if there are Christians living in Sudan. Many Americans learn about South Sudan through knowing lost-boys first. Lost-boys bases in USA or Australia formed non-profit organizations to serve in the field of Sudan rural areas and these based non-profit organizations get backup support from the churches. Lost-boys Foundation in every State where lost-boys reside was offering great services at the early arrival of lost-boys, and these formed foundations were aimed at incorporating lost-boys into American lives society. Lost-boys foundations got a lot of donated goods from churches, and on behave of lost-boys free services and gifts were donated to lost-boys.

Lost-boys are Leading American churches to build water wells, funds children's schools as well as help in any humanitarian assistance in Southern Sudan. Many churches in the United States help lost-boys get jobs and creating networks that offer others assistance through education and social networks among lost-boys in various States. Many churches attended by lost-boys donated clothes, cooking stuffs; used computers, beds, chairs, as well as money and all donations were either forwarded to foundation or went direct to individual lost-boys. Majority of lost-boys were not happy with Foundation or with some others volunteers who collect money by the name of lost-boys and hardly gave anything or little to lost-boys who went to various churches seeking assistance. It was name lost-boys has become a project creation name where many lost-boys foundations could easily raise huge amounts of money in a short, limited time lost-boys still fresh with long tragic history of a long odyssey and motivated donors to give and Lost-boys Foundation raises money to support lost-boys and its operations.

Lost-boys/lost-girls sports, fun, vocations and leisure time activities are the most restrictive as busy school, work and other important commitments didn't allow in such a limited time to those time obedient lost-boys or lost-girls. Many high school lost-boys participated in the game, mostly soccer and basketball, and it is a great achievement for lost-boys who got scholarships through their strong demonstration expertise in soccer or in basketball. Lost-boys formed soccer teams across every State of living, and their team tournament with other African soccer team across the USA. Nigeria, Somalia, Liberia and many other local soccer teams compete with lost-boys various States soccer teams. Many lost-boys do play valley ball with a local States court, and although very few lost-boys play basket ball, they mostly intermingle and play either local or joint college basket ball team nearby their residency.

Many lost-boys past their idle time by playing dominoes as well as other indoor games like playing cards and computer games are the most time spend playing game for many lost-boys. Taking weekends driving across neighboring States for visiting is also common for lost-boys who are living in the Southern States or in Australia, where lost-boys attend many weekends traditional Dinka dance performancess or some other Sudanese events conducted everywhere in Australia. Many lost-boys spend their weekends drinking beers, liquor, or socializing themselves in one central apartment. Lost-boys gathered and spent many hours talking and discussing political topics as well as conversations that are directed at American politics, lifestyle, as well as American democracy, which lost-boys critic. Taking vacation to other part of the country is very rare for many lost-boys as very few lost-boys visit other States only when there are important events like wedding, SPLA meetings, Mayo 16, sports competitions or drinking events of friends. Leave of absence from work is the best time lost-boys spend well on visiting their lost family in Sudan. Lost-boy would take leave of absence from work, commonly from three to six months. The long visit to village in Southern Sudan was full of searches and locating long-lost families, and the time spent is another adventure of individual leisure time roaming in Sudan.

Night clubs, parties, stripping clubs, bars, as well as many other African social entertaiments places, are common places where extreme pleasure seekers lost-boys would be found. Very few lost-boys go to weekend's American nightclubs, but many lost-boys attend Sudanese parties as well as Liberian parties. In some local night clubs, or African parties, lost-boys are known as trouble makers or fighters even in spite of gate guards or policemen. Relaxing time after work is spent watching seasonal basketball competitions or watching soccer's seasonal African Cup of Nations. Watching movies in the movie theatre is a rare time spending, or not one of the lost-boys funs as they used to love watching movies in the camp. Lost-boys were outdoor people in Kenya, but now they are tame to be indoor persons who love to stay indoor for whole day, either watching TV or sleeping or busy with school work. Intellectual lost-boys love to attend concerts, plays, drama school festivals or other school activities or games competitions across the country.

Visiting neighbor lost-boys is very commonly as they donot make an appointment to visit other lost-boys next door but just walk to the door and knock and if nobody is present inside, a door wouldn`t open. Majority of lost-boys spend most of their time listening to SPLA maritial songs on Mading Aweil dot com. Listening to their Terap batalion songs or other Sudanese guitarists is a pleasure of fun to comfort a stress, out lost-boys. Many lost-boys do not listens to American rap or other music but listen to only African music. Black American rap music is considered misleading or not understandable by many lost-boys, accept the underage lost-boys or youngest one who mingle their lifestyle in African American lifestyle and want to be called or look more like young African Americans with durek on and pants down on the end of butts as well as rap goes on.

Lost-girls living was rough upon early arrival to US and mostly affected by nightmares of the recent Kakuma girl-controlled lifestyle, which has left them with a fear logic of control and made them stay up as good girls who don`t go to night clubs, smoke, drink or play around boys. Foster parents used to encourged overage lost-girls to date and get to know boys tricky ways of lying, not until lost-boys started dating and take these shy lost-girls out and show them how to do it. Few lost-girls end up in marriage with lost-boys who have arranged marriages in Dinka's way of matrimonial marriage. None of the lost-girls became heavy drunkards, abused drugs, or even became a bad girl in any way. Lost-girls sociality was still under guard by her fostered parents, relatives or her fostered brothers who were living with her in the same family. Since number of lost-boys out number of lost-girls, lost-boys quarrel and fight over lost-girls until one fatal case happened in Seattle, as well as many more attacks recorded in northern States where majority of few lost-girls were resettled. Lost-girls socialize themselves on rare visited across town or are escort by their related brothers. They could visited different States attending any Sudanese events, but after being permitted by either related brothers or fostered family members. Lost-girls were the most obedient girls as many white fostered families in the north complemented their culturally obedient behaviors and called it a the most successful lifestyle compare to white girls way of life achievement.

Many lost-boys or lost-girls easily intermingle with Americans of different ages, but majority of overage lost-boys find it difficult to socialize around Americans, even at work or schools place these anti-American social behaviors has become anti-social issues as many lost-boys believe that Americans overlook lost-boys as the same way other foreigners overlook Americans and these claimed has end lost-boys up not agreeing with Americans in any simple conversation. In any social places, lost-boys would sit together or close to another foreigners or immigrant friends as they try to avoid Americans who might be saying something that could park up a stressful day. Anti-social is an event a big concern between Africans and African-American compared to African with White America. Lost-boys fight in any apartment shares with young African-Americans boys, or even at school or at work, lost-boys and African-American boys never get along together because of their different communities background concepts. It seems to be the same reversed claims where lost-boys accuse African-American boys of mistrust, disrespect, abuse, bullying and curse words, overlooked as well as the same is claim said by young American where few white boys seem worse compared to black youngsters.

Many lost-boys drink, smoke, date black girls, white, Sudanese, and spanish as they go out and stay alert in a believe that life is running hell out of them. Nine years in Kakuma camp was a human sociality waste, and in a refugee camp where lost-boys couldn`t afford to purchase local brew liquor araqi, {*mau chol or mau xeer*} or even find a girl to date, somehow the opportunity they have found in USA or in Australia where beers are very cheap and a purified one they can drink for many years without deathly or complicated healthy problems compare to Africa where unpurified liquor can kill an addicted alcoholic man in less than one or two years of continual drinking. Lost-boys date black American girls more than they do white girls because lost-boys neighborhood is always surrounded by the black community in a place where white residents moved away from black people populated areas. Lost-boys in the northern States face troubles with white girls, and that child support or domestic 911 issues has led many lost boys in the north to quit living in USA as they moved back to Sudan. Many lost-boys fear socializing around or with black American girls because of mistrust and fears of trouble compared to how comfortable they could socialize around Spanish or with white girls. Pleasure of fun, love, adventure and honeymoon enjoyment in America or in Australia was mostly geared down and up by moody, antisocial, lost-boys who went through many changes in human happiness and sadness transformation.

cxl

3   . On the barefoot onto the vehicle and into the airplane

Before the first cock crowed in the dawn morning of September 2000, unusually, small white plane was zooming over the camp *ashantee huts*, as the underage minors on the flight list looked up with hope of their flight arrival, surprising them to have it landed down in the dusty airport of Kakuma town. A door-by-door bye was hurriedly done by leaving minors as they greeted friends, colleagues, or relatives before heading to the UNHCR compound, which was a couple of minutes away from the minors `group of residences. Underage minors rushed as they increased their steps and walked to the UNHCR compound as they marked the first list of the first-morning flight. Outside the UNCHR compound gate, by bye, relatives kicked in last hugs, kisses, and last words accompanied by bye to minors who were leaving the camp behind. Relatives and friends whipped tears as their loved underage were leaving the camp. Underage minors were accompanied to the airstrip by their friends, relatives, and colleagues as the huge crown of the refugees gathered outside the fenced UNHCR compound or camp`s airstrip. Overage minors started their flight on Feb 14, 2001, after underage minors had left the camp to the USA. Insecurity caused by Turkana gunmen was getting worse as some of the leaving minors that morning would be ambushed and shot, robbed, or beaten up by Turkana gunmen between the minors` group and the UNHCR compound. Turkana gunmen were perceived their mind with the wrong concept that minors were leaving the camp with small handbags full of money given to them by the U.S. government so that they could flying to the USA. As minors were scheduled to arrive UNHCR compound in the dark dawn morning around 6:00 am-7:00 am, the risk was high when minors walked to the compound alongside the empty and dark dried seasonal river where gangsters and Turkana men robbed minors with backpacks and handbags as well as harmed them on leaving the day with their accompanies on the way to compound. Attacked minors on their pleasurable leaving day had to miss their flight, and the next flight would be scheduled after the recovery of the wounded patients.

Minors walked from their respective groups of residences to the compound. As they arrived compound, a watchman would open the passengers` gate after minors were shown gate pass letters of appointment. The front entrant compound gate was overcrowded as the huge refugees' multitudes stood there with hands hung over the back of the netted, wired, barbed compound fence. Compound fence was shadowed by the accompanying groups of leaving minors` friends, colleagues, relatives, and other refugee watchers. At the gate, INS officers stood there with a list of leaving minors` names. INS officers would called in minors' names and precede them to JVA check-in names. In the reception room, minors were checked into small UNHCR buses to carry them to the Kakuma airstrip. In the UNHCR compound, elderly refugees Sudanese women opened their Bibles reading and sang Dinka hymns in the ears of minors who were quietly set in the buses. Elders' Sudanese women wipe tears over recited Bible verses to minors while buses left the Kakuma UNHCR compound to Kakuma airstrip. The crowded front gate was cleared as buses dropped out of the compound to the stony airstrip of Kakuma. Minors were waving and peeped their faces out of buses` windows while the crowded roadside refugees waved back in tears to minors.

Missing flight dates in Kakuma was a common issue, as many scheduled flight names were left empty under no-show flight files. Some minors went to Sudan after they received INS INS-approved letters, as well as some went to other Kenyan towns or neighbors countries to pass a word of bye to friends, colleagues, or relatives, knowing that the flight scheduled date would take longer than the minor's camp away visitation. Some minors who went to Sudan were reported as slain after the government Air Force bombed the SPLA-liberated town of Narus, Chukudum, and other liberated areas minors visited before their flight scheduled date. Missing minors on the scheduled flight lists were reported to have been killed in a government attack during a visit to liberate. INS reacted by pressuring UNHCR to pay finality for the death of minors as UNHCR was responsible for allowing minors to go into the hostile fire hell of Sudan. On the flight date, minors had to fight over names sold, purchased, and names occupied where names' owners fought names` occupants as the compound gate closed minor's names conflict cases with policemen that forced a picture minors to take flight seats regardless of names` owners. On the flight dates, some minors were attacked in the camp by some refugees whom they had a conflict with over issues of girl pregnancies, debts, or other disputes in the refugee camp. Some minors were trapped and blocked from coming to the UNHCR compound as their enemies prevented them from going to the USA. Policemen responded by forcing attackers to break to allow trapped minors to reach the compound for a flight uplifted to Nairobi. Minors rescued by policemen were delighted and happy to get their flight scheduled before reported missing.

The guarded stony Kakuma airstrip was secured by Kenyan Policemen scattered around the crowded airstrip fence. A huge crown of refugees covered the fenced airport around just to watch minors boarding the plane. Minors` buses were waved at by the roadside, walking multitudes of refugees until buses reached the stony airport of Kakuma. As minors buses entered the stony airport, the crown ululated, waved, and cheered over the leaving minors as the accompanying friends, relatives, and colleagues of leaving minors peeped their faces through barbed-wired airport fence just to say bye to their loved one boarding the plane. Minors took last snaps of their friends, relatives, or crown refugees and rounded the fence as well as byes with tears caught up.

Minors lined up before the plane step, each carrying a handbag or backpack. INS officers called each minor name as minors stepped up onto the plane using short ladder. The plane hostess or assistant directed minors into their seats and showed them the use of a fastening seatbelt. Seeing the plane close in the minors and flap its wings, elderly women carrying Jesus' cross with Bible sung and prayed, refugee youth waved, and young women ululated with the noise of cheering as the plane left off the dusty Kakuma airstrip. Kenyan residents of Kakuma town were surprised by the huge crown of refugees that came to say bye to their leaving minors' boys on daily flight schedules. It was a surprise to other African national refugees in the camp to see minors being loved by their Sudanese refugees in the camp after they left for USA resettlement. After the plane had flown higher, dusty airstrip was deserted by refugees as the crown walked back to the camp to their respective groups. Minors waved down the crown as their plane took off the dusty airstrip of Kakuma. The crown looked up and saw the light of hope as tears shaded their eyes, both minors and Sudanese refugees.

As overage minors started flight schedules, the number of minors scheduled for day flights had increased from forty-six to a hundred in two trips of the day. The morning session left the camp on the first-morning flight at 6:00 am-7:00 am, and the second flight would take off at 2:00 am-3:00 am from the camp to Nairobi. Although the plane reached Nairobi in one and a half hours, the minors were exhausted and tired as the first-lifetime flight was a rigid exercise of tiresome that shook up minors butts. Honeymoon shocked minors when in the air over the camp shanties huts as their plane zoomed away higher. Some minors got very quiet as memories rang their minds in mid of non-stop in no final home fleeing. Minors` minds rung in recalls of barefoot trekking across deserts thousands of miles from Sudan to Ethiopia. Nevertheless, Red Cross vehicles convoy that uplifted minors from across Sudan trek to Kenya, and then minors thought about the flight fled to the USA. It was a quiet summary of the fleeing series from on a barefoot trek to convoy vehicles, and then into flight fleeing to the U.S. Some minors were optimistic as they kept talking, and discussion went on from pointed hands down on the ground seen items as well as how Nairobi would look like in the first city visited.

Many minors were very pessimistic on the first time step on the plane, keeping quiet, nervous, and moody of sad face was a sign of fleeing danger. Minors had to hold their seat firmly with a high scarcity and fear of thought that the plane was going to be crushed or fall as the plane took off or landed down. Many Minors vomited, peed, sweat, or got sick on the first time plane trip from Kakuma to Nairobi as a result of fear and scary moving up and down plane from stony airstrip of Kakuma to Wilson or Kenyatta airport in Nairobi. It was fun, but minors got sick as the first flight was like the first vehicle convoy trucking nine years ago when minors recalled Kosangor Red Cross uplift them up.

Reaching Kenyan airports in Nairobi, the minors were very happy and very sad in the Kenya sky as the fact of seeing the beautiful, well-developed Kenya's heart Nairobi was an adventurous in pleasurable look and, at the same time, was a shame of backwardness in my minors' hearts as they imagined their native land. Minors' thoughts all went back to the beginning of the flee since, from the barefoot trekking to the vehicles uplift and to then in flight fleeing. Landing down in Nairobi airports and, minors found their IOM personnel waiting with a wide sign written IOM. Minors lined up in the airports as they sneaked out of plane with dust still in clothes from Kakuma. Minors walked in lines headed by IOM personnel leading into the edgeless, tall and wide building, where minors kept looking and glared at the strange first buildings in the airports. In was a big surprised to Kenyans in the airports as they just kept their eyes and lips open on the watch of the tallest, skinny, and deep dark color Sudanese who appeared to never been in that city before. Minors were led to IOM airport check-in as the line was longer, and IOM personnel were busy checking them in. Kenya citizens looked and stared at the minors as the day of seldom appeared of deep, dark skinny boys arrived in Nairobi and Kenyans couldn't believed the minors. Walking in a lines with very small hand or backpack bags, minors were led into matatu buses where they boarded to Gold Medical Centre where they had to be given vaccination medicines, food, and last stand accommodation before an out of Africa flight.

Wherever place minors fled to, they found it learned new stories of comparisons, minors always almost learned something different in their pathways of destinationless fleeing. In the Matatu buses, minors basted up tough comparison discussions as their eyes were facing out of the Matatu windows. Minors kept points tallest, beautiful, and all developed areas in Nairobi as their buses were passing by in the city. Nairobi was the most beautiful city minors ever seen in their life as they the compared present with flashback of their bushy lived Southern Sudan. Many cars racing side highways, beautiful roads, tall buildings as well as developed landscapes, all made minors stirred up their thought as some minors said, "We can't compare our Southern Sudan with just part of Nairobi; as Southern Sudan was colonized by two colonies that can't be compared to Kenya." "We don't even have one of these tall buildings or this tarmac road in Southern Sudan {pointed out one minor at the building}." "If Southern Sudan had happened to have one of these long tarmac roads with tens of these cars on it, the war wouldn't be fighting now, or we wouldn't end up here." They discussion went on and on as minors swore their hearts for education as their own solution for the backward and left-behind Southern Sudan. Some minors were just keeping quiet and felt shocked at what they had seen as well as pessimistism was a factor in their sloughed mind as well. As some minors wiped tears on the buses. Minors discussion never stopped until Matatu buses reached Gold Medical Centre, where drivers ordered minors to get down and find a place inside the fenced gate to place their bags on and sit.

The watchman closed back the gate after matatu buses re-entered out, and he asked minors to find anywhere inside the gate to sit on or shelter under for the day, or slept for the night. Minors had lined up as they nurses called them in for medical given out. A medicine given to each minor in the line was to be swallowed in the presence of the nurse, as the medicines were for the malaria, cold sickness prevention, and tablets for weather changes. Some minors complained about how hard the medicine tablets were strong to be chewed as sugar cane, but the nurse asked the minors to chew and swallow this medicine and drink full cup of water. A young Kenyan lady called minors to an open meeting ground where she explained housing upstairs, bathroom locations, mealtime, as well as orders of not getting out of the gate. Minors lined up for food as the cooks scoped rice, cabbages, kale, beans, and *sukuma wiki* with meat onto plates. Minors set anywhere on the ground as they ate their meal. Some minors ate while standing up as they rested down on the green grass floor. As minors were eating, they never stopped discussing in their Dinka, where topics weren't limited to their special fleeing and resettlement changes of little-known destinations. Some minors complained about Kenyan cooking styles, and the kind of food cooked as a meal wasn't the Sudanese cooking style. Some minors didn't want to eat fry *sukuma wike* with *ugali*, complaints were raised as minors dumped a whole plate of food into a dished bin, eventually, cooks shouted at minors to wash plates and place them on the rack or placed the plates into sacks for easy collection. Minors ate to their fullness of their little stomach in Gold Centre.

Minors hung around inside very small fenced gate with two store building apartments. Minors weren't permitted to go out as the watchman was set on the gate. Minors who had their friends, relatives, or colleagues in Nairobi, came out to meet them at Gold Medical center, where minors received shoes, clothes, and other things. Some minors received advice and missed words from their loved ones, who peeped their faces outside the bare bed-wired fence while talking to minors. Other minors had a chance to waste their Kenyan shillings by exchanging them in buying something as the by-passers sellers were called to exchange food on sale over the fence. Minors gave some shillings away to other Sudanese in Gold instead of carrying Kenya money to the USA. As the Sun disappeared, minors had to get into lines again for the evening dinner of *Sukuma Wiki* and *Ugali*. Minors ate their dinner and hit the way upstairs or downstairs to find beds in rooms where beds were double stacked on each other. Two strange minors had to share one bed. Blankets, bedcovers, and other beddings were distributed by housekeeper, and minors had to share one bed. Two minors teamed up when they barely knew each other and acted to sleep as bedmates. Minors kept talking while lying in their beds, as the pleasure and happiness of miracle resettlement fled was very adventurous, and optimistism caused minors` minds to discussion about everything in fled life. Minors don`t sleep overnight because of endless conversations that kept other minors awake. Minors' nightly discussion and conservation topics were circles about politics of Southern Sudan, development, about Kenya women in Gold, and about pessimistic or optimistic life that would be encountered in the USA. Some minors wouldn`t sleep as long the light was lit on in the room, or when someone went out or in the room, others would be awake. Other minors stayed up watching TV on channels like War Africa and other news channels that revealed war issues in Africa. Minors felt enthusiasm about how well Kenyan women received them and were well treated in Gold Medical Center.

As the second trip arrived at Gold Medical Center, the first trip had rested already on the ground outside the apartment's yard. Minors greeted themselves as two trips met and exchanged in Gold Medical Center. Minors greeted and talked about the great city of Nairobi, as far as adventure of the first flight stories made minors laugh at themselves. As the number of minors increased in Gold Medical Center, minors began to face bathroom problems. Two to three poor toilets were overfilled, and water couldn`t run down anymore, eventually, minors hadn`t anywhere to have a long pee. Many minors hadn`t taken baths since there weren`t enough running water or even shower heads. Some minors used to urinate on the back of the fenced gate just like they thought it was still Kakuma refugee camp. Minors complained about the stingy and smelly bathrooms as well as the poor sewage system with nowhere to have showers in the overcrowded Gold Medical Center. Kenyan ladies who were working in Gold told minors to use buckets kept outside the bathroom to draw water from the tap and use bucket water to flush the toilet after use, and even flashing toilet with bucket water still wastes stool on the floor of the bathroom and still water didn`t run down at all. Minors were advised to use buckets of water drawn from the tap for bathing in the bathroom. Minors lined up to wash their faces and brush their teeth in the morning as well as some minors were drinking hot milk tea with unbrushed mouths due to cooks who rushed milk tea to minors' bedsides. Minors laughed at Kenyans as some Kenyans ate breakfast with an unbrushed morning mouth, which minors considered to be unclean mouth. Minors weren`t used to morning milk tea for breakfast. Some morning milk tea with bread was neglectable as cooks were surprised by these boys who didn`t eat every prepared food, not knowing that minors' stomachs had grown narrowing for many years.

In the evening, after dinner and before the minors went to their two-boy shared small beds and, the night got longer in the discomfort bed of the two boys. In the morning or evening, IOM officials drove in with a full van of minors' clothes. Minors were lined up, and name by name IOM officer called their names out as each minor was asked to tell his clothes and shoe sizes, but minors hadn`t any idea of what their clothes, or shoe sizes would be measured to what number size. Many minors didn`t know their clothes or shoe sizes, but the IOM officer used his civilized mind to imagine what size of clothes or shoes would fit a physical look minor. Each minor got his imagined size of clothes one pant, one shirt, one cap, and a pairs of shoes with a big written letters on "USRP." The minors initialized letters as United States Refugee Program. As the Sun was running down to the West, minors were very happy, chatting, laughing, joking, and rushing with their received clothes as well as trying them on and off with high level of fun. Minors received departure package with inclusive documents for traveling, flight date and time from Kenya to Europe connection via USA. Minors showed off smiling faces and revealed teeth which never been smiled upon in the camp. Some minors trips were scheduled to leave from Kenyatta airport at 5 o'clock, as early as in dawn morning, and since minors didn`t sleep overnight, they were likely to be the first to wake up before the first cock crowed. Flight-scheduled minors were woken up at 4 o'clock as cooks got ready milk tea with bread for leaving minors. Minors wore their uniforms, as some minors drunken milk tea without sugar and bread without butter in the dark dim light.

Matatu minibuses arrived in the dark dawn as minors were urgent to line up in the chilling cold morning. The IOM officer called each boy listed name onto the bus, but some minors were still drinking milk tea without sugar but got rushed by the IOM officer, who closed buses doors and ordered buses drivers to drive until the main gate of Kenyatta airport. The sky was dark, and stars shining white, as well as the shining city of Nairobi, were just in front of minors' eyes when peeping out of the bus windows, and it was enough to view the entire city. High Rise Estate was brighter than anything else as minors passed several city traffic lights before the main gate of Kenyatta airport. Even in the dark dawn night, minors never stop talking. Rather did, they stopped looking out of the buses' windows, as well as discussion went on with mixed topics of comparison between well-developed Kenya compared to Southern Sudan. The city was shining with lights in everyplace as well, as it appeared beautiful when minors compared it with Kakuma city of refugees. Minors arrived at the Kenyatta airport as buses drove them up the gates where IOM officers led them to check-in counters where assessment of their traveling documents was reviewed and approved. Minors walked in lines from counter to counter and from small room to room inside the airport. Minors stared at the white transparent glasses as the wall of light-building glasses was almost knocked down by the head unknowingly as minors walked after the IOM officer to the final terminals. Passengers and Kenyan workers in the airport stared at minors as minors looked like sports teams going to play abroad. Some minors would be asked for the bathroom, but no pointing direction would be given by the IOM officer, who took the minor by hand and walked him into the bathroom as others would follow one minor in the direction of the bathroom. Minors set down at the final terminal to wait for their flight to get ready, other minors trip would wait for six hours before the flight got ready to fly up. Minors would watch awaited white passengers, who were enjoying themselves with drinks, eating, or playing games, while quietly or sleepy heads minors were just sitting idly on long waiting seats. The high-rise airport platform that made giraffes visible in the nearby forest; minors were watching giraffes loitering in the green pasture park zone close to the airport.

After a tiresome awaited flight, the IOM officer got the minors ready and went into the lines for the Kenya Airways door opened for passengers. Getting into the plane was done with priorities, high class, middle class, and the last class. A huge number of white passengers went onto plane and filled the front seats of the plane. The second entry was the middle class, which was a mix of passengers like Asians, Africans, and others who filled up the middle part of the plane seats, and the third group of passengers was the last class, which was composed mainly and only minors. Minors were lined up and check-in lastly as they were seated in the far back of the plane. Each minor was directed to his seat by the flight attendant, had a seat belt fastened for him, and his handbag or backpack was placed on his lap. Minors enjoyed the comfortable soft seat and felt the pleasure of the first big plane in their first-lifetime adventure. Minors smiled and said few words while other minors wore pessimistic faces. The plane rose higher in no minutes, and minors wondered how quickly and fast the big plane flew higher without a storm of shaking like what they experienced with a small plane that took off in stony Kakuma airstrip with a storm of shaking shock. Nairobi landscape aerial was beautiful as minors looked down upon the city of Nairobi where their hearts looked down upon Southern Sudan at the same time. Nairobi appeared shining, and it was well developed, making minors believe the city's modern construction as the best one of the world developed city. The plane entered clouds and out as minors saw the beautiful landscape of the green natural grassland and the beauty of African land. Northern Africa appeared as heaps hills of desert sand. Minors kept looking out as they were enjoying the pleasurable adventure of their yearly fled.

Flight attendants and hostesses served drinks and snack food on the plane. Snack food and soda drinks placed on the small table in front of seated minors would remain there until flight attendants returned to recollect and took it back. Hungry minors tasted the snack food and soda but leaved as it was. Minors named snack food in the plane as a colored food because of its green vegetable salads as well as its simple color looks. Soda tasted like champagne, and every edible in the plane was nasty as minors` mouth taste got used to beans and hard water in the camp. Many minors just looked at the snack food and soda drink and left it the way it was for flight attendant to come back and recollect it. Hungry minors who had tried to eat snack food and drunken soda were vomiting on the plane and finally got sick. Some minors smelled the food and swore that their parents had never eaten food like this before and, so why should I? Minors joke in the plane as they amused themselves by drinking Western beer by tasting soda in small tins. Some minors refused to drink soda as they considered it a Western wine, and they were cautioned in the camp by elders not to start drinking alcohol on the plane before reaching America. The only thing minors tasted on the plane was sweets and water, something minors know in the camp.

Hungry minors just gazed and stared at snack food in front of their small table while showing no interest in eating snack food at all. All passengers on the plane ate their snacking food and drank soda, except minors who had refused to eat snacking food, which they believed to be food hadn`t eaten by their parents. Passengers in the plane amazingly stared look at the minors and noticed how village minors were in the plane and how the physical appearance of minors and the nature of not eating snack food were all negative perceptions views placed on minors by other passengers as well as minors were a brand marked of uncivilization. Visiting the toilet and leaving the toilet unflashed was a stingy aired work in which hostesses or flight attendants had to flash down minors` mess in the bathroom. Passengers turned away as they tried to visit the unflashed toilet for the branded named minors couldn`t recall the instruction directed to them on the no-experienced toilet used orientation day in Kakuma camp. Huge number of white passengers in the airplane got it straight into the back of their minds that minors wouldn`t be blamed for toilet missed as many of these white passengers just came from visiting bushes under tree toilets in many visited African villages.

Connecting different flights through Western Europe via the U.S., minors took long day flights, ending with passengers stretching their legs in a tiresome mood as some minors already fall asleep on their comfortable seats. Hunger in minors added more exhaustion and tied sleepy minors to stay up with the pleasure of the first flight traveling that kept them smiling with empty stomachs. Minors yawned in a quiet, mixed look of pessimism and optimism. In spite of the white passengers` fun in the plane, minors remained sited quite like a beaten-up soccer team returning home from a defeated loss tournament. White passengers snapped pictures of their family members, or flight backbenchers group of minors. White passengers chatted, laughed, joked, and played. Whites seated in the plane showed a lot of adventured fun while minors remained faced down in moody home leaving. Some minors snored with a lean head or hanged a low head over their chin, but one couldn`t wake up even when a plane went into a wave break over the desert wind of North Africa. African music played in Kenyan Airway plane aroused sound adventure in minors as it suggested last time heard African soft music in an African plane. Kenyan flight attendants came close to minors for counseling, advice, and encouragement. Flight attendants, "You had suffered a lot, but the lord permitted you to go to the U.S. for a better life." "You survived a cycle of war, fled, and hardship. May the Lord bless you in your new home, America", said the flight attendant. "God has a plan for you, but don`t forget to come back home after the completion of your education," commented the flight attendant. Flight attendants continued the conversation in the air; "don`t forget the Bible and your country, and please just concentrate on your education and return back home to relieve our suffering people." Flight attendants met each minor on the flight as advice and encouragement went on from seat to seat. The flight attendant's advice meeting was very welcome by each minor, just like the last community elders meeting advice in the camp. Minors loved being advised as their head node movement was a signed agreement that shacked off pessimism and fear of fled to an unknown next place of refuge. Minors murmuring next to each other in their Dinka dialect as they appreciate and thanks Kenyans flight attendants for being nice and concerned for them, and the love of Africans shaded part of minors' hearts in connection to African love of oneness.

Delight and smiles hit tired minors, as the flight overflown shining city of Western Europe where minors connected their flights to the U.S. The shining lighted city of Amsterdam was heaven in my minors` first spotted city in the dark dawn evening as the flight was landing in the directed colorful, lighted airport. Minors woke each other up and started murmuring amongst each other as some were pointed down the flight window and felt the joy of the shining spotted beauty European city. "Look! Look! And look! Awesome city of Europe and how beautiful their heaven appeared before Americans paradise city". Minors cheered their adventure as well as white passengers cheered home welcoming, but neither passenger was looking at the other as the long seated was shaken off. Minors faced ear bursts as the plane was landing. Minors felt no air in the plane as they felt their ears burst and couldn`t hear the sound of their murmuring. Some minors shouted and were scared that the plane was nearly going to crash since no passengers heard each other as the plane landed low to touch the ground of the airport. Inside the plane was cool and breathless as minors held their breath up in the adventurous of face out watch of the beautiful airport. Spotted burning light flames around the airport and the edgeless view of the large European airport had enlightened minors' smiles. The booming and roaring of the plane as its back wheels touched the airport ground gave passengers broader smiles; white passengers clapped their hands as minors initiated clapping their hands too in celebrating the landing of the plane safely as nobody knew the pilot's mind or plane mind that would have landed somewhere in misfortunes.

Tired minors had to wait for huge front passengers to get matched out of the plane as minors murmuring talked continued looking out as well, as pointed at different strange-looked objects, buildings, or anything strange materials in the airport viewable area. Last minors were always the last to get out of the plane in their backward seats in prioritized seated planes. As minors walked out of the some couldn`t differentiate the body of the plane and the airport hall where the plane docked as they walked into the airport concords hall. IOM officers would wait in the airports to receive minors just as they entered the plane or at the corner of the airport hall, where IOM officers would shock minors' hands and lead them to the next connected flight or waited rooms. Minors walked in line or sat in lined-up chairs in the airport as their flight tickets got check-in for the next connected flight to U.S. Minors didn`t look at where they going as their IOM officers lead them in the airport hall ways minors kept their eyes wandering around as they gazed at different wall design of the airport floor and the interior.

People in the airport got surprised as they looked at the minors; some people got close to the minors and asked, "Are you an entertainment team or a sports team?" Minors in uniforms looked like a sports team and were watched struggling, stepping down or up in the airport escalators or elevators. Minors got connected from plane to plane as they took naps in European airports. Minors' adventure was staring at different dressed European citizens in the airport. Minors dwelled their adventure on comparison of Southern Sudan via, and Kenya, Africa via Europe, as development could be seen in the airport buildings and designed high-tech construction. Looking at the most modest European cities from an aerial view to the airport exploration, minors murmured that Europe is more developed than Africa as minors concluded that Kenya is more developed than Southern Sudan. Many minors felt not happy seeing unjust and no equality in world development.

Entering into a connected flight, minors wouldn`t differentiated whether they re-entered into another flight that brought them from Kenya, where they had just got out from, or they entered into the new flight that would take them to the U.S. Minors lined went into the plane last as the first, second, third or even fourth class seats got seated; than backbenchers, minors would walked into the plane by lines directed to the back seats by flight attendants. As minors seated in the flight that connected them to the U.S, they eventually realized that a flight that fled them from Kenya to Europe was smaller with no TV, or other equipments compared to the flight that connected them to U.S. Minors murmured about how comfortable and big was the flights that connected them to U.S, as the small Kenyan flight got no TV, newspapers, comforters as well as miles, weather check and others good things. Minors would be tired and slept in a loud snoring sound that bothered other passengers on the plane. Minors covered themselves with a little bedding on their seats. Some minors had fun watching TV, and estimated miles, hours, kilos, or feet height of the plane. Minors wouldn`t see anything as the flight went higher and higher.

Some traveling batches of minors went hungry between connected flights to flights in Europe to the U.S. without eating anything as they kept refusing to eat snack food on the plane. Minors felt hungry, and they tried colored snacks and drank soda, which caused some minors to vomit on their little parcel bags. Soda tests like spirit or beers as many minor passengers dislike soda. Instead, they perefered water. It was a long tripped flight when some minors connected the flight from Kenya-Europe and finally to the U.S. in a non-stop connection. Some minors slept in the plane till they reached U.S airports unnoticed. In the flight from Europe to U.S, minors were still in the back tail of the flight, and although huge number of white American passengers were seated in the front part of the plane, minors were still seated comfortably in their backbenchers' seats. Minors were a symbol of scary looks as American passengers in the plane secretly gazed at them as well as snooped at them in a shot of a strange look. It was difficult for minors to feel easy and feel at home the inside the plane with American passengers as far interactive of the eyes was full of interpretable meanings. Minors murmured at each other as one returned back from using the bathroom, where he was stared at by seated American passengers. In the plane to America, minors discussed how European passengers' eye contact with them compared to American passengers' eyes contact, which set uneasiness in minors as far as welcoming home in American air was felt by minors. Minors felt not welcome by the sign to read in American eyes contacts.

4.   Welcome to america! The found home for the lost-boys and girls of south sudan

Welcome to Found Home! America! As many signs written welcoming lost-boys across US international airports, but the found home turn shortly into found homeless home in America. Another comparative aerial view from the above over the look of American town escapes of New York, Boston, or any flight down the city as multiple KLM large European planes tripped minors to American cities in every connected flight to the U.S from Europe. Every connected minors' flight from Europe arrived in the U.S at a different time as minors' pleasure of looking down to enjoy aerial view of the cities was affected by what time the plane arrived in that city, but still, minors would find something strange in the city to gazed or stared at in any arrival city time. Regardless of the roaring stomach and snappy yawns, minors woke themselves up as some minors had seen the viewable town escape from the American city. The pleasure of coming home to the promised land aroused minors' joys and happiness, and sticky teeth could be seen smiling as minors viewed out of the window like kids as the flight lowered down steadily. Minors remained covered in the plane as little cold stole the joy of their fleeing adventure of exploring the American sky with an aerial view of the city escapes. Some American cities were foggy, and the whitest snow covered anything on the ground, as minors couldn`t have a pleasurable view of the developed city. It was a winter time, and minors fleeing time were altered wrong as thought to be different than Africa.

Landing down in New York and to meet New Yorkers was a mixture of home-welcoming smiles with the open lips whereas a face showing a level of pessimistic escalation. Minors stepped out of the plane in line as usual, and in view of New Yorkers looked at them like sports boys who were visiting America for an entertainment joke of either a soccer tournament or Ndombolo ya solo performance. Minors who got resettled in New York met their Caseworkers standing with pictures for identity to receive their client minors. Minors resettled in different States would meet their IOM officers to take care of them in locating the next connected flight terminal as well as check-in for the next connected flight to their final home. Minors never stop touring the hallway of the airport by staring and gazing their eyes around every corner they turn into. Murmuring was heard as minors urged among themselves on how big and well-modernized the city of New York airport compared to those of the European airports which left behind. Those minors who arrived in the nighttime wouldn`t get a chance to tour the just like the day arrivals did. Minors who arrived on the cold night in the New York felt a freezing coldness that marked their first time of cold experience.

Night arrivals would meet their IOM officers, who took them to hotels for a night, as far their connected flight would fly them to their final home destination in the morning. Minors had to eat meals and sleep in different hotels for a night before their morning-connected flights, but each minor budget was paid by IOM care. In some hotels where one room had two beds, Western Hotel was used by night arrivals as minors enjoyed their first sleep in America, in a comfortable hotel. Most minors wouldn`t sleep for the whole night, as many of them stayed up for honeymoon in the beautifully decorated room that was full of modern life each minor had never experienced before. Some minors prayed, read the Bible, or chatted for a time passed before their bedtime. It was an adventure of fleeing as many minors fell in love with everything in the room. In the hotel room, minors touched the mattress bed, and they appreciated how soft it felt and how comfortable they felt it after laying on it. They sleepy relaxed on a soft mattress bed as they compared it with their sawdust bed of Kakuma with holes filled with bedbugs and other small insects bedding in minors mud beds. Minors turn on/off bathroom shower tap by error and trail. And in the morning, when the hotel officer rang the phone to wake minors up and call them down for readily airport uplift, minors wouldn`t pick up the ringing phone. Some minors would get lost in the huge building of the Hotel as they walked up and down breezeways without finding way out to the office or leading downstairs. Their buses were awaited to the take them to the airport where their terminal flight would connect them to their final home States.

In different States, minors catch different flights, minors from the same State connected flight to their home State. Minors felt cold and very cold on the plane when they didn`t even have sweaters or cold clothes on. Minor cuddled themselves up inside their back seats with only a piece of cold cover seat clothes used to cover them. Still, minors wouldn`t eat no snack food on the plane, but some minors got used to it than. Getting landed in different States of their final home, minors would meet with their Caseworkers waiting for them at the airport. Pictures or photos of minors were presented to minors in the airport as minors surprisingly found themselves in the hands greeting of their caseworkers who received them by introduction.

Many Caseworkers spoke Arabic, Kiswahili, or African English accent for Southern Sudanese minors` easy communication. A group of identified minors would walk away with their caseworker, as many resettlement Agents presented themselves at the airport to receive their minors. Some minors would still have to connect flights to their final home, but some minors connected flights to their final State within the States without help from IOM officers, which was a big disappointment to minors who lost in the airport. Minors couldn`t find their terminal and check-in in the absence of IOM officers. Lost minors in the airport would ask Americans in the airport for terminal directions, but minors received negative feedback confusion in communication where many Americans wouldn`t communicate or understand minors at all. Some minors had to connect two to three flights before their final home State, and that disappointed lost minors in the airport felt like catching a flight back to Kenya. Minors walked the airport hallway looking for their awaited terminal for their flight, but they didn`t know where to wait, and as they tried to ask Americans in the airport, communication was a big problem. Minors were upset as the cultural shock got into their mind. Sitting in the circle, minors discussed cultures and how Americans just looked at them while they walked the whole airport with faces of lost people and no bypassed American who even sympathized to stop and ask minors if they were ok. Minors were frustrated in the lost airport where they couldn`t find their connected flight terminal. In the flight-connected airports, minors saw black Americans, minors murmured as some suggested stories told in Africa about slavery as well, and minors discussed how black Americans heard stories in Africa. Minors discussed how they heard that black Americans hate Africans and might kill Africans in the USA. Minors discussed scary stories about black Americans as they were sitting waiting for their connecting flight to their final destination home. Inside the airport, it was very cold for minors, and since each minor didn`t wear sweater, or double clothes, they seated close to each other while awaiting flight at the terminal. Minors talked with other Africans resettled to the U.S. from different parts of Africa, and also awaited their flight at the terminal.

Minors lined out of the plane and walked out to the main concourse, they saw a big sign, "Welcome to America," as well as Welcome home signs were held up by resettlement agents as well as pictures of minors presented by resettlement agents to amazingly welcoming minors home. Caseworkers from different resettlement agencies, held minors' pictures up as well as minors were called out by names as caseworkers identified them with pictures. Minors responded to their correct names and pictures as well as greeted the caseworker by handshake.

In the airport, minors whose names fall with one resettlement agent were to leave with their agent after picture identification and name confirmation. Minors received staring and gazing eyes from Americans as some minors reacted by murmuring among themselves, but the airport was overcrowded in a way that minors felt was a standout welcome gusts. American citizens in the airport surprisingly looked at minors with curiosity as some Americans asked minors, "Are you coming to the USA to play any sport?" or What is your visitation about? These tall, dark skins, slim with small hands or backpacks with no luggage, were minors. Minors would hug and say goodbye to each other as friends got separated and carried away by different caseworkers. Friends, relatives, and colleagues minors were separated by different resettlement agents as the matter brought changed in the camp to have minors file the form of living together as friends, or relatives after they got resettled in the U.S. Caseworker drove away with four to six minors from the airport after identification using their pictures. As minors walked to the parking lot with their caseworkers, they were surprised to know their caseworkers as a foreigners or immigrants as they thought to be. Inside the car, minors kept their eyes out of the window, viewing everything visible and comments as they discussed issues of heavenly America and poor Africa. Minors saw every strange and unpopular building, car, person, and every street, traffic, and rail. In the northern States, snow was a big surprise to minors when every tree was covered by what minors called white ashes (snow). There wasn't a tree with green leaves, and the ground was covered by white ashes as well as minors felt very cold as they wore no warm clothes. Minors were shivering with cold while the caseworker's car was heating up, and they rushed to drive minors to a warm clothes store.

Minors were very happy as they left the airport with their caseworker. They were speaking Dinka as well as conversing with their caseworker in English full of African accent. Americans who heard about coming of minors as they had little knowledge about minors' epical history came to the airport to welcome minors, and together with caseworkers, minors felt the joy of being hugged by a welcoming group of American friends. Minors felt happy, as if their lost parents and relatives received and welcomed them to America at the airport. Minors felt like they found their lost parents on that first day of arrival to their final State home as they were warmly welcomed by their volunteers, caseworkers and other Sudanese. Minors who had their names titles changed to lost-boys were also in the airport to welcome new arrivals minors. As minors and lost-boys met in the airport, it was a warmly welcoming and meeting as they greeted themselves in the Sudanese way----padding the shoulder, strongly hugging, and shouting while speaking Dinka.

Lost boys and minors hugging and padding their shoulders as Americans in the airport watched them with a gay mood of amazement. Minors' adventure of window outlook had just begun in the city they called heaven, where they pointed fingers at the tall buildings, highways, and other strange-looking things as conversing in Dinka while caseworker droved them home. They had seen the reality of the city beyond whatever city they bypassed in Europe or in Africa. Some minors would still question themselves if this is the American land, if Are we in America yet, and if it is the only country called heaven. Traffic lights amazed them, as well as many major highways with many multiple streets and roads full of so many racing cars of different sizes. Minors tried to grab attention on how

American cities looked in comparison with the fact they already knew from their movies and news perception experience and what people said about experienced America sighed of look.

As the conversation went on between minors and their caseworkers, volunteers, or lost boys, minors were driven to the food store first or clothing store to either buy food or clothe themselves. As they hit food stores with caseworkers or volunteer American friends for the first time, store employees or customers would turn their faces and stare attentively at new arrival minors. Minors walked into the grocery food store and amazingly saw the first life grocery food store, color and all decorated kind of food. Minors kept their eyes busy looking at unusual or unpopular kinds of food and different designs of the packaged food and how it is stored or stocked up on unique shelves. All customers wore warm clothes, but minors hadn't have warm clothes on the accepted T-shirt uniform written on USRP. Minors were cold, and some were shivering. Other customers stared and took a quick look away at minors as the first shopping went on. Caseworker directed minors to a seemingly African or international food store or department side store where minors would choose to buy beans, lentils, flour, rice, oil, cabbages, milk, eggs, juice, and other simple food which they knew how to cook, but declined broccoli, kale, and other American food types. Pushing the shopping cart was the first learning lesson from day one, as the buggy was filled with a lot of food, minors hit the registers, and the caseworker had to pay huge amounts of dollars for food purchases as minors stood watching. American customers in the paid register line just took a quick stare and gazed at the minors, very strange looking the tall, slim, and dark, skinny African boys who just arrived from Africa. Opening the car door was a little embarrassing to minors as the caseworker had to hold the car door for minors to get into the car, and the caseworker had to fasten their seat belts down too, or else it would be a police ticket in other States for riding without seatbelt.

Reaching home to apartment complex, the minors were so much joy to unload their food out of the car trunk and just walked into an apartment where the caseworker opened their apartment door. Minors felt happy to see inside their apartment as the caseworker toured them around the apartment rooms. Apartment orientation day was at first as the caseworker walked minors from the corner of the kitchen, living room, bathrooms, and bedrooms as well as patio outside or balcony. Minors were oriented by their caseworker on how to store different food in the refrigerator compartment, cook, clean, and serve food or microwave food refrigerated food. Stove usage was important in the orientation, as well as a fire extinguisher with a smoke alarm device. Turning on/off the stove as well as the oven was the first lesson in the apartment orientation. How to use a water tub, dishwasher, and waster, as well as an opened and closed refrigerator, was another lesson covered. Minors found everything in their apartment as if they had just come back from a short visited vacation. They had a sofas set and a TV in their living room, they found cooking and dining wares as well, and their refrigerator was filled with food. Their bathroom had toilet tissues, towels, bathing soap, lotions, toothpaste, brushes and many more. Bedrooms have beds, bedcovers, quilts, and other good things for the room.

Minors were shown how to use the bathroom, toilet, and shower turn on/off, as well as washing hands after visiting the toilet. Flashing the toilet, and use of toilet tissue and toothpaste were the lessons covered in the bathroom in the day one welcome orientation. Minors were very happy being warmly welcomed to their final home State as well, and seeing their first apartment was an enlightenment of joy. Minors set to cook and eat as they celebrated their honeymoon in their hearts with a few lost-boys whom they exchanged words in Dinka as far as a new home in America was a concerned of reaching the so-called arrival at heaven. Welcome to America, the land of bills with opportunities that are not free, commented already settled lost-boys to new arrival minors as they conversed on the first visit day.

Already resettled minors whose name title changed to Lost-boys welcome new arrival minors by warmly visiting them with volunteer American friends' free ride. Lost-boys met new arrivals and chatted as well as they conversed mainly in Dinka about Kakuma lives, asking about friends they left behind in the camp and all sorts of strange things they have seen or met on the way of adventurous travelled cities along the flights connected countries. Lost-boys brought some food, clothes, or other things to new arrival minors, and sat together in the living watching Fox 5 news channel as well. As the conversation went on about what happened after crossing the Nile River and how to pay bills in America. A living room was full of gatherings of lost-boys visiting new arrival minors, and the room was full of laughs, giggles, as well fun of the beginning honeymoon started. Lost-boys show new-arrival minors how to cook and use certain thing in the kitchen as well as caution new arrival minors to expect what is not true about America out there, and a few months of life experience started to be told by already settled lost-boys. Lost-boys bought calling cards for new arrival minors so that minors could call friends or relatives back in Africa to let them know about their arrival as well as calling Africa had just begun on day one to forever.

Sudanese communities welcome Sudanese Lost-boys across the country as it was like cooking a Turkey and having it for arrival minors' dinner as a sign of commemoration of welcoming Lost-boys to America. Sudanese refugee families who were resettled from Egypt, Ethiopia, Kenya, as well as in any part of the world formed communities, churches, and unions across the USA as well as across

Australia. These Southern Sudanese families were resettled before minors, and now minors were welcomed by Southern Sudanese families. Young Sudanese men who were resettled from Egypt way pour into arrival lost-boys apartments for visitation as news on coming lost-boys already hit Sudanese communities across the USA. Lost-boys were welcomed by Sudanese churches on Sunday as well, and parties were thrown to welcome lost-boys to the USA or Australia. Lost-boys were very happy to see how adorable they were loved and cared for by Sudanese communities. Minors left the Kakuma refugee camp in bye bye party and landed down in America or Australia for welcome party. Lost-boys were invited by Sudanese communities across the USA as well as taken as part of the community members. Some individuals in the Sudanese community considered lost-boys as not lost-children as they seemed to know a little history about lost-boys; other Sudanese individuals got confused about why these boys were named lost-boys. Some young Sudanese considered lost-boys as child soldiers as well as others believed lost-boys to be born out of refuge lives or lost their parents during a long struggle. Although there was confusion going on in the Sudanese American community trying to define the exact history of lost-boys, there were very few or no one ever asked lost-boys for a reality explanation of the epical odyssey of minors. Northern Sudanese families in America or Australia heard or watched the news about lost-boys arrival, but few or none show concern or interest in welcoming or meeting lost-boys.

Besides parties thrown by Sudanese communities in welcoming lost-boys to America or to Australia, American volunteers had played a major role in welcoming lost-boys to America by throwing parties where food was prepared, a lot of drinks and pop music went out, as well as dancing called the floor. Many foster care American families for underage took their newly fostered minors around by visiting relatives with them and showing them some beautiful, fun places. Overage lost-boys were welcomed by their volunteer American friends by taking them out to many white people's churches on Sunday, to schools, to friends, or to beautiful, fun places, as well as taking them out for a dinner or lunch. Spending time with lost-boys was crucial as many volunteers stayed with new arrival lost-boys for couple of hours. "We have been waiting for you all these years, and finally, we are pleased to receive you, said Cindy from Atlanta, Georgia." Good Samaritan volunteers or fostered care parents always visited new arrival lost-boys and enquiry them or asked them who was not feeling good, who was sick, or got any problem. Volunteers spend money and time on new arrival lost-boys as that makes lost-boys feel at home. Resettlement agencies welcome lost-boys by meeting with officials, having lunch or dinner together, or having director of the agency come to visit lost-boys and spare a little time in their apartment. Some Good Samaritan caseworkers would organize parties or take new arrival lost-boys out for dinner or to church on Sunday. Although some resettlement agencies don`t even see lost-boys for week after their arrival, some agencies take care of lost-boys by visiting them every day and taking the sick to the medical center or taking them out to visit other lost-boys` apartments.

Many lost-boys attended churches every Sunday for the first time after arrival. Lost-boys go to any first church they were introduced to regardless of which church they were attending in the refugees' camp. Many lost-boys were attending Episcopal Church as well as Catholic; very few came from Baptist churches. Many churches heard lost-boys coming news from different broadcast channels, and eventually, many American churches rushed to bring lost-boys to churches. Many Americans who heard news about lost-boys arrival in their city, rushed to where lost-boys apartments were located and quickly made friend with lost-boys as well as brought them to their churches. Some lost-boys attended two to three churches in one day Sunday as either a volunteer, caseworker, American, or individual Sudanese took them to church on a series of prayers. Lost-boys faith was booted up, and they became close to God as any church they attended doesn't matter to them with the unexceptional of the mosque.

Every church lost-boy visited, they were given Bibles, and each lost-boy ended up with five to seven Bibles from different churches attended on different Sundays, or on one Sunday. Some churches, like Jehovah's Witness, started knocking on new arrival lost-boys doors and set down praying and worship with lost-boys in their apartment. Bibles were distributed to lost-boys in their apartment, just like clothes given away to each lost-boy by their volunteers or fostered care parents. Some individual lost-boys purposed to set up church of their own and to have lost-boys pray in their own church. Episcopal Church or catholic lost-boys began to pray in small congregations of ten to fifteen in rented schools, community libraries, or in city hall. Newly small lost-boys churches were rapidly filled and attended by the Sudanese families every Sunday as the congregation began to swell in school class.

In the face of the stranger, every new look was like a sign of cultural shock; new people around, the food, new place, money, dressing style, language use, culture, and even news on the local TV was disturbing new arrival lost-boys. Humans are used to daily things they see, feel, sense, and like, but anything new is always an extraordinary shock, and that is what happened to lost-boys on their first time arrival to the USA. The first thing that got lost-boys confused was the position of where the Sunrise and Sunset. Waking up in the morning and expecting Sunrise to be very hot from the eastern side of the earth and watching it going slowly to settle in the western part of the earth, Lost-boys missed that when some of them end up not seeing the Sun at all. Some lost-boys see the Sun when it is about to set in the west because they were now in the west, so the Sun comes to them instead of leaving them from east to west.

The weather change affected lost-boys health as the cold was a new experience in the first time lives of the new arrival westerners. Many new arrival lost-boys were sick of cold flu, freezing and sneezing snort out of their nose being affected severely by daily cold from the raining ice stone of snow. It was worse for lost-boys resettled in the northern part of the USA as some lost-boys don't go out at all. Lost-boys stayed indoors for days, expecting cold and snow to halt before they could go out to purchase groceries or go to work. Lost-boys missed enjoying the evening walk along the Turkana trachea-dried seasonal river of Kakuma refugee camp. Missed green local Kakuma shrubs tree of *Peggu* and *Acuil* tree as lost-boys used to hang around branches of the trees at the bank of the dried up seasonal river of Kakuma camp. Loitering between groups and walking to Kakuma town was missed by the closed indoor lost-boys who got nowhere to visit or were confined to living indoors rather than outdoor living of African style. It was a stressful and boring living as lost-boys bear it all from fresh.

Major cultural shock occurs in American public transportation where one can visibly see all American races in the open of how each race dresses, talks, acts, and can be differentiated from there. American public buses, metro transits, and transit stations were they best places where lost-boys easily learned characters of each American race. In the evening, a gathering of lost-boys in their apartment living rooms would discussed how African-American in the public buses stared at them or gossiped few words about them, how white Americans were very concerned about asking them and got close to know them, and how moderate were Latino American as they don't seem to belong to America. Just like African-American, some Africans who met lost-boys seem to be less interested in lost-boys, even not saying hey. Some would bother to disturb lost-boys by gossiping or post-starting cross-eyes.

The only group of race that lost-boys appreciated and associated with was white Americans, who could stop in a minute to ask lost-boys "Are you the one I saw on the TV?' are you lost-boys of Sudan?'; that conversation never ends there as exchange of telephone numbers including addresses was involved. Many lost-boys collected many white American friends compared to very few or none of the black Americans who were friends to lost-boys. Many lost-boys distanced themselves away from black Americans just like other Africans in the USA do, as they believed that black Americans just shared negative name with us but stayed rude and being hostile to Africans living in the USA, causing black people separation across the black people world.

American lifestyle of control level of conversation has killed the African way of random talk conversation, as lost-boys came with a used African way of borderless communication to strangers. Many lost-boys American friends complained a little that their lost-boys friends asked too many questions and wanted to know a lot or talked too much. It was homesickness to lost-boys who missed their home of the motherland, Africa. In the public buses, young Americans, especially teenagers, were more troubleshooting compared to aged Americans; furthermore, young black Americans were more troublesome than aged black Americans. As lost-boys categorized American racial ages, finally, lost-boys associated themselves with white American youngsters who didn't mock, openly gossip, or stare at them just like young black American did. Women's dressing styles shocked lost-boys the first time they arrived in the USA. Sexy dressing style to kill men around was a question of protest in lost-boys mind.

African women seem to be more respectful in a dressing style that would cover men's eyes with sensual parts like protruding breasts, exposure of good-looking booty, or public kissing, as well as any other sexual mood provocation. Lost-boys didn't feel easy to see American lovers walking hands in hand or kissing, hugging, or talking erotic in public. Lost-boys were shocked by a question posted on them by some Americans: "Are you gay partners?" since many lost-boys were still practicing African men's way of walking hand in hand or hand around shoulders, which seemed normal in

African brotherhood way of body touching, but in America, lost-boys were considered gay partners on the street walkways.

Lost-boys were used to listening to radio British Broadcast Corporation, Voice of America, and many other local African radio stations. It was a shock when indoor lost-boys were confined to local city TV channels or local city radio stations that don't broadcast news about America, Africa, or any other part of the world. Lost-boys quietly protest against the media for growing damn and damper by not learning anything from the national and worldly news. Leaning on money usage and getting to know American money units was easy for some lost-boys who came across very many foreign currency exchanges from Dinar, pound, Birr, Shillings, and to Dollar. Some lost-boys stumble by not calculating exact changes, so it was difficult for lost-boys to get jobs as cashiers on their first arrival to America. Food was another shock to many lost-boys who lived away from international food stores or international products that sell African food and other products. Many lost-boys were shocked by using unusual American products like toothpaste or toilet tissue. Some lost-boys bought a tree toothbrush {Acuil *toothbrush*} from a local Somalia store and used it to brush their teeth as they were not readily use to toothpaste and plastic toothbrush yet. Lost-boys purchased dried beans, rice, milk, eggs, okra, peanuts, goat meat, mudfish, oil, and flour as the best food to cook and eat. But broccoli, kale, collard green, butter, and quash were types of food out of new arrival lost-boys food lists.

New city place was amazing to lost-boys as it wasn`t a cultural shock but an adventure of a change. Large parking lots with many cars surprised lost-boys. Upstairs, mall elevators or escalators were stumbling tricks to many lost-boys. Wide freeways or large highways were a scary driveway to some lost-boys. Learning new things to use was a welcome-to-city life message to many lost-boys. Too much abundance of everything in lost-boys eyes caused them loss of appetite in want and needs on the first arrival time. Lost-boys flown away from refugee camps of scarcity to American cities of abundance lost their appetite for any want or need as the fact that their eyes and hearts got satisfied to the point of not wanting to purchase clothes to dress nice, or even eat decent food than just taking lunch by eating cookie and a cup of tea. Lost-boys style of dressing was to wear a suit and tie on iron skin neck, and many lost-boys seemed to be professionally dressed in suits when they hadn`t a field of professionalism.

In spite of hashed cultural shock, lost-boys had a chance for fun and upgraded mood honeymoon for their special adventures in the new home of the last Promised Land. Lost-boys enjoyed the adventure of meeting new American friends, mingling and chatting with new people who met in the churches as well. As students from various colleges or universities loved to converse with lost-boys as unheard strange life story of lost-boys attracted them many American friends. Fun to tour downtown, visit other lost-boys, and add the adventure of free rides from volunteers as well as other Sudanese with cars which could ride lost-boys around the town where lost-boys could amazingly pay closed look at tall and different designed buildings, highways, and other buildings. Learning computers and mingling in ESL class was adventurous for lost-boys. Shopping was also pleasurable for lost-boys, especially in the shopping mall, where some lost-boys enjoy the pleasure of climbing the elevator or using the escalator. Lost-boys enjoyed a new apartment and living in new home as watching TV was the first adventure in the history of the lost-boy.

It was of help to lost-boys when they were grouped in the camp by the JVA and resettlement agency resettled lost-boys in group of three to five in two or three bedrooms. Turn of cooking routine and cleaning duties was easy and quarrelsome to many lost-boys who were living as roommates. Some lost-boys wouldn't like to cook or miss their routine duties, not cleaning the bathroom or vacuuming the carpet, or else some may not want to cook when their turn cooking comes in a round. Eventually, lost-boys got into an argument, and others fought as a result of the duties conflict. It was an amazing story of the first 911 call when police stood there listening to the narration caused by the fight. Some lost-boys were very cooperative and cared for themselves, especially those who were roommates or came from the same sub-tribe or related by clan. New arrivals lost-boys who couldn`t stay together would get separated by the resettlement agency, or other lost-boys could decided to leave the troublesome one and join other group of lost-boys as roommates. Some lost-boys would drink or smoke when they first arrived in America, and their roommates' lost-boys wouldn`t like that if they both didn`t drink or smoke. Lost-boys who had never been friends or who barely knew each other in the camp came to meet in their final home State as a resettlement agent resettled them and rented two or three bedrooms for them. These new faces lost-boys who were strangers to each other, wouldn`t live in peace as sharing bathroom, kitchen, living room, and other things would brought in a problem of arguments and fighting. Many lost-boys were very hashed and hostile on the first day of arrival to America; they were very hot with Kakuma heat where they ought or readily to fight at any time. Some lost-boys taste the jail from day one in America and yet happy spending their honeymoon in the jail.

5. Unaccompanied minors became lost boys

Simple question of "Where are you from" was hardly get answered by new arrival minors in the first reception, where caseworkers, volunteers, or Americans` friends would inquire to know where boys came from and whereabouts where parents or lost-girls. It seemed easy for lost-boy to answer that they were from South-Sudan than to say they were from Sudan, or even easiest to say they were from Ethiopia, Kenya, Uganda, or from U.S., for they have lived in these countries more than ever in Sudan. This marked Sudan as a mostly unknown country to many lost-boys. Where are your parents? It was a shocking and tears-dropped questions many lost-boys wouldn`t answer, and this particular unanswerable question furthered and led to the naming of unaccompanied minors as Lost-boys of Sudan. It was a series of naming and names changed when it came to Lost Boys epical odyssey of their exile living, or anytime they launched into a new flee or entered into another country as asylees or refugees. Lost-boys recalled from the moment they used to be called Village Boys, and in the lonely apartment of Boston lost-boys, they flashback memoirs of being a Village Boys whose destination ended up in America in the mid of an endless odyssey.

The name Village Boys changed when Fugnido and Itang refugee camps were modernized into big refugee camps for the externally displaced Sudanese as well as SPLA expanded and became very powerful with tens of thousands of battalions where Village Boys were trained as another battalion, " the Red Army." The name Red Army became a common military ID name batch for the current lost-boys in the 1980s-1990s, when SPLA was the top rebel leading power in Africa. Jec al Amer in local Arabic became a name of identity to minors' parentless military-trained children soldiers of southern Sudan. Every woman, man, girl, or elderly refugee in the camp would yell out Jec al Amer or call out to the Red Army in any kind of that sorted name. Although, there was Jec al Assout {Black army}, Jec al Amer was the name love and easily pronounced as well as easily called when a minor child soldier passed by a distance.

The Terap Battalion was another name given to Red Armies minor child soldiers after SPLA officers determined a reason for keeping this large number of minor child trained soldiers in the camp for the purpose of feeding them and helping them grow up so that by one day, they will be released with armed to fight the common enemy at the warzone battlefield of any specify enemy-occupied towns in Southern Sudan. Terap {Seed} was a name given to Red Armies in general when the school opened in Fugnido refugees' camp in 1988, where majority of thousands of Red Armies were refugees. The Red Armies, who were school children in the day and became child soldiers in the night were, also became Terap of

Southern Sudan. As many names multiples, it was ok for Red Armies. SPLA soldiers went to the war line, fought, and must captured the enemy strong strategy with enough food to feed the left behind Red Army, who were baby soldiers reserved in refugee camps. SPLM begged or put out begging appeals to all worldly NGOs, governments, international communities, faith-based organizations, UN, or other worldly children organizations to provide food, clothes, and education supplies to baby Red Armies. The logistics of SPLM put Red Armies first in everything as well as Red Army welfare was taking in a comprehensive manner.

Since majority of the Red Armies went to under trees churches on Sunday, it became an attractive scene for U.S and UK church missionaries to fry on the Red Armies as when the Red Armies dressed up in normal clean clothes and went to either Catholic or Episcopal church and set down on the lined up stones or trees benches to worshiped God who they could only understand by Dinka and few Arabic prayers. At the same time, the Red Army was also called "Selected Children of God" as Abunna Matong from the Catholic Church and Father Girma had named Red Armies in the Fugnido refugees' camp. Children of Living God was a name given to Red Armies in the Episcopal Church after mass baptism and had built a long huge hut temple within the church-fenced with Chilim shrubs for community as well as it became the entire Sudanese refugees' worshipped church in the camp.

Even in the Kakuma refugee camp, where Minors' names became popular, Children of God had linked minors to all faith organizations and many churches from Kenya or the entire of Africa where churches flew into the camp and established small churches for worshipped with minors. Even it became a title of fund raising on Western TV churches Ads showing worldly Hungary and suffering Southern Sudanese children, who were in need of food, clothes, and water. The endless naming of lost-boys had been following them in any lost direction of the Odyssey as the epical historic continues. Any new name lost-boys adapt in the new country of asylum do not really bother them, so long they find peace and temporant harmony in any refuge place. Those who are not lost-boys and the Sudanese community could complain about the names given to lost-boys, and some would be willing and ready to change the name at their expense, but the owner of the name is not entitled to change his name other than lost-boy.

Lost-boys recalled and remembered when they were used to be called Minors, meaning that they couldn't produce babies with any woman. The name minor means "underage," although some of the minors were twenty-five or thirty years of age, but living in the minors group marked them as minors too. The name Minors was to replace the name Red Army, and since the military organization living lifestyle of sixteen thousand parentless refugee children was established in a country that didn't support SPLA militarized refugee camp, the Red Army became demilitarized in the Kakuma refugee camp. Kenya became the second country where the Red Army name was changed to minors after they became true refugees of refuge. Many Minors who enlisted SPLA forces from Kakuma in 1993-1999 were military retrained, armed, and called AllahJabu, Jamus, Koriom 2 as a long their liberation warzone militarily named change in continual liberation. The hungry lost-boys in US or Australia would sit down and recall the name *"Ajuel, makoro, or chokoro,"* the name used in the series of hunger or poverty refuge boys who had nothing to eat in those days of starving refuge in western Ethiopia camps. The local Anyuak residents could see Village Boys {Red Army} collecting leftover or thrown away food in villages dumpster so that boys could feed in the serious hunger of 1986-87 as in the recorded event in the Lifeline Odyssey of lost-boys.

Local Anyuak inhabitants used to call Village Boys *"Ajuel,"* when collecting locally brewed wine residual dumped on the dumpster places around villages and eaten during great hunger in Fugnido camp in 1986-87. Makoro described Red Army boys who used to visit Toposa villages or trade with local inhabitants of Kapoeta, whereas many Minors who fled Kakuma hunger depression to Nairobi city became *Chokoros* in the homeless city center of mass street children. Many unaccompanied Minors join bad companies of street-children, thievery, or homeless in Nairobi-based asylum carton shelters. The odyssey of Sudanese Lost-boys would continue with endless naming until the deceased of the lost-boys generation.

Their endless journey started and would be continuing from Village Boys to Red Army and from Red Army to Terap and from Terap to Minors and from Minors to Lost-boys, and the naming list is indefinite. The current name is lost-boys, and still, lost-boys are very optimistic about their next name changes to something else as long as refuge hasn`t come to an end. Lost-boys recalled all the events linked to their naming as that triggered tearful memoirs on a long-suffering odyssey in an emotional moment state of the mind. A long line of series events of naming, lost-boys would recall them a jungle lives, rebel living, refuge camps, parentless, orphanages, war children, great hunger, epidemic diseases, dead comrades, and many sickening ill thoughts memoirs that interrupted lost-boy happy, moody day at work or at home.

Lost-boys was a collected given names to describe the majority mass number of southern Sudanese boys who got separated or ideally lost their parents, relatives, siblings, and other buddies aged from six to nine years old during hostile civil war in Sudan from 1983-2000, whose their lost odyssey ended them up being resettled in the United of America and Australia from late 1999 to 2005. Lost-boys were also called by the name of their geographical, environmental town, places, or area where they got situated. There we have lost-boys from Australia, America, or even the UK lost-boys, in every State in US or Australia, lost-boys got State names like Lost-boys of Texas, California, Nebraska, and Georgia as well as every State out of fifty US states must have a few group of lost-boys families, just like Red Army, who were named after geographical area like Itang Red Armies, Fugnido refugee camp Red Armies, Zinc 1 and 2 Red Armies, as well as Dimo Red Armies, or Molly Red Armies. Naming lost-boys by the town or place of resident had been a common acceptable thing by lost-boys in their odyssey of lost epical history.

Since there isn't any naming, renaming, or name changes without disagreement or an agreement in any way around, Lost-boys faced many arguments or fights over disagreement of the new naming names and being bother other communities around about the names change in lost odyssey of lost-boys. A change in lost-boys names caused many disgust agreements and disagreements within lost-boys and with the outside community. Any naming or renaming in the African tradition is done by offering the blood of the sacrificial lamb or goats, where a clan or family members get invited and set together to discuss or select the right names for the son or daughter. Lost-boys names selection was done like that. It wasn't individuals naming but given as general association of events in the odyssey concurrent of the lost-boys epical history. The organization that was dealing with lost-boys in assistance provision must come up with a name to use in the suitable project of raising fund to help lost-boys in right title. Lost-boys naming scheme depend on what kind of assistance was rendered or what were they issues at stakes or what party was associated or alliance with lost-boys. Red Army was given by John Garang battalion naming officers to alliance and associated trained reserved young southern child soldiers in the refugees' camps. Minors was a refugees naming given for ration assistance provision and rendered cared of underage children in Kakuma refugees camp. Anything to do what lost-boys events or what lost-boys were doing contributed to naming and created additional reason to be named like being a school children in the refugee camp had given name of Terap or refugees school boys. The name lost-boys were given to Minors to answered big question of where were your parents, relatives, siblings or whereabouts did you came from.

Among other factors related to name changes was disagreement among lost-boys themselves when their names title were switched changed in 1988 from a Village Boys to Red Army. Some Red Army who did go for military training were joined into as Red Army regardless of their inner argument of why should untrained Red Armies should get along with trained Red Armies when there was so much argument between these two Red Armies comrades. Some Village Boys who arrived at refugee camps in

Sudan late in 1987 were joined into Red Armies groups and trained for incorporated with Red Armies. These new joining in groups of Village Boys used to face criticism from true Red Armies on how they lived group living in an untrained village lifestyle. Red Armies from different geographical areas didn`t trust themselves as far as getting a long or mingling Red Armies became difficult in the hands of the SPLA officers who did the integration of Red Armies forces. Fugnido Red Armies were the most majority and considered themselves as much disciplined than Itang or Dimo Red Armies, who were considered to steal, misbehave, be shabby, and act with less self-esteem compared to Red Armies in Fugnido refugees camp who act responsible, self-esteem, less military trained and inexperience. Those Red Armies who went to the war zone frontline and returned to the camp for integration faced many challenges of not getting along with Red Armies who had never been at the frontline to see the enemy face.

Minors in the Kakuma refugee' camp got divided along the line of true underage Minors and overage minors who impregnated girls in the tribal group communities in the camp. Minors who lived in fostered cares or in the camp communities didn`t get along with true minors in the minors groups because of the differences in ages and the life preferences. Even in the US or Australia, lost-boys from different States don`t trust themselves unless they lived together before, there seems to be a fear among lost-boys in some States who are considered more drunkards, prostitutes, jobless, drug users, or even those lost-boys overheard to come from a States where crime is high were scared off by some other States lost-boys.

Some lost-boys do not like the name lost-boys as they think this name was given for a degrading purpose, and some lost-boys who got their parents alive and know where their families live dispute the named lost-boys. Many of the lost-boys considered this name as devaluing themselves and degrading their self-esteem and integrity of their manhood in the Sudanese community, or in American society. True Red Armies understood the true meaning of why they named lost-boys, and many of themselves didn`t dispute or disagree with issues related to being called lost-boys. Lost-boys became general names, just like the Red Army in 1980s or 1990s that, describes any young Sudanese man who looks young physically with a deformed, intelligent old man's ideas and talking styles. Many young Sudanese men who look alike just like lost-boys were considered and called lost-boys, but they would either dispute the names or dissociate themselves away from names or groups of lost-boys. True Red Armies and fake lost-boys debated the name lost-boys, but true lost-boys won.

The community was the centerpiece of a major naming disagreement where the Red Army remained isolated from Itang or Fugnido refugee' communities' camp. Since many women or young men in the Sudanese community mistaken and misinterpreted Red Army or lost-boys as a name used to describe those children whose parents died, orphans, homeless, villager parents boys, or a description that devalued Red Armies or lost-boys in any way was unacceptable by lost-boys. Those Sudanese who got resettled through Egypt to the USA or Australia began to ask why they "called you lost-boys."

Sudanese communities don`t like the named Lost-boys and always ought to change the name lost-boys to something else, as well as claim that Lost-boys were lost. They know where they came from, and they have their parents back in Sudan. The name lost-boys served as an Identity that Identified young SPLA veteran boys in unreachable destinations of the epical odyssey. Some American or Australian communities or individuals don`t like these young Sudanese men in the odyssey to be called lost-boys as they would prefer different names. Lost-boys responded back to young men, women, or girls who used lost-boys as a term to devalue themselves in the Sudanese community or those who watched documentary films or read histories of individual lost-boys and used it in disrespected manner.

Even the fact that lost-boys names have become a controversial issue, there was still a window of opportunities gained through the use of these generally projected names. True Red Army, who were true lost-boys, do not disagree or else defended names lost-boys because they had been reaping the advantage of being named differently and in general for the purpose of assistance and other provisional needs,. NGOs were flown in, camps opened, clinics opened, schools got built, food was provided, and all necessitates were provided under the use of the projected named Red Army, Minors, Students, or Lost-boys. Some young Sudanese men sneak into group of lost-boys so that they could also reap all the goodness minors were getting, including resettlement benefits. Even many young Sudanese men got resettled to the USA or Australia after they accepted or surrendered themselves as Minors or used names lost-boys.

The name lost-boys was generally used to define the purpose of assistance, where many individuals wrote hundreds of funded projects, whereas funds didn`t reach the hands of lost-boys. So many NGOs appeal to millionaires on behave of the lost-boys projected names where little funds reach lost-boys in assistance. Lost-boys projected names have been used to benefit individuals or NGOs or even certain lost-boys who gained benefits of assistance from external sources. The names lost-boys helped lost-boys to control, identify, manage, assist and get to know themselves in terms of living together, organization, love, and survival out of solidarity. The named lost-boys united boys as post-conflict civil war veterans and brought lost-boys closer to the created SPLA chapters across the

USA, Canada, and Australia. Lost-boys names were very beneficial to Sudanese communities across the world, where many families got served because of the assistance that came from the names of lost-boys. In spite of the jealousy of individual Sudanese, they community remained united under the named lost-boys as many services could be easily provided by any offering sources under the title called lost-boys. Some elderly Sudanese men love the names lost-boys and always welcome lost-boys into the community with pride, love, and congratulation. The success of the Sudanese community in the refugee camp was dependable on Minors, or Red Army, and the same applies to Sudanese communities in the USA or in Australia, where lost-boys service is organizing the community services and bringing it support from external sources of other communities for appreciation.

Australia started resettling minors after the September eleven hit of the Twin World Trade Center, eventually halting the minors' resettlement of minors to USA. Australian resettlement agencies started taking in remaining minors to Australia as JVA switched from US to Australia minors' resettlement. Many minors got resettled to Australia with their families or in the grouped minors by the resettlement agency. Following the same channel of the US lost-boys, Australian minors got the same name changed as their brothers in USA who have became Lost-boys. Australian government agencies supported lost-boys just as US resettlement agencies supported lost-boys here in USA. Although lost-boys got names changed after a series of every journey to new country of asylum; changing names from Red Army to minors or to lost-boys didn't really change lost-boys problem, or way of living rather lost-boys remain the same in nature or ages.

Changing geographical location as journey of lost continues could emerge or accompanied by names changes too. Many lost-boys bypassed very many tribes a long the way on the range passing Murle, Anyuak, Toposa, Turkana, Boya, Didinga and more across each visited country. What remained the same in lost-boys as the name kept changing with the change in geographical movement was the accent, styles of wearing clothes, as well as many lost-boys retained Dinka dialect or it original accent from either being Dinka Bor or Dinka Ngak or Bhar el ghazel. Some Red Armies spoke Anyuak, or Amharic language during the mingle time of Ethiopia 1980s, or many lost-boys spoke Kiswahili as they were taught in Kenya for nine years. Even if lost-boys hit the new country of asylum they remained unchangeable in cultures or not very many changes applied as that was very different when came to the USA or Australia, where many lost-boys changed in an English accent, style of dressing, and little alteration of cultures. Too many changes applied, no permanent change on many lost-boys temporally living in every country of asylum seem to fit lost-boys for a while, and because the new journey would be called in as the odyssey continues, lost-boys wouldn`t learned anything either being a culture or language of that country fluently. Many lost-boys adapt and easily learned in any foreign country of asylum as in Kenya.

Many lost-boys seem to be missing out a point under pessimistic way of trauma hit in America live when they thought of no more fleeing movement as America become the destination and a final home place where lost odyssey ended. In the back of some other lost-boys mind, there still a place of the last destination where this odyssey must end their journey. Lost-boys know that America or Australia is another country of asylum in the row line before the final destination home of the odyssey. Many lost-boys believe that going back home to Sudan makes the end of the odyssey as from where you started it out must be where you ended it up. Some lost-boys believe that you must either die and get buried here in the US or Australia or find way to heaven where last odyssey home place would be restored by God the father.

The next new name after lost-boys would be marked by the next fled, where lost-boys must flee in the collection of the individual as group of lost-boys to the next or final destination in the still continual odyssey. Many lost-boys were aware that America or Australia was not their found final home because they still facing too many challenges than ever before in the epical history of odyssey. After the stressful work lost-boys would gather in the weekends evening to celebrate the stressful gone by week. Talking the future life was all that lost-boys could discuss as far as where the lost odyssey would final ended. Going back to Sudan would seem to be ending the odyssey as many lost-boys felt like the have reached the end of the entire world and now they have seen nothing important in the world or a paradise world on the earth. They believe America and Australia are two different countries everyone in other part of the world wished to see or live in, but lost-boys found out that proven perception has nothing to do with a proven true odyssey.

New arrival minors chat with their caseworker for a while in a living room shortly after arrival from Africa; where minors and their caseworker jot up few words of introduction in welcoming lost-boys to new found home. Some minors got welcomed by their former unaccompanied minors whose their named title changed to Lost boys, since they been in America for some months, they served as first advisors to new minors in term of cooking stoves lesson. New arrival minors would got advice from former minors or American volunteers on what to cook and how to do cooking in the new kitchen in that very first day of arrival. Minors rest in deep sleeping as their bed where already prepared as well as their room was set up with bed, quilts, bedcover and pillows before they even arrived home. Many explored their apartment rooms after departed caseworker.

Curiosity was number one minors' spirit as they love to move freely and in exploring adventure of the new fled refuge areas as for the case of their first home in America. The first evening meal of super or dinner food was tasteful enjoyed by new arrival minors for the welcoming gusts food as Sudanese called. Minors who were sited in temporary hotel, Jubilee camp, or in temporary States had to eat meals from there before their relocation to their new apartment home. From three to fourteen days, new arrival minors would stay temporary in Jubilee, other States, or may be in the hotel as the resettlement agencies got prepared for permanent apartment home relocation. Jubilee camp was mainly another Kakuma camp as minors thought it to be and other resettled refugees had to stayed for a period of time in order to learned English, job searches lessons, cultural orientation and other learning bases before they got to jump into the American city life. New arrival minors in Georgia stayed Jubilee for a while, as in other small rural town situated outside the city, and minors would seem frustrated being placed in another Kakuma looking-like area.

New arrival minors in Jubilee or in hotel, set quietly after meal as they discussed fear of isolation and lonely living of soldarity they had faced as far as mission of their placement in hotel or in Jubilee wasn't cleared and didn't get into their mind as explained to them by their caseworkers. Volunteers and Lost-boys visited new arrival minors in temporary placement places; it was a fun when new arrival minors met their former minors in the hotel or in Jubilee. As volunteers and visiting lost-boys left, new arrival minors were left in a loomed of loneliness again as the evening fall.

Some minors stayed in Jubilee for three months for a completion of their cultural orientation. Underage minors were resettled by their fostering Americans families and than it was a happy time interacting with white kids and played around in own home where fostering parents check their happy time by counseling underage with issues like home sickness, cultural shock and other life transformation issues. Underage lost-boys settled right with their fostered parents as far few lost-girls were taking care by foster America parents. Overage minors hit America as many cities got a number of minors' resettled overage minors. Deep sleeping and scary snoring were the first characteristic of the new arrival minors as they got tired of the connected flight trips, plus not eating a real meal in the airplane for a day and half.

Cooking in the first days of arrival was a tough arguing and a confusing routine duties as many Lost-boys didn't knew how to cooked in the camp and couldn't on arrival days in U.S; it was a must for them to cooked plus considering the factor of what kind of food to cook. New arrival minors opted to cooked lentils, peas, bean and *ugali as* every day meal or some minors' cooked dried corn mixed with bean, as they used to eat in the camp. Maize was the particular kind of gorilla soldiers food cooked as daily meal in war zone areas and at the time when the Red Army trekked jungle bushes. New arrival minors were helped by already arrived lost-boys who knew little on how to cook, cleaning and even used of Laundromat or used of dishwashing machine. Volunteers also help new arrival minors to cope up with everything that was frustrating them in their new founded home.

Deeply sleeping was longer more than twelve hours as some minors wouldn`t even got up on their bed, as it was cold and chilling all the time day and night for those who were resettled in cold States. In the cold northern States, minors would cuddled in quilts for a day or night, or worse when caseworker didn`t turned on heater for them. Minors were bored by staying indoor a whole day as well as night, as they thought about Kakuma where they hanged on branches of trees or sited under trees airy open places. New arrival Lost-boys set in living room watching TV and browsing TV channels to watched what they had no clues. Most of the time they listened to their cassette taps for elderly advice which they brought from the camp as well as time were passed by listening to Dinka songs and others Africa music by artists like Awilo Longomba, Koffi Olomide or SPLA revolutionary song. New arrival Lost-boys listened to SPLA martial songs as well as Red Army`s song of their SPLA military, SPLA battalions revolutionary or Slama Musica of Sudan. Memoir flashback was the hope of the Lost-Boys as they gathered in joint one apartment to chat, conversed, shared honeymoon and listened to their 1990s Terap battalion songs, or SPLA battalions' military songs of Koriom, Intifadha, Muormuor, Jamus, Eagle and other more battalions. Sudanese youth and families visited Lost-boys as well as American volunteers spent time with Lost-boys to accompany new arrival unaccompanied minors.

6.   Lost boys in the 3rd promised land {usa}

In the black American apartment neighborhood, the rested new arrival lost boys in Arlington, Texas, thought and counted on the number of barefoot journeys travels and wildness they had gone through and now in exile, seemingly land of bills called America. The new arrival lost boys had placed another bet on the new fourth refuge country named America as well as thought about the last or next destination country of another refuge. Lost boys have imaged where the next fleeing journey in the odyssey might hit after the refuge city of America in what is so call found home. Lost boys weren`t sure enough until September 11, triggered their next fear and a warning that signaled the next expectation for the next fleeing status for another asylum after American refugees cities. New arrival minors recollected and did a flashback on their terrific epical history, and only they could think were counting numbers of the refugee camps and countries of refuge as well as number of fleeing treks on barefoot, trucking convoys, or plane trips. Hope to restore lives in the final land of asylum seemed illegitimate for the final destination at the first time of entry to America, and it was a theory conversation in the lost boys ending next fled.

In the historical ladder of fleeing journeys from Sudan's southern villages to western Ethiopia, {1986-1991), back to the southern Sudan jungle {1991-1992}, to Kenya refugee camps

{1992-2005} and again to America and Australia {1999-2005}; Lost boys gustily counted their promised land in a series of Sudan, Ethiopia, Kenya, and the two found homes of America and Australia. In their evening gathering conversation, lost boys believed that America was their final promised land, until September 11 raised a red flag of the next flee warning case where the same common enemy triggered fire on lost boys again. Lost boys who were boarding the plane flying to America were the last to be the final end of the boarding journey to America as the lost boys enemy hit and brought down to ashes two Twin Towers trade centers. It was obvious as it wasn`t a big worry to lost boys who got used to their enemies attacks and the spell of that chaste and ambushing mean used by the enemy along their destinationless fleeing journey.

Australia is believed to be another promised land where lost boys got another found home as they got resettled there after September 11 attack collapsed minors' resettlement to the USA. Both Australia and America became the third Promised Land in the lost boys series of fleeing odyssey and countries of epical asylum. Lost boys begin to see and feel the same life thread, devil, enemy line, headache, weight down by life in America and in Australia after the end of three to four months of cultural shock. Although lost boys compared and weigh every new fled tragic malign in the new country of asylum by different degree of trauma affection, America and Australia life-threatening is the best moderate lost boys can count on compared to the rest of the other previous fleeing odysseys which were full of the hostility of dead. Lost boys had hardly or never believed America or Australia to serve as their final found home. Many lost boys believe that in every new country of asylum, their journey halts in the waiting room, which they consider to be a hot hanging in place of a tightens life-threatening. Lost boys compared the last country of refuge they had just escaped from with newly America or Australian lifestyle, where each country of asylum weight a tragic life lost in the lost boys epical odyssey.

Lost boys in America or in Australia count on how tightens life turns out to be as it was expected to be better. Surprisingly, better life expectation loses their taste as it is moderately getting worse in America, where men's wallet is the only source of life. Most lost boys believed that America or Australia was their finishing lifeline or Sudan would be the next extended ending country to finalize a long destination, less fleeing journey of refuge and asylum. Lost boys living in America or Australia see living on daily bread is getting toughest compare to the lives they had lived in the Kakuma refuge camp in Kenya, where cups of cereal, wheat flour, oil, lentils, and salt were provided free of charge, in addition, water, medical care, housing and education were also provided free of no dim charge by UNHCR, LWF, IRC and World Vision as well as many other non-profit organization were concerns. Moving on is the motive of many lost boys as well, and moving back in total life failure was another motion for failed lost boys, which is obvious to many lost boys who had learned from the epical fleeing history. Many lost boys had lost lives or perished along the fleeing path as well, and more lost boys are now losing lives in homeless American homes.

Lost boys toughest life-trauma in America or in Australia can be counted on collection of single friend roommates living together in one rented or mortgage paying house or apartment of living. Furthermore, lives of lost boys are center on jobs and work-related issues, education, faith, future family life, America's social environment, community affairs as well, as major factors in calculating ages next chance of survival is a thoughtful lost boys major concern. The first trauma that hit lost boys shortly after their three to four months honeymoon of living in a rent free apartment paid by the resettlement agency, food stamps, and other necessities was a storm of mistreatment from some resettlement agencies. Some resettlement agencies which help resettled a number of lost boys from Kakuma refugee camp to America had shortly lost appetite for taking care of these new arrival lost boys.

Caseworkers from these failed agencies had nowhere for visitation to lost boys apartment of living, nobody would take these abandoned new arrival lost boys for shopping, or someone to show them coin Laundromat places, or even find them jobs or take them out to fill application for their ID, Social security or get lost boys jumpstart. These abandoned new arrival lost boys would stay indoors either idly sleeping or watching TV for weeks. No telephone call or no friends to talk them, as these abandoned new arrival lost boys grew lonely and in solidarity, they felt their first cultural shock as it was a bitter taste of the American lifestyle at the end of a short honeymoon or in a mid of lessen money of food stamp. Most lost boys were struggling with their expectations of America and what they have witnessed as a true America. Most lost boys expect to come to America and find jobs immediately to work and fund their dreams of earning as soon as possible, but those lost boys who had failed in the wrong hand of bad resettlement agencies had to stay in the rented apartment till their lease, light, water or food stamps got cut off before one out of five lost boys got a job to pay bills or expenses for living. Some resettlement got lowly paid jobs to most lost boys who hadn`t any experience in anything other that building a *makuti* hut and watering the kitchen garden of okra in Kakuma refugee camp. Lowly paid entry-level jobs started at either $5,6, 7,8 per hour in restaurants, manufacturing plants, retail stores, warehouses, and hotels were the best jobs for inexperienced new arrival lost boys as well as other American job seekers ready to work.

Many lost boys hardly paid off their monthly expenses or

bills after they were employed part-time or had no job at all. But sharing an apartment as roommates helped lost boys in any way where many lost boys save hundred of dollars. Early first employment of new arrival lost boys was the toughest one, and it started from orientation class of ESL where lost boys got oriented on how to fill out job applications, conduct a successful interview, maintaining scheduled job hours, and budgeting money earned from the job as well as time management.

A great shock of depression hit lost boys as they entered into new world of job function and maintaining chances of employment through employment history background checks. Although, lost boys spoke fluent English, the dark, skinny African can be compares with other Sudanese and had no better than any other refugees who came to this country from any part of the world, but lost boys were much better at defeating interviews over other refugees because lost boys were very optimistic and organized when it comes to interviews and jobs performance. Accuracy of conducting interviews, filling out job applications, and maintaining employment were among classes taught by resettlement agency caseworkers or job coaches who helped many lost boys to cop with job employment in the most indirectly hidden racial American or Australian code of discrimination. Employers chose to take lost boys interviewees because of their demonstrated energized power and readiness to work manual work. It was an amazing thing to many job fair employers to see lost boys as a group of young, energized, tall, smooth, dark-skinny Africans who are passionate and optimistic about working, and for the first time to see extraordinary young black Africans once again in America or in Australia.

Many new arrival lost boys were escorted or taken to attend interviews or job fairs by their resettlement agents or caseworkers. Employees in many resettlement agencies were complaining about the lost boys stubbornness, that lost boys had no patience in job searches and other needs, and they wondered why lost boys acted in demanding way or immediate way of wanting jobs now from resettlement agencies. On the job fair day, lost boys could be seen finishing up with many filled-out job application and walking around helping other refugees of African filling their job applications. Many other refugees who speak French, Spanish, Arabic, Bosnia, Somalia, or Kiswahili were helped by lost boys either filling out job applications or in job function communication. Caseworkers help lost boys in the hiring process, or caseworkers serve as staffing services to lost boys and employers. If there was anything new hired lost boys didn`t do right at work, employers would reach news to the resettlement agent or boys caseworker who brought them to the employer. First eight hours in the new job were toughest in tiresome shock to many lost boys as a change of work challenge began to start taking place.

A week in the new job was full of complaints and long rests of sleepiness to many lost boys who were rocking away laziness and idles of the recent futile refugee camp lives. Many lost boys would sleep for ten to twelve hours per a night or a whole day after getting off from eight hours of tiresome work. Long sleeping hours were the only way tired, lost boys could ease off stressful, tiresome job jumpstart and a restful way for another next day to work. African time clock had to be switched to the American busy time clock, and lost boys faced terrific trouble in keeping and respecting the alarm clock on the table. Coming to work late, long lunch or break was very common to some new arrival jobs holding lost boys. Employed new arrival, lost boys complained about pains in their legs, stomach, neck, back spinal, and most parts of their joints and bones affected with striking pains due to long-standing of eight working hours.

Socializing at work was another issue, although many lost boy don`t associate themselves with their colleagues who are American co-workers, but they easily do with other refugees, foreigners, or other immigrants. Lost boys easily mingle with Spanish co-workers more than they do with American born employees. It is like a new group of new Americans versus oldest group of Americans. New arrival immigrants Americans seem to be very skeptical about oldest immigrant Americans as both lack trust to have connection or relation of living. Interaction was very intense as lost boys would mingle or socializing themselves at the lunchtime or break with other employees of their reserved types like Mexican or other Africans.

Using public transit was a key for lost boys to get to work for the first time, so caseworkers consider reliable transport as lost boys used public buses or transit as the only way to get to work. Although, lost boys got tired after eight hours of work, they could either respect the alarm clock or get to work late because transit comes at the stop at the designed stop as it is timed. Missing bus or transit stop time was very common, and many lost boys waited for long minutes before they could catch another bus or transit. Lost boys who got jobs in areas of the town where buses or public transit could not reach would take rides with co-workers or quit that jobs. Some lost boys were very aggressive and even sometimes provokes bus drivers to anger on the hand argument on payment or exchange issues.

Lost boys walked to bus stations or transit stations in groups, and that scared transit police or even the retail store police or apartment guard. Public transportation was the cheaper means of transport for lost boys. Even when some lost boys have saved money that they can afford to pay for a car, the rest of the lost boys still use public transportation up today. Many lost boys stick to public transportation since the first day they entered America because it can be afforded rather than car insurance and maintenance. Some lost boys whose driving licenses suspended under the influence of drugs or alcohol meant to use public transportation.

Getting off from the transit, lost boys started gossiping in sharing stories of the public transportation, how transit ride sharers looked at them, and what they overheard from those who were in the transit as far as their skin color and physical was concerned. Lost boys considers original American, either white or black, to be more racist.

Americans like to have a space in between, but lost boys would get in between as they got used to Africans overcrowded nature. Public transportation is the most overcrowded ride at rushing hours because it is the mean of transportation which is a base for affordable ride to low income Americans as well as new arrival lost boys. Sometimes, lost boys got to walk some short distances in between shopping stores or to bus stops or even walk to work distance where bus doesn`t reach; and in a cold or extreme weather, it was terrible in northern States where chilling cold always chill on ride less lost boys who awaited buses or transit in the cold freezing weather.

Some lost boys walked to their nearby working places, and since lost boys were still active in walking, some could walk a distance of 35 miles going to work and came back without a thought of any paid mean of transportation. Many lost boys bought their transit pass tickets a head of the time and use them before expiration date of issue. Public transportation was the only first means of affordable public transportation for lost boys and other day to day jobless, non-driving license, and low income Americans depending on public transportation. Public transportation helped low-income lost boys to save money as well as it does to many low income Americans who pay a dollar for transit rather than paying for gas or car insurance.

Lost boys who bought cars after three months after their arrival in America were at risk of stress as their faulty driving record hit high in a situation where police tickets hit them at a high costly rate. Speeding, accidents, drugs, drunk and drive as well, and bad parking were all source of lost boys license suspension. Many lost boys got many driving faults and had their license taken away by the police as it was very dangerous to those lost boys who had caused tragic deathly accidents after drunk and driving. Paying car insurance, title registration, emission test, car maintenance, and gas was very costly to low income lost boys or jobless who couldn`t afford their car loan payment end-up losing the car to auto-loan or car finance, as many lost boys do voluntarily repossession.

Lost boys who have cars can help their careless roommates giving them a ride to work or taking them for shopping, as well as others share the same car. Buying expensive cars from ten thousand

and above was the favorite of lost boys from the earlier time they came to America, and that altitude didn`t last as lost boys got into America lifestyle system of spending. Lost boys drive from State to State for many reasons other than a weekends drinking celebration, weddings, meetings, visitation, or SPLM chapter important day. Many accidents were caused by lost boys during their early driving learning experiences as they hit driving on Interstates highways and other traffic jam boulevards. Lost boys were considered by the county police department to be enthusiastic youngmen who lacked proper driving experience and order of law. Many lost boys got charges of drunken driving, driving signs or rule violations, and speeding, as well as red pickups.

Many lost boys went to courthouse several times until their wrong-given driving police ticket got clear. Too many arguments were raised by lost boys to policemen when pullover at faulty drive.

Many lost boys complained that police were not fair to them as some policemen would stop them and issue a ticket for racial discrimination rather than a valid ticket for reckless driving. Many lost boys would argue with policemen at the stop drive on the issued ticket, as many charges were disagreeable. Many lost boys would drive without States insurance or even without State driving license as they end up being thrown into the jail by the police. Man lost boys don`t show a sign of being scared when meeting or stopped by a policemen, they always find a reason to argue and disagree with a policeman.

Driving records that hit high tickets and accidents are charged a high rate of insurance or expelled by the insurance company, and this punishment has reduced lost boys driving faults for the better, or shaped some lost boys to drive without passing red lights in a very careful caution. Many lost boys loss their driving licenses for good as the State police required Hugh amount of money to be paid on the accumulation payment on the suspended license. Some very careful and cautious drivers lost boys have been driving very carefully and have no driving faults record, and that project them to pay less insurance rates on their cars. Driving was the most tragic thing the first time lost boys entered America or Australia, but this tragedy died down as consequential punishment reached its highest in learning lost boys. Now, many lost boys drive safely, and many got no license to drive or drive illegally, sometimes to get beers or liquor home in the dark time when police can be dodged around.

It was about time when the servicing power of assistance was placed or transitioned to lost boys hands so that they couldn't feel the weight of feeding themselves in new American life. Resettlement agencies which were helping lost boys for a set period of time, almost three to four months of free servicing by paying rent off, light bills, free rides for shopping, and other services, had to say bye by to old arrival lost boys for a chance of helping new arrival lost boys. Moreover, volunteers and others helping friends disappeared from lost boys sights. Although, underage lost boys and others overage lost boys had to stay in the homes of their caretakers or fostered parents, they also had seen elimination in some of the free services and assistance offers to them. Many of the lost boys were opted to start living without any volunteer, caseworker, or American friends due to that services ceased by resettlement agent. Leaving the volunteers, resettlement agencies, and other American friends was a shock, since many lost boys were still very dependable or bottling feeding on volunteers, helping American friends, or caseworkers' services. Not only did lost boys loose important guardians like volunteers or caseworkers, but they also lost many friends due to time factors and having no free social life sociality, which has just started in the mid of mixtures mood of honeymoon and a stressful shock.

Another thing lost by lost boys was government assistance support like Medicaid, food stamps, match grants, and even resettlement of other camp minors had come to cease due to the September 11 attack. Every free service was switched off or turned off in a situation where Lost boys begin to see oneself as a true, independent, responsible Americans who are dealing with life in America as the old immigrant Americans. Many lost boys seemed to be losing control of themselves as the monthly free services came to cease after three or four months of the lost boys arrival from the Kakuma refugee' camp. Many lost boys were very overwhelmed in the first three-four months of their arrival.

Having Lost boys starting life in America with eight hours of five days of work, school work, and caught up in adjusting to resting via busy hours in shortening longer used to sleeping of African as that was the beginning of the traumatized American life jumpstart. Even lost boys who used to take care of themselves in the camp turned to be careless in those few months' bits taste of America's bitter lifestyle; carelessness mount later, but it began when boys don`t do hair cut, nail cut, used deodorant, washed their clothes, eat healthy food, wore clean clothes, used cologne or even dressed-up professionally on the days of attending interviews.

Transitioning themselves from Kakuma refugee's camp lives to American City living style was kind of a mocking issue. In the Kakuma refugee camp, no refugee could ask another refugee what kind of clothes each wore, or no other refugee could determine if the other refugee had mismatched clothes or even walked barefoot. Lost boys switching point from a refugees lifestyle to an American city lifestyle wasn't easy at all, but a slow change came in as a result that lost boys responded to criticism daily posted by laughing, starring, and jokingly speaking American who always run their freaky mocking words on lost boys who looked like Nairobi chokoros or homeless a cross U.S cities.

Starting from a minimum wage, lost boys first jobs in their lifetime and first job in America paying little at the beginning and rise elevated wage bar, but expenses of bills and rent were made permanent. In the first three to four months of arrival, many lost send a lot of money to Africa, particularly in the Kakuma refugee's camp or Nairobi, where their friends, family members left. New arrival lost boys would loaned or asked for money from known lost-boy friends already resettled in the States before them to purposely send this money back to Kenya as a servicing need to help those left behind was a priority number one. Many lost boys send money via the camp's local fast-growing Al-Barakat International Bank, where refugees in the camp lined up to receive money from lost-boy senders.

At a goodwill assistant, many lost boys would even send money to a collection group of friends just to inform friends of their safely arrival to America. Every single night, a hundred phone calls rang from Africa, and it rocked the lost boys' apartment as lost boys don't sleep anymore. Lost boys gave their number away to many friends, relatives, and even strangers of their clan residing in the camp to call for the hope of support from the boy, who is expected to be earning a lot of money in the USA as their thoughts went on.

Many lost boys didn't sleep, but stayed up as a call receiving secretaries of his own night. Due to time variation, when it is night time in Africa, it is a day light in America, and lost boys rest from any African phone calls. Lost boys apartment turned out to be a calling center at night when lost boys friends and families could line-up for a call at the local camp international caller. Lost boys at lower levels of minimum wage couldn't save money as they kept spending the whole of their earnings in Africa over, balanced their savings or used their budget in all little they were making at lowly paid jobs. Volunteers and caseworkers had shown lost boys assistance to open their bank accounts across America, and lost boys hardly saved little due to too much sending many to Africa. Many lost boys would send more than five to seven hundred dollars every month, and this sending left many lost boys surviving on cookies or biscuits snacks as permanent meals of lunch and dinner. It was a weight-loss boys life beginning as lost boys first entered into American life.

The first taste of life in America was a very bitter mix of lost boys' adventurous honeymoon and life transitioning cultural shock of high levels of stressful trauma. A controlled life of staying indoors with fewer socializing places or less time to mingle with no public Americans was the first cultural shock lost boys confronted. Managing time on school, work, sleeping, resting, and friendly visits was another new experience that added the burden of a shock. Mingling in the public of America was full of so many strangers' eyes staring and gazing abusively at lost boys, and many lost boys would sit quietly in their apartments discussing how American perceived them to be different dark-skinned black creatures.

Maintaining jobs and employment status was very fragile as many lost boys loose temper easily and readily to fight off supervisors and many other co-workers whom they felt distrust and dislikeness at the workplace. A long refugee's stress had deformed lost boys into a less angry management lifestyle. Many employed lost boys easily kick, punch, and throw down their bosses, supervisors, or co-workers. Many lost boys complain about being discriminatively underpaid, over-supervised, overlooked, perceived negatively, insulted, bullied, humiliated, attacked, and even ignored by managers at workplaces. In the evening, as lost boys return from work, a group of roommates sit in the living room or group of a visiting friends discussing how interaction with Americans becomes one of the most difficult things in the world. Lost boys sough of distrusting American co-workers who seem to have problems understanding boys' heavy African English accents.

Many lost boys lost their new jobs, but were still under the control care of other roommates, and since there was no more resettlement agent to find jobs for lost boys, lost boys could only find jobs through social networks, jobs staffing, recruiters, and school jobs placement. Lost boys who lost their jobs were taken care of by their caseworkers where some got no care in searching for a second job, being driven around for a second chance to get another job, or what to do next after losing their job, a question of Hitting Street of homeless found home. Lost boys do have conversations across the States in sharing talks on the topic of experiencing America in different States. Sharing life experiences and facing it toughest were topic of mind discussed by lost boys.

Lost boys complained about how bitter America's living turned to be in the mid of its beginning, when lost boys started facing work or American racial discrimination factor on the public places. From State to State, lost boys, colleagues, and friends called each other as well, and they conversed on issues of honeymoon mixed with seemingly cultural shock buried inside dark, skinny racial discrimination. Some lost boys wouldn't even take a bath after getting off from work, as they were complaining about how tiresome they were and opted not to cook or even eat anything rather than they chose to go to bed and remain in bed until a time to go to work woke them up. One may slept for ten to eleven hours before the alarm clock forced them up. Since lost boys were not concerned about eating healthy food or balancing their diets, they had an added burden of unhealthy states in addition to a weak health that came with them from Kakuma camp. Some lost boys would eat donuts or had a cup of milk tea as a lunch, or some may eat junk food for the sake of hunger rather than healthy eating.

Lost boys started getting more independent after the recovery from the probe of cultural and trauma living style transitioned to become a true American. It wasn`t easy for lost boys to get jobs or even go out there to find jobs, as many lost boys complained about indirectly being discriminated against in the process of pre-application or job interview screening by those hiring managers. Some lost boys complained about how American typical co-workers or managers used them over the fact of their hardworking ability, and that included over supervision, over worked, and taking advantage of hardworking lost boys ability in any assigned tasks within the company. Expecting promotion and raise was empty expectation to many hardworking lost boys who accused supervisor of the American type of mistreatment, discrimination, harassment, or not treating them equally with either white or black Americans.

Since lost boys do industrial, manufacturing, and production jobs, many lost boys face jobs affected side due to their physical health nature. Some lost boys who work in cool places of production plants, complained about pain in their long-time wounded or fractured bones affected by the cold. Heat and other chemicals affect lost boys in chemical production plants. Many lost boys got hired in groups and worked together as union of workers by the same company, which was impressed by the lost boys epical history or their hardworking ability.

It was easy for Lost boys to work together in one company and share their feelings while working as co-workers compared to those lost boys who complained about co-workers being different and mistreated them in a different way that discriminate on how lost boys got perceived negatively or sometimes gets mock at by some other co-workers because of their unique physical appearance. Many lost boys quit their jobs or end up being fired under what lost boys described as an indirect racial discrimination act, which is not been introduced as a law yet in America.

Living expenses were equated as lost boys, reducing the amount of money sent to Africa to minimum. The prioritized first budget becomes bills to pay and some other loans like car monthly payments. Living as a collection of roommates saved lost boys heel lot of money, and many lost boys were able to purchase their first car in the first three to five months after arrival to America from the refugees' camp. Many Lost boys rarely purchase cars by loan, but love to pay cash on used cars as many Africans do get a used car for a price range from three thousand to eight thousand dollars as they believe to be free from loan interests lenders.

Some Lost boys saved tremendous amounts of money, but other lost boys who used their money on dating American girls, drinking, travel, and sending money to Africa have little savings compared to typical lost boys who don't smoke, drink, dates, but only stay focus on working, schooling and saving. Many lost boys pay a lot of their money out for their school tuition, or tuition of the children, or family member sponsorship in Africa. Many lost boys send a lot of money to Africa or Australia in support or establishing foundation of marriage to specially called in-laws families while preparing for wedding. Lost boys, who are living with girlfriends or married as their wives joined them in the US, seemed to be spending a lot of money on rent, mortgage, bills, or in-laws support in Africa compared to those groups of lost boys who are still single roommates. Some lost boys send up to ten thousand dollars to their families in Africa so that their families can purchase many herds of cattle and become riches or use those cows for marriage. One cow costs about three to four hundred dollars in Dinka land, and these cows are used to pay marriage dowry or serve as source of being riches in the Dinka cattle boomers. Many lost boys tried to break these barriers of a cultural way of living and spending uselessly, but it hasn`t come to be true.

7.   Lostboys grew lostmen: education is a key mission

Education has been a dreaming key destination for lost-boys, since from the genesis of the lost-boys creation. Education needs fulfillment is a lost-boys dream that emerged from the village all the trekking way to America. From southern Sudan villages to eastern Ethiopia, village boys trekked thousands of miles in the hope of their education search, and they did get education offered in under-trees classrooms in Fugnido, Dimo, and Itang refugee camps. It was a dream of education that moved hungry, thirsty, tiresome, and sick village children of nine to ten years to cross the desert and semi-arid jungle for three to five months barefoot trek to Ethiopia. It was a dream of education that encouraged Red Armies to go through gorilla military training in Dimo, Fugnido, and Bilpam. Ambition to become a Doctor, professor, teacher, and even an engineer has moved minors across the hellish trek of the most dangerous African refuge life all the way to the USA. It was a dream of education that strengthened the hearts of those Panyido village minors to bury their brothers in unopened graves under trees left away the body in Panyido overcrowded camp during cholera outbreak. In the hellish bush schools of Pachalla, Pakok, Narus, Moli, and Palataka, the Red Army became a seed of education planting where a community of Southern Sudan bases their hope for tomorrow's reconstruction and development of the war-destructed Sudan.

All the way along on the path dream, the main dream of lost-boys has been an education, NGOs, UN, SPLM, and many other organizations have helped lost-boys to achieve their dreaming education as a key to their main living for life. Minors only lived to see another day in Kakuma's hellish life only when they could barely attend Makuti school classroom. Education is the only mother and father to orphans, minors, the Red Army, and separated children of war like lost-boys in most parts of Africa. Lost-boys were the first and maybe the last generation of African refugee children who had that free opportunity education offered by LWF and other NGOs to have minors studied from primary school to secondary or even Kenyan colleges, which were fully supported and sponsored by organizations like RADDA Barner, JRS and churches. A living hope of education has been a key life support and courage that survive lost-boys all along the pathway of their tragic odyssey in epical destination less journey. It is this dream of education fulfillment that spreads lost-boys over the world as seeds disperse by the planter. It was this special dream of education that took and brought lost-boys to South Africa, America, Australia, Norway, and other part of the world. Long live lost-boys dream of education. A child without mother, father, and relatives can survive by education alone.

They were told to leave their exercise books, pens, school

bags, learning academic books, and exam papers on the table and go away to do the process so that they could come to the United States of America. " in my country, there are a lot of examinations to take, too many classes and semesters to score, so do not worry about these small camp examinations," he told them while they were sitting on the floor in under trees minors meeting, John Livingstone resettlement sponsor. Minors put down their pens and left KCPE as well as KCSE Kenya national examinations so that they could do process of resettlement to come to America for further and higher education. Education was on the top number one priority list for minors in any interview they had attended with JVA and INS. Minors came to the USA for the purpose of education, which is a very different key issue of why they come to America compared to other African citizens who come to America for the sake of a better life. The one and only word that comes out of the mouth of four thousand resettled lost-boys across United States is EDUCATION.

Stepped down onto American soil in New York, lost-boys held handbags or small backpacks with only a few African books, the backpack had nothing else in it than just a few books or papers. It was an amazing question when the Red Army hit a bush-to-jungle bush escaping trek without or with a backpack made of tent-patched pieces and filled with exercise books and papers. From Fugnido refugee camp to Kakuma refugee camp and from Kakuma refugee camp to United States refugee camps, lost-boys all along the way carried nothing in their backpack than a Bible and a few books and papers. Meeting caseworkers, American volunteers, and agencies in the airport, lost-boys, the first words of greeting and handshake were education, education, education. The message of education has spread across the United States, where every single lost-boy lives in the USA. After a complete minor's resettlement to the USA, there was a sound of education complaints around lost-boys apartment, church, party, and even in the lodge. The continuity dream of education restarted shortly after lost-boys arrived USA, and continuation of classes was the first expectation in many lost-boys minds, which wasn't the case as job search became first rather than education classes resumed as a continuation from the left classes in the camp refugee education. Many lost boys thought that the system of education in America was the same as that of Kenya so that they could easily come to the USA and resume classes from where they stopped and left in primary or secondary Kenyan school.

Many lost-boys made a loud crying noise after their arrival to the USA as they were demanding to go to school immediately after two to three months of arrival. Caseworkers, volunteers, agencies, and friends get lost-boys started with ESL, computer operation, and job search classes. Peers of lost-boys attended evening or morning ESL classes of levels three to seven and computer classes as well as job search and interview tip classes. Many resettlement agencies founded a project only for lost-boys education, starting up from ESL to job and from job to GED through college admission. After lost-boys scored high in their ESL classes and got jobs from agencies, the next step was a High school diploma, GED, TOEFL, SAT, and high-end college admission. After one year of arrival to America, many lost-boys passed the level of ESL, and the majority got admission into many American high schools. American high School admission required lost-boys to present their primary school report form, and high school entry test. Many lost-boys were admitted to grades nine, ten, and eleven as their high school tests determined them.

American friends, caseworkers, and lost-boys Foundation bought GED, TOEFL, and other examination books for lost-boys who were ready to study and hit a test room. Many lost-boys study after work and prepare for GED many passed the GED test and earned their high school equivalent as they were excited about going the way to college. Those lost-boys who failed some GED five tests would be required to repeat only the failed tests. Those lost-boys who failed GED class entry test were taken back to level six or seven ESL classes. Many lost-boys were also admitted to adult learning classes or adult high school academics, where they obtained their GED diploma. Many lost-boys find it difficult to understand the way the American teaching style was very different from the African classroom teaching style. Many lost-boys who went to American high schools came home from school with many stories of complaints and protest about how young American high students their classes started overlooked, backbiting them in the classes. High school lost-boys included underage lost-boys, faced a questions of mistreatment by classmates teenagers American as lost-boys students were considered very old to be in high school and being laughed at due to their most dark skin, skinned, heavy African English accent and had no lower teeth, added more humiliation and peers group harassment. Many high school lost-boys students consider high school in America to be the most stressful learning institution for non-born American high school students. Lack of discipline and respect from American born high school students is always a cause of cultural shock to non-American born high students who are more reserved and disciplined when it comes to class, and teachers respect in a quite respectful class of an honor teacher. Disagreement between American and foreign born high school students is debatable.

As many lost-boys graduated from high school, completed their GED across the United States, and then come to college and university admissions as the cries of lost-boys education continued. Applying to college and university in America required lost-boys to submit SAT scores, High school diplomas, GED transcripts, TOEFL scores and College entry test scores. Many lost-boys passed all the requirements to their school of admission, and huddle was a college entry test that required English and mathematic proficiency knowledge at a college level. Many lost-boys went through another frustration after most public colleges required them to repeat ESL classes in college or university of admission as foreign students are targeted for English as a second language.

Some lost-boys got college admission after they submitted TOEFL scores with their African high school report form from Kenyan secondary schools.

Many lost-boys who have graduated from high school or held GED joint technical colleges and public associate degree colleges across the country, as well as majority of the lost boys, joined the USA Army, Air Force and Navy across the country. Many lost-boys academic intention was to finish their associates, bachelor or technical college so that they could further their master's and PHD studies. Disciplines in computer science, law, political science, business administration and nursing were the most admired first programs of study chosen by many lost-boys. After five to seven years in America, many lost-boys serve as graduates with associate, bachelors and some with masters degrees. Across the country, there are more lost-boys graduating every year from high schools, colleges or from universities.

Financial aid has become a main source of lost-boys tuition funding, as well as federal student loans, grants, and scholarships. Scholarship is awarded to lost-boys who practice playing basket ball, or who scored higher GPAs in high school or college. Majority of lost-boys pay their tuition either by financial aid mean or out of their own pocket. Many lost-boys students applied and joined privates' schools where they would get huge financial aid or loan that pay off entire degree tuitions. Public universities and colleges charges low tuition fees, and many lost-boys could end up paying their own tuition fees out of their pocket. A credit hour per a dollar is of lower rates charge in public schools compared to highly expensive private schools credit per hour rating. Many lost-boys who completed associate degrees in public school have ended up paying around twelve or more depending on any community college they attended.

Many lost-boys students who have finished their first Bachelor's degree in private schools have already loaned up to fifty thousand US dollars and regularly paid back federal education in monthly installment of two hundred to whatever amount agreed to pay per a month after graduation. Interest growths are big factors in a place where interest itself doubles the amount of the original principal federal loan or subsidized and unsubsidized federal loan. Paying back a federal loan is a slow processes that incur huge financial interest over a period of longer time. Many university or college graduates who do not have enough money to pay back their monthly installed federal loan would appeal for a grey payment period or deferred payment suspension or pay less than that proposed by federal lenders. After graduation, students get their degree papers, and the case of paying off loan remains with federal education loan. Unlike many developing countries where your degree remains with them until you pay off last cents before you take it and hang it on your room wall. Many lost-boys went to Africa to work and still pay their federal school loan here in the US. It would be hard for those graduated lost-boys without jobs to pay back their loan.

Many lost-boys students took a whole federal or loan bank tuition that would cover at less three or four years' degree, including living personal expenses in the school dormitory. Such a huge federal or bank school loan for study yield high end interest, and paying it back would take longer processes. But if the plan goes well with student to get a job in his/her graduated field, he/she could pay the student loan back at once or pay exactly monthly installment. Since entry-level jobs are always temporary, causing distraction from academic school continuation, lost-boys students decided to stay in the school dormitory and have federal loans take over control of tuition and personal expenses pay off in agreed period of a degree time ending. Since lost-boys hadn't no parents or relatives to pay their tuition fees or support their personal needs or other expenses, just like the majority of American students, many lost-boys end up dropping out of universities or colleges because of unstable entry-level jobs and lack of financial support difficulties. Many lost-boys students lost hope in education as financial support difficulties emerge and lack of support from anyone, and that forces boys to abandon school.

The first primary problem with many students of lost-boys/girls is American way of teaching, studying, grading, testing, examining and passing scores. Many lost-boys students fail tests, and exams, repeat classes or end up with underscore grades due to that American grading system or way of learning is completely different from their previous African system of teaching or grading scores in Kenya. Lost-boys are still rigid with African or British ways of teaching, grading or way of scoring examinations, but Americans system of education is completely different from that of Africa or the Far Eastern world. African system of teaching is based on instruction where instructors put the notes on the board, teaches, lecture, and students are free to not interact with each other or no discussion between students or less question and answering between students and a teacher. Many African school systems of teaching is of less student interactions or teachers.

Multiple choice examinations or testing is not very common in some African schools where dried questions hit the examination, and students are expected to completely answer toughest mathematic questions without a calculators. All exams or test questions will come in terms of true or false, desciption, explanations, discussion or put in order. The American way of circling students' discussion, class random question responses, class presentation, class participation, class peer learning and even group assignments is not the system of learning lost-boys got used to before they came to America. American school grading, where the overall passing score is determined by how long you talk in class in the last semi-semester, or how much did students interacted with or discussed assigned topics in class. This grade scoring system leaves lost-boys students with fewer hundred scores on less portion of examination or dried test questions and ends up failed portion of discussion or class participation. Talkative students score high on discussion and less on tests.

Many lost-boys students' do not like to open their mouths in class discussions because they are shy, feel offended, or do not like the way they sound when other students react to their heavily accented English or oppose their responses. African students like to receive teaching with notes taken and responses by scoring high on the dried test or examination questioning time, not by doing in class-group assignments or group discussions, which they consider less proven of what students learned. Many African students assumed that the American way of teaching, learning and way of examination is the easiest way for students to learn in the world. Grading scores on class discussion, group assigment and class participation are considered free grade scores by many foreign students. Unlike developed world students, the third world students do learning by paper and pen as well as by questions and answers as a proven acquired knowledge of students passing score examination. American examination timing is too quick and not right for foreign students who spend a lot of time repeatedly doing the same examination over and over again, not because of the test difficulty but because of it quick time factor.

Another overlooked factor in the American grading system is grading under the interest of racial discrimination. A dishonest white teacher would rank his three students in a class depending on his/her interests driven under hidden racial factors. A white teacher would mark scored high white students, second Indian/Asian, third African-America, and lastly Dark, skinned African students, including Lost-boys. The same is true for black teachers, but foreign professors have different viewpoints when it comes to this racial grading discrimination. Lost-boys students' complaints that failing grade is ninety percent hidden racial discrimination against victim students being racialized. Many lost-boys students believed that their dark skin color had something to do with how low their teachers scored their grades or ranked them last in the class where they expect to be ranked higher depending on their claimed overlook well performance in the class.

Many lost-boys also believed the continent or country of

origin has been playing an overlooked role in how low their teachers' undergrade scored on their tests, examinations or overall failed class scores. Sitting in uncomfortable class where classmates laugh, joke, or do amusement on one dark-skinned student in the class, is a cause of failing class to many lost-boys. Classmates bully or play racializing jokes around lost-boys because of their skin color and continent or country of origin, and sometimes, fights broke out between African-American students and African lost-boys students. Negative perceptions of the community have crept the way to school in a way where some teachers or schools would still overlook students of their overlook community at the level of racial hatred but in a hidden, defendable way. Lost-boys students become the last most racialized students when white students treat them low, African-Americans treat them low as well, and Indian or Asian students treat them very low, too. Many lost-boys students quit school for good because of hidden racial school discrimination.

The percentage scoring of American education system is very high compared to the Kenyan education system of percentage scoring. The average failing grade in Kenya is D, or fifty percent of the overall average score. D is the failing grade in the American grading system, and that is several percent of the average total scored per examination. Setting grading per credit hour per examination is not fair for how much a credit hour for a dollar, and this hidden factor has demoted or wasted many students' tuition money as lost-boys students are among American students society. Failing grade below 2.00 GPA is a must for some school expulsion, and many lost-boys students quit public school because of this freedom that move to private non-traditional schools. Problem of grading, teaching, learning and examination timing in the American system of education has discouraged and dropped many lost-boys students out of education and lower academic performance across American schools. Very few determine lost-boys students' work harder to achieve American students' standard level of competence and reach graduation date as job level of competition in America.

Many lost-boys transfer their credits from college to college or from university to university, and that is freedom for transferring lost-boys who are facing hurdles in their current school. It is an advantage to lost-boys who are for the shortcut and want to cut money by cutting short their education in a way that they get admitted in those diploma, certificate and short courses colleges of eight, nine months or one year technical colleges. Some of the short course disciplines are ranging from diplomas or certificates in paralegals, nursing, computer courses, mechanical repairs, plumbing, painting and more. Many lost-boys who had attended Job Corps were awarded their high school diploma and certificate in short courses in plumbing, car repairs, nursing and computer courses. Online high school diplomas or short courses were taken by lost-boys who had attended Job Corps or do online studies at home. Lost-boys choose to take any shortcut courses or college programs of study depending on their preference without utilizing American standard use of selecting program of study after analyzing the job market. As far as the African way of learning is concerned, many students choose their careers, or program of study depending on their family preferences or field of study likeness, as that is the case with lost-boys too. Lost-boys education is not limited to a high school diploma, short course or high studies for a PhD.

One of the most touristic problems lost-boys/girl students encountered with is choosing a program of study or major in any discipline. Many American do not hold PHDs because they chosed program of study or return to school for only program or major in a study field that is job marketable for top hiring with high earnings in the American job market. Lost-boys with African viewpoints of selecting program of study were completely different from that American students' way of choosing a program of study. African students or Asians studying in the USA chose a program of study just like lost-boys, because they chose a program of study depending on their parents' preferences, field of their interests, field program of their strengths and their peers' friend field of interest. Many lost-boys students choose a field of study or major in any study program with the intention of what they would like to do back home in Sudan, regardless of what they would do in America, they would rather chose a field of study that they would have interest in doing in

Sudan.

Lost-boys students' do not even evaluate top job market degrees or see school counselor before they could jump choose the field program of their studies; eventually job degree market in America depends on what skills or studies are needed to get the job done in a specialized industry. Nursing has become a central piece of study across the United States, but none or few lost-boys students are interested. Many lost-boys students would take humanitarian or political-related programs of study as their epical odyssey focus or speak their mind about politics and humanitarian services. Lost-boys students switch majors and fields of study frequently before or even after graduation to fit their preferences for hearty education. Overtaking more classes as well as dropping classes or paying more tuition has been a result factor of changing field of study or transferring from school to school seeking a specialized program of study. Lost-boys students do very well in programs like political science, history, computers, law, business education, sociology, mathematics, geology, and religion studies, as well as criminal justice. Lost-boys students do not worry about getting job or not in any chosen field of study, as the fact that they want to advance further studies in any chosen field of studies as well as do more certifications related to the same professional field.

Lost-boys are experiencing too many problems at school,

name it from any high, college or technical school, lost-boys and girls are treated by American-born students in the same way that Kenya-born students treated lost-boys students when lost-boys used to live in Kenya. Many lost-girls and boys complain about degrading scores, under-graded, overlooks, and not being liked in the classroom by either a teacher or American-born students. It was a quote of the hate and segregation when many lost-boys residents of the southern States of the United States complained and revealed evidence of most hate by black African-Americans. The top range black hatred States for lost-boys are Texas, Mississippi, Alabama as well as Georgia, where many cases were documented, including the author's apartment attack on September 11.

Communication was the first problem lost boys and lost-girls underage experienced in American high school classrooms. The school cultural shock started when the American English accent became a problem where none of the lost-boys and lost-girls got to hear anything that came out of the white or black teacher's mouth or, even worse, with niggers on the main street. There is nothing bad like lecturing to an audience who has no ear to listen, and presumed listeners would be given intensive examination on what was lectured, and a teacher expected them to pass. It was hard heard for lost-boys to understand what African-American with local non-standard English said more than it could be compared with what local villagers Whitemen would have to said.

Many lost-boys students ought to take their discriminated low, graded examination papers to court, and a will of mistreatment has been a silent voice as it is between black African-American and white teachers or professors.

Lost-boys, mainly from the Dinka tribe in Southern Sudan, love to speak their mother tongue as any other African, but that first language has killed growth to make lost-boys students the best learners of American English accent or encourage them to quickly learn well-spoken standard English. Majority of Lost-boys would have been speaking many languages by now as their odyssey journey has passed them through many corners of the worldly people who speak different dialects or other language. Speaking in Anyuak, Amahari, Toposa, Turkana, Kiswahili, mule and mainly English would have been an advantage to bilingual lost-boys. Because SPLA Red Army system was the most controllable system that kept the Red Army in fence without interaction with their neighbor tribes or learning their surrounding language of their refuge land residing native people.

Scoring low grades also contributed to time management factors, in a situation where the African time arm clock ticked slower than faster ticking American clock. Lost-boys students face occupation of time, and budgeting time become a number one big problem with many lost-boys. Breaking down twenty-four hours into pieces and having lost-boys, students use it for their success as follows; a time for work, time for studies, classroom time, sleeping time, family time and taking a nap time. It is hard for many lost-boys students who couldn`t manage this time to break down and finally end up dropping out of school and becoming Chokoro number one at the city underbridge home. It is double harder for lost-boys students with families or children to even go to church, spend time with their families, or play with their children. Assignments late or, coming to class late, or going to bed late are factors of late students who can`t manage too many programs in a single time, that eventually ends them up quitting the one less important program that qualifies to quit, either education, family, or job. Many lost-boys students would rather stay with their family and opt to quit school or have a wife working that allows them time to study.

Another major factor is lost-boys students` age that, which is correlated with many other aged man problems. Although learning is ageless, but man's age goes with the right time needs, and a fulfillment of an old man's heart desire is uncontrollable measure. Many lost-boys students are above thirty years of age, and the determination for education is a key success of hope that keeps them going and pushing on stressful days of life regardless they have no wives, children or families to care for. The adult mind is not as sharp as a teenager's mind, and now learning of creaming every professor lecture or quick memory of the best student has begun to fade away as lost-boys students are getting older in every second year of their degree studies. Many lost-boys students started quitting and transferring their less accumulated credit hours from public to private schools due to how harder are studies in public schools compared to easy private schools that push students to the next level of class as long as students score lower grades with no pressure for demotion.

Many lost-boys students join the adult education system, which is non-traditional school system in America where old age, single parents, and responsible students need little freedom with fewer assigments, flexible schedule class hours, less pressure grading and promotion. Lost-boys students become part of the American adult education system, whereas learning becomes much easier for aged lost-boys students. School performances dropped with a few lost-boys who do not participate in school activities, registered clubs, school trips, and tours. Since lost-boys students get less time to even nap, there hadn't no time for school activities participation, and many of them are objected to assigments and taking online classes which at less saves them little time. Some lost-boys students applied and joined online universities and other online courses so that they could unless spare little time drinking beers on weekends, if not visiting long time no sees friends. American adults aged are less good with academic studies in public schools compared to private schools that also suit and fit adult lost-boys students to graduation date.

In the back of lost-boys, students mind are thinking about the desire for a woman and getting marriage as well, as age also demands a family and education at the same time. Aged students occupy their limited lifetime with too many programs that ought to be accomplished in no time. It is harder for lost-boys students to get everything in one basket and try to enjoy without a painful struggle. Having a family, a job, and a full-time semester of classes is a brain-drain out the task to do, but many lost-boy students sacrificed their long-time goal to be done with school regardless of what circumstances are in place. A two-year associate degree would be completed in four years, with limited time depending on how many credit hours a class one takes per semester. Due to their age factor, many lost-boys quit school for good and got marriage to a beautiful Sudanese girl and started making family as well as strife for a happy family out of education. Lost-boys two main goals is to either get education, or get a wife, or both, but many lost-boys end up not giving or satisfying both sides to the maximum. Age has become a factor that causes lost-boys students to drop out of school for good or have both education and family together at one time. Just like many young American who are in colleges, lost-boys do work-study programs so that they can pay their bills, rent and also pay support to their found families back home or in Kenya or Uganda. It was hard to do work-study as some lost-boys stopped schooling for some semesters so that they could work two jobs to pay for bills or car loan. After working two, getting money and paying off credit card debt or car loan, they could return back to school and start from where they left. Some lost-boys students would struggle to get a job after getting laid off, fire or loss their jobs, so they would stop going to school for a while until they got a job before resuming school again. It has become unstable learning until graduation day when students are assured completion.

After graduation, then come to a job to do in a field or program of study. Just like any other American graduate students who struggles to find a job in a field of studies, lost-boys graduates are faced with the same devil inside lack of experience, not sound meet resume, or no job after graduating in the field of study. Graduated lost-boys students must get internships before they can start working in their graduated professional field, but complaints arise when professional jobs are white people occupied or under control by single race company that wouldn`t allow a rarely and stranger look lost-boys to get a professional job unless there is a network of friend connections. In America, professional jobs are highly racial factor, and one can get a professional job where your race goes or in a company that is not of institutional hidden racism or discrimination in a hidden code of defense. Many graduates lost-boys become the last victims of professional job unemployement, and with degrees that federal loans demand pay back, lost-boys graduates are left with no choice but to go back to Sudan, where they belong. Lost-boys lost social networks with their former American volunteers, American friends and even have no American colleagues, which eventually leads lost-boys to no connections at all.

Many lost-boys graduates complained that American interviewers perceived them negatively based on accents, names, and physical dark skin looks. In an American cultural way, a man that does not sound like American or with an American English accent is perceived to be nothing compared to where she/he come from. Non-accent American English speakers are perceived to have low verbal, written and well communication in spoken English, meaning he/she cannot do a professional job right. Many factors lead to the complexity of graduated lost-boys not to get a job in their graduated field of specialization, and these factors range from their skin color, accents, native African names, lack of job, racial discrimination and wrong specialized field that is not listed or listed last in job market lists. Many graduates lost-boys would either go to Sudan to seek job opportunities, work entry-level jobs, self-employed or go back to school for further learning in master's degree or resume studies in a research field of Phd. Many graduates' lost-boys go to South Sudan to do their internship and later come back to America to find a job in special field of their fit education, but still many wouldn't get hired, or hired under salaries as compared to discipline areas in actual pays scale. Lost-boys iron heart in academic education has inspired many youths Sudanese in many States to go back to school as well and many other African youths are motivated to resume their academic school learning as lost-boys curiosity in education move them. Lost-boys epical life history has already hit young American students, and motivation is highly encouraging frustrated high school droped out to drop back into school as lost-boys get admission to high schools and colleges across America and that motivates hopeless students.

Education is the mother of hope to many lost-boys, even those who are not at school, or stop going to school would still sing song of education in their heart and minds, dreaming of finishing school. The school which many lost-boys started before 1983, and even right now, many lost-boys hadn`t completed college Bachelor's or associate degree. It has been a war after a war, refugee camp after refugee and, asylum after hiding and in between wasn`t a peaceful time for education. Lost-boys students who hope to earn Ph. D.s are at a stake of high motivation as their old age is nearly approaching. Education is the only key that kept lost-boys living all years in the odyssey. In a refugee hardship life or at frontline place where you have never seen your parents, relatives or friends, education is the only key to success that could reward us back all the losses or whatever losy-boy misses in their early lifetime. Education is lost-boys life and a key to opening the dead door of opportunities and the way families happiness.

THE ODYSSEY OF SOUTH SUDAN RED ARMY:

THE LOST BOYS AND GIRLS OF SOUTH SUDAN

Series-4

THE RED ARMY OF THE UNACCOMPANIED MINORS ON THE 5TH EXILE EXODUS FROM KENYA TO WESTERN WORLD.

INSIDE: EPICAL STORY OF SOUTH SUDAN LOST BOYS / GIRLS (FORMER RED ARMY / UNACCOMPANIED MINORS REFUGEE FROM KENYA. ON RESETTLEMENT TO USA AND AND AUSTRALIA

Mapwar Mabor Pur

cclv

Contents

Page Blank Intentionally

CHAPTER 2

THE LOST BOYS AND GIRLS OF SOUTH SUDAN EDUCATION YIELDS NO BENEFITS IN THE WESTERN WORLD AND SOUTH SUDAN.

1. Good News for Excellent Governance of South Sudan.

1.1   Schools are Part of Academic Progress.

Excellent governance for an excellent government is a seed that grows, breeds, and broods in lively sources such as in an authoritative family, school, society, association, faith base, and community organization. The leadership knowledge for an excellent government is a behavior, knowledge, skill or a natural wisdom acquired from rich sources mentioned above, and the source must have excellent longevity history on its deeds of goodness. The school is a theoretical source of leadership that develops and molds students for future leadership qualities that would enable a good governance system. A well-defined system of education can help the nation raise healthy future leaders, and those well-learned future leaders will establish excellent governance for a rich nation. The academic school teaching of deliverable speeches, law school, religious education, history, and political science, as well as other leadership disciplines, would breed well-taught and quality-acquired students for future leadership in high government positions. A school teaching non-science traditional subjects and humanities is of great help that raises well-bred future leaders. In today's democratic system of government, raising qualified leaders from healthy systemic sources is a great success to excellent government. Bringing up the best leaders dependent on education as an academic leadership school is a key for a well-governing government.

1.2   Faith Bases Are Centers for Worshipping and religious mindset.

Every constitution is backed up by people of faith, and every faith is a rich feeding source for excellence in government. Faith-based education, organizations, clubs, society, family, and associations are rich sources for future leaders, and these future leaders would lead to well-defined governance. The constitution of the United States is a Christian backup of values, while the constitution of Iran is an Islamic backup system. The faith-based centers encourage every family to go to a holy place of worship and declare faith in divinity that a good government will be led by leaders who are sworn in using the Bible, Koran, or any other holy faith book. Religion teaching is based on excellent leaders for an excellent nation, and that phenomenal religion act has bred and molded religious students to become those who have acquired leadership qualities. Religion orientation of excellent governance is a central to the national constitution, and many leaders must have qualities of the main religious traits that encourage people to define an ancestral government ancestral. Faith-based organizations are important in electing leaders who represent party religious values as well as choosing the path for a well-defined government that will defend religious values.

1.3   Community Organizations creates a modern pluralistic society.

Community organizations are the heart of small government, and a national government is born out of a community organization. Community organizations are a rich source for qualified future leaders. Community organizations are the base for a humanistic organization full of many values, cultures, religions, concept, and leadership teaching supports. Since community organizations are based on particular people who share the same language, lifestyle, culture, and way of life, it is not certain that a community organization impacts and grooms leadership ability in young youth. Leaders who grow up with leadership qualities from a supportive community organization are always specific and secularize their leadership powers in a specific community or related society. If we have excellent community organizers, we can also have excellent leaders who can serve as excellent governors in any system of government that supports a community-based organization. Good leaders are bred from the ground root of a well-raised community with strong leadership powers. If we have elderly organizers who can educate the new generation of youth to act and acquire all leadership qualities from good organized community, it means that a country or a nation will have an excellent governing system.

1.4   Society Unions or political Parties are pillars of successful governance for a great country.

The only ideology campaigns preached and demonstrated by a good society are excellent governance that promotes peace, prosperity, development, and social goodness of that particular society. Society unions are the source of supportive education for government future leaders. Meetings, solutions to disputes, and society welfare are a few agendas that are carried out by a good society union. Society unions are more advanced in leadership ability than community organizations because a society union deals with a variety of agendas, including incorporating societies' economic sectors, trading, society pluralism, tribal, racism, and faith differentiation, as well as dealing with people of different backgrounds. A party is more than a society union because it works against or supports a country's government. Many good leaders emerge from excellent parties. Good government supports its country's parties financially as well as encourages each party to do according to the country's constitution. Excellent leaders are raised within a well-established policy party. A party with ideology that goes against people must have its top positions occupied by leaders who are minority or have community-based leadership ability. Society leaders are basically easily upgraded or promoted to a particular party, and society leaders, based on ability, work very well and fit in any governmental position due to the fact that a society is a small country from where a big country emerges. Party or society leaders must work to show excellent governance or educate youth to learn and adopt the fountain base of quality leadership that will progress tomorrow's leaders into a well-governance country government.

1.5 Government is made up of multi-parties of unions and organizations.

Depending on the type of government system in the country, faith, and community, society or party organizations are groomed, directed, supported, and coached by the ruling government to pass down its policy or extend its laws and mission to reach people at the local level. Government is the last level of power in a country that has the power to decide regarding what to teach and educate citizens about or what not to tell its citizens. Government has the power to create or recreate its citizens from what will go with a government system of ruling, constitution or way of life created by the government laws and policy. Citizens of the country who leave their country of origin for another country and later come back seeking a position in their country of origin are likely to cause alteration of the constitution and the way people live as long as they gain power in the ruling government. Defining the present country's constitution and the people's way of living in another country's constitution and way of life is the most dangerous change in assumption. Many good leaders are raised and adopted with leadership qualities from the present government that encourage the system to breed its citizens in orienting them to become what the government thinks is a good way to become, whether for capitalism, communism, socialism, dictatorship, or democracy.

1.6   Associations and Clubs are pillars of successful education institution.

Schools or society associations and clubs are great in creating the baseline of leadership growth for teenagers and youths of young age. The baseline level of leadership begins with the knowledge quality of conducting meetings, delivering speeches, asking questions, being the sole solution provider, writing minutes, organizing a small group of followers, and spending time working off for people or what a small group of people want to have. Offering your time off to work for people and providing free services starts with small school clubs or high school associations. Our children learn the simple leadership baseline when we allow them participation in school associations and clubs where they practice and create posters with insightful imagination of becoming tomorrow's leaders, and that vision could survive for a longer dream to come. Leaders of tomorrow must learn the basic leadership qualities from simple small school clubs and associations around their ecosystem environment. The gifted talent of leadership from God who loves kids or teenagers can be improvised, encouraged, and sharpened here by knowledgeable parents who observe the gift of talent in their kids. Just like kindergarten kids' clubs and middle school associations are important to American kids, mind development in leadership ability and creating a baseline for tomorrow's leaders is also important.

1.7　Individuals' Leadership Ability starts from a great, loving and successful family.

As mankind is created with a sensual inner ability to create and sharpen his/her own ability and talent, it is easily and commonly known that many leaders are not born leaders but become leaders. Individuals sharpen their daily creation of themselves to become leaders of tomorrow, and many youths do this practice of becoming tomorrow's leaders depending on their parental and friends' inner needs and mentor's or coach's encouragement or support for leadership in a successful life career. It takes and picks up youth by simply attending school, church, party, club, or teacher meeting in the nearby surrounding, and this is how many individual teenagers and youth learn to sharpen their leadership qualities. Sometimes, it starts out as a game or in a gathering of a small group of friends or players where human sense of care jumps into the mind and progresses individuals in the long-term life careers of leadership without knowing it. Some youths adapt to become leaders after they go to school or first learn leadership classes on topics of presentations or speech-delivering methods. Some youth might find a job or become experienced with a job where leadership ability is encouraged and some companies make leaders, and leadership pushes many employees to become leaders even if they haven't even thought about leadership.

2. The Three Disagreeing Doctors of South Sudan (SPLA-IG, SPLA-IO and NDA)

Dr. John Garang De Mabior—with political ideals on the movement struggle for South Sudan's independence, New Sudan and a vision for united Sudan as well as East Africa's vision of unity.

Dr. Riek Machar Teny Dhurgon—with political ideology concept of South Sudan's independent and superior self-determination and creating government of South Sudan fit with N. Sudan.

Dr. Lam Akol Ajawiny—with political insider ideology with a mindset that believes in fairness, equality, and justice democratic system of rule in South Sudan and peace of living in Sudan.

Other South Sudanese Disagreeing Doctors:

Dr. Benjamin Bol Akok—with ideological faith in successful guerrilla warfare by selecting the best route that could enhanced successful warfare in the 1990s when SPLA/M was in a critical situation and in need of change to assist recruits with less severe training. This decision to his tough political thought eventually buried him in the rebel hands of debate to the catacomb.

Dr. Salva Kiir—with ideology of fairness, justice, and equality in the democratic system of South Sudan, governing one statehood on self-reliant government and independent States.

Dr. Yusuf Kuow—with the political ideology of New Sudan taking over Khartoum, powers and rules Sudan democratically and creates equal opportunity for every Sudanese in Sudan regardless of their black skin color, faith or even regional place of origin in Sudan.

Dr. Mamut—equatorial-headed political agenda in South Sudan's self-determination as a country of prosperity and growth, favoring vast Equatoria region of South Sudan in rules and respect.

Dr. Malik Agar—with Blue Nile-headed political agenda of a democratic system of independence in a statehood that hosts all tribes in South Sudan, respect, equality and love for all South Sudanese.

3.   President G.W. Bush Got Ambushed

3.1. Act of September 11 Attack

The act of terrorist attack on the twin towers was nothing else than a test to put the newly elected president into hot water and let the world see how he was going to react in bubble hot butts. It was clear, and a link is even clear to Mr. former president G.W. Bush, that terrorists act as friends with him, and the worst enemy is your best friend whose trust betrays unfulfilled promise. If competitor Al Gore had won as the president instead of G.W. Bush, it would have had helped terrorists not to demolish the Twin Towers, or maybe it was just because Bush became the president that he was given that prize after his honeymoon in a white horse. That was the first ever ambush any newly elected president could handle, and that was why rampant war hit the wrong target at the triangle of Saddam Hussein. Well, Americans still hope for the better because their elected president is prepared to face the country's challenges from day one in the Oval Office.

3.2. The War on Terrorism declared on Lost Boys and Girls of South Sudan

I had been in just two weeks in America, and I was there that morning sitting in my ESL class when my white ESL teacher rushed into the class with the news that the Twin Towers were now being bombed and the country was under attack, although it was not clear what had happened. The class was dismissed for the day, and only after everything was clear about the attack would we resume classes the next day. My mind was unable to understand terrorists in the American business; all I could easily recall were Arabs whose persecution led me to flee for refuge in America. I went to work that evening at DeKalb farmer's market, where I worked to make money, and returned home late evening after work, and as I had no car and there was no bus, I just walked back to the apartment. As I approached my apartment with my roommate—we were both from Africa—we were ambushed just as President Bush was ambushed on September 11. About seven to ten young African American men suddenly started stabbing, stoning, and beating my roommate and me over and over again. We struggled to run but could go nowhere. Those young men accused us of the terrorist attack on the Twin Towers. President G.W. Bush got ambushed by that war on terrorism, and he hasn't ended the war yet.

3.3. The Saddam Hussein fade cast a dark shadow on Lost Boys and Girls of South Sudan

If G.W. Bush died, he would meet Saddam Hussein, and I'm sure, hopefully, Saddam would explain to Bush where he had hidden his NBC weapon of mass destruction. I have a reasonable doubt that Saddam has left his NBC weapons hidden somewhere else in the world; luckily, he is not going to come back to visit the world soon.

After September 11, Iraq was the last country on the list of targets after G.W. Bush scratched his head to think where the hell on earth should be bombed for retaliation. Bush thought deeply, and after quickly calculating profit and loss by mentioning a few countries names to be bombed, like Sudan, Somalia, Iran, and Libya, he thought about Afghanistan and perhaps Iraq. Saddam Hussein had ambushed Bush, and it was a hit and run, but little devil Bush couldn't be a hit and run of Saddam; it resulted in a real deathly accident. Too many South Sudanese lost lives to Saddam's NBC weapons, and Bush was a witness to that. Many Lost Boys of South Sudan served in the United States of America military and lost their lives in the Iraq and Afghanistan invasion wars.

3.4. Taliban recurring war switch from Russian to Americans

Taliban are a headache to the world, even to me, who has never seen them, or maybe there is an economic reason behind the Afghanistan war. I have seen Russians in that country before with their Kalashnikovs, and now with the M16, they are loitering everywhere as the Taliban are the soft top target before a hidden real agenda. The war on Osama bin Laden is the hidden agenda of the war in Afghanistan, but G.W. Bush got ambushed by the Taliban, Bin Laden, and what was underneath Afghanistan. There was no Taliban or Afghanistan war before G.W. Bush. All the blood spilled by American soldiers on any land of the world is a newly planted seedling, and it will reap three times as it ripens with time. It is good for America to carry on with its two presidents, a president who messed up and scared the world and the next president who restored peace and happiness in the world. Taliban ambushed G.W. Bush, and Bin Laden has not been found yet with all those CIA personnel and later found and killed.

3.5. The troubling U.S. immigration system makes a case for global terrorism.

The U.S Immigration system has never been bad and links with terrorism as it did with G.W. Bush. President Bush must do something about the flooding of immigrants into this country where terrorism is growing out of new joints in Americans way of life. Reformed immigration policy was the strategy response that Bush outlined to fight back the ambushed immigration war of the world. Bush tightened laws, policies, and the immigration process to America, G.W. Bush also built a tall bordering wall dividing Mexico away from North America, and the wall left no window for Mexicans to peep looking into America or even jump over it. Isolating Mexico by building a bridge or divided wall on the border is deleting Mexico of North American territory and making Mexico sort to be a part of South America or Central. Bush Administration was ambushed by immigration issues more than any other president in the history of America. There was a lot to do to fix America's immigration issues, part of which was President Bush, and that included even offending immigrants as Washington was flooded with Protestant immigrants. We can see the Spanish going on demonstrations a lot more here in America than they do in Mexico or in their native countries.

3.6. Bush Faces John Kerry as it does today with the Joe Biden Administration.

John Kerry or John Edward had posed many headaches to G.W. Bush as his campaign was so wordy and violent, with tactical ambushing of Bush in the White House. Just like Hillary Clinton, who lost the presidency to Obama because of her long bites, John Kerry lost too because of his nonadjustable heat. It was a tough fight between the two men, and G.W. Bush, who had gotten used to being ambushed many times, won the battle with John Kerry. As the disaster of Katrina ambushed Bush too, it was another advantage to Kerry as Bush was in the middle of wild correctors to bring him down from his throne. Obama has ambushed Bush too, but it was too late for the morning hyena running away to hand over its kills to a hungry lioness. Obama ambushed Bush and hit him on the head with a dodge knuckle hammer, and that was why John McCain couldn't stand against Obama first. Bush was and will be forever a victim of many ambushes in US presidency history.

3.7 . Bush's House is the same as any other U.S. president's house.

Likewise any other man's house, President Bush Jr. was also ambushed by his own family issues, and it was tough fighting to correct the issues in the small government called family, the country, as well as in the entire world. His twin daughters' issues were the same as many kids' or daughters' issues; seeking parental love, warm family gatherings, and true gifts from the father was not much demanded by the Bush Jr. Daughters. Bush Jr.'s housing mortgage, his budgeting salaries, and his expenses contributed to another ambush on former president George Jr. Bush. More money you come across, the more problems you see. Bush had more financial problems more than ever before. He was not a president. His wife, Laura Bush, was another ambush on Bush himself. The First Lady needed something more than what was in the White House, and the president got to crack his head in the midst of world war to find something unique to please the First Lady that time between day and night.

3.8.   Americans Ambush President Bush Jr as any other U.S. president.

It was a tougher fight back as President Bush Jr. got into a triangle of American trust in a way that American minds doubted, and yes, they had voted for him twice but now want to impeach him out of the Oval Office. Americans rose over Bush and tried to shake him by the neck as he was a culprit known for lying, cheating, fighting and was a racist and did not know how to handle the country's problems, causing more trouble to Americans. I lost my job because of the Bush Jr. war issue. As an American president, he was ambushed by Americans due to the mishandling of Hurricane Katrina, war in Iraq and Afghanistan, tax policy, immigration issues, jobs, foreign relationships, domestic issues, and energy issues. It was a critical time in Bush's life to experience and feel the grief of the nation's citizens over the act of terrorism killing and recession destruction at home; it was the right choice by the brave president to save a nation from its collapsing economy. Terrorism arose here in America.

3.9. Middle East Ceaseless Crises middling into Lost Boys of South Sudan lives.

As the Middle East crises always ambushed every upcoming American president, the Middle East in President Bush Jr.'s time was very critical in the sense that Israel got attacked by Hezbollah and the Palestine and Iran uprising. Bush Jr. was ambushed when the Middle East crisis intensified as far as the Far East was also concerned. President Bush Jr. did try his best to fight back Middle East crises by developing the peace process between Arab brothers, but it was left on the table forever. Middle East crises are a test and a taste for every American president, and these crises will never go away until one out of three things will happen: the coming back of Jesus Christ or Prophet Muhammad to judge over the dead and living Middle Easterners, extinction of Palestinians by Israel fire, or if America provides new final solution to settle Israel and Palestine war. Middle East problem is an American problem; terrorism starts from the Middle East problem, and it's a world issue.

3.10.   N. Korea and Iran keep America on top as future enemies of the state.

I didn't know that I would be sitting down here between South and North Korea while writing these pages. I am now being ambushed by Kim Yong of North Korea, just like Bush Jr. or, currently, Obama. It was very critical as North Korea got very harsh with the Bush administration at that time, and little cooled now in Obama's time. North Korea, Iran, Sudan, Venezuela, and many other countries posed an ambush on Bush Jr., and now Korea is the number one topic. Testing its missiles on America's birthday was a major provocation, and its critics have pierced the bones of human Bush Jr., but because too many war frontlines have been created by the Bush administration, there would be no more war with Iran, Korea, or even Venezuela. Nevertheless, after a wait, America will conquer the whole world one day. Now, there are many uprisings against America everywhere, even within America; Africa, Asia,

South America, Middle East, and every foreign is getting upset with America. We will see the next war on America after terrorism, and that war will be disastrous.

4. Building a World of Characters is building a successful person with legacy

4.1. Building a World of Character within a Person (The Lost Boys of South Sudan)

Where do personal characters, personalities, positive values, and virtues come from? Isn't it that a person is a piece of developmental living thing that grows just like a tree and picks up his/her form of character on the cause of changes in developmental growth? A person of character is a positive person of the right attitude, and a human who possesses genitival virtues resembles one of the parental characters or else you're growing up in an environment or lifestyle could deform you to be a person of your own character. You acquire positive character by being born naturally out of your mother's womb with goodness in how you respectfully treat the world with obedience and dignity. The character in you shows to the outside world that you greet every old man, old mother, and every grandfather in any race just the way you respectfully honor your extended family who are of old age. Your personal character allows you to see the outside world as you're inside family house, only if you love your family more than anything else in the ideal world.

4.2. Building a World of Character within a Family leads to building a great community.

Is there any good character in a family that attacks another family, robs, and steals or is a racialist? Is there any better family that feeds the homeless, poor, hungry, thirsty, and peasants out of their single-house refrigerator? A family character must be built on the image of the father who is coupling with the true natural mother. If there is a true natural love in that family since the family creation, then there should be family character on how to raise healthy-minded children, and the character of a united great, loved family lives long. A family of positive virtues is characterized by a healthy and happy family atmosphere, and that happiness can diffuse the neighbors' environment, and every neighbor may get the chance to catch the spirit of good family character. Pay your neighbor's bills, shop for their groceries, and help them get a job. Visit the sick, counsel the neighbor couple, share BBQ cookouts with your neighbor families, and be a supermodel for families.

4.3. Building a World of Character within a Community leads to building a great nation

A community is a collection group of families, and every single family in an ecosystem of the community must come with its well-known character contribution in order to build up one good known community of a character. The best-organized norm community is the living soul of a healthy nation. An organized community must emerge from the original lengthy living norms, culture, beliefs, taboos, and lineage, which for long lives have been respected. If there is a virtue-characterized family next to another family that makes up a positive community character, then there would be no crimes in any neighborhood, and there would be no racism, tribalism, fights, mobs, killing, and sectionalism. A community of a character reinforces another ruined community and defends neighborhood communities by providing clean water, contributing food, improving health problems, and helping at any disaster time. The best community is characterized by mercy, respect, assistance, love and hope, progress, unity, responsibility, wealth, cooperation, peace, courage, and all goodness to be successful.

4.4. Building a World of Character within a Plural Society leads to building a great country.

A community is a group of families that share original character in one accented language, culture, lifestyle, belief, taboo, determination, religion, or common mindset. Unlike community, society is a group of communities united under one common lifestyle, mindset, one second language, second culture, or belief, as well as one determined goal. If there is a positive character in society, there would be no American bowl of salads today.

Otherwise, racism, discrimination of color, religion, accent, mindset, and culture wouldn't be present in the ideal world of character. An organized society is one where leaders are born, and it possesses virtual values of its norms, rules, policies, laws, and correctional characterized cultures, as well as its forges lifestyle. The best society of a character is the one that fears God with God-fearing characters as well as with powerful leaders' management. A character society is a caring one, loving and peaceful, with a high responsibility to give out assistance.

4.5. Building a World of Character within a Nation is a progressive way to sustain active governance.

A person of character is the one who makes a family of a character, and families of characters make up a community of character as well as the best-characterized society is born in the most blessed nation of true character. A nation represents a small world of a character, but the positive characteristics nation stem from a small characterized nation called a family. If there are more rich-value characterized families, then the best community is established, leading to a well-built nation. Before building a nation of a character, you might have to build a family of the best character first or else you are going to cast your own fate of foolish wisdom to harm the health of an emerging nation. A most powerful nation emerges from a family of character, and the best leaders or presidents are born out of the best-characterized families and in the best-characterized individual parents. A nation of a character is the one who donates, provides reliefs, supports, and gives to others.

4.6. Building a great World of Character within the World is a great way to prevent world wars.

The United States of America is seen as the number one world troublemaking nation, but imagine if it disappears from world affairs. What do you think would happen to the world? The USA gives hands in spite of taking hands; it has satisfied the range of a characterized nation. A nation of character is one that feels sympathy, is concerned, loves peace, provides counseling and assistance, and is willing to negotiate as well as respect and dignify other nations' affairs. If there were many nations of excellent character, there would be no nightmare dream of the Third World War, or else all world conflicts among nations would terminate right then. That one ideal world may be at peace only if every nation is a nation of excellent character through fear of the world's Creator, dignifying every human race, respecting and obeying boundaries of our cultures, religions, beliefs, lifestyles, mind-set concepts, good faiths in our international business, and providing assistance to ourselves as one world of peace, love, prosperity, respect, dignity, and fear of one earthly Creator.

5.   The Animal with a Political Mind is a politician.

5.1   Judgmental Mind

Mankind is living a human being lifestyle different from animals because of his judgmental brain that tells right from wrong. However, some people are judged by the judge after they have committed a felony and have run into making the wrong choice instead of doing the right legal thing always. The human judgmental mind is the central source for making life easy, and that has elevated the human animal to a high-thinking animal before any other creature created by God. Too much human judgment is not compatible with life and contradicts religious values and faith in forgiveness, and you should not judge too much or else you will always be judged by the same law. If every person were born with the same mental judgment capacity, there would be no judges or court cases, even crimes, because every person could do something morally legal and right always. Judging the human mind always knows the right moral legal thing to do, but the hardest part is the action of legality.

5.2   Rational Mind

Judging, reasoning, and sorting things out is the full mental capacity of the human being to be called a rational animal. Human beings' mental capacity thought of care, love, right, wrong, spiritual feeling, anger, sensual senses, faith, and recognition of the Creator is the centerpiece of human rationalism. The difference between a human judging mind and a rational mind is that the judging human mind is very much concerned about what is morally legal right and morally legally wrong. On the other hand, human rationalism is about reasoning, analysis, choosing the best alternatives and rational acts in support and a supplementary brain function that reinforces the judging mind's function ability. Mathematicians and scientists used their rational minds with less force than their judgmental minds to create the work of scientists. Rational human thought saved human face from the shame of dignity, respect, honor, and faithfulness, and it also created links between humans and the Creator.

5.3　　Pursue of Struggle Against Successful Life

The human judgmental mind and rational mind make man direct his way of life between living alternatives for survival. Every time man falls on his knee against the struggle in life for survival, man's rational mind acts so that man finds an alternative choice to correct life's problems. A judgmental mind encourages, strengthens, and pursues hope and gives man an iron heart and mind to fight against life's tough problems without surrendering, giving up or failing to produce and commit to the solution to solve life's problem. Pursuance of struggle against life is a will survival of every created creature, but man leads the way ahead when it comes to life's struggle for his needs. Irrational animals struggle every day to find what to eat and drink and for the safety, treatment, or even protection of a young one. Man has got the upper hand in providing life's necessities to work for every life's difficult problems and to enhance easy ways of life as rational top animals among animals.

5.4　Image of God in Him and Her.

How close is man to God, or how close is man to the devil? God presents his image through mind and soul in man, and man can act not to be exactly like God but to be like his love creature. God created man with the insight that man can see God's work in himself as well as around him. The presence of God's image in man allows man to believe in God and have faith in religion because God is present in man, and man is present in God. God looks, feels, thinks, acts, and judges like a human being, but he is God with super extraordinary power more than the little he presented to man. God gets upset like man, and God destroys like man does. God judges man's actions just as many men today are trying hard to judge God's creation and criticize the Creator's way of creation. God has given man a judgmental mind, not to turn on him on how wrongly man judges, but good reasoning judgments to recognize that the Creator and man make life easy.

5.5   **Distinctive Creation of a Mankind.**

Man created or made many cars, planes, and clothes in different sizes, colors and styles as well as God created men in different races, colors, languages, and many different ways of life. It is advantageous to God to see his different creation variety, but to man it is the worst to have differences as a centerpiece of man's cause of conflicts. Differences in man's languages, religious faith, lifestyle, regional, tribes, nations, races, and cultures are what cause problems in human actions in life, but there is beauty in the differences, as God, the father of varieties, is the only happy Creator seeing his varieties covering the earth. We can accept differences and live in peace, sharing the benefits of all human differences— black people, white, Latino, Indian, Arab, and every religion is the love of difference and variety of living. God brings peace among his racist sons and the living world by his grace. A distinctive variety of creation is the beauty in God's eye and in a man who loves God.

6. Uncontrolled Out of Control
6.1.Uncontrollable Person in the Family

A family that falls into a pitfall pool of drug abuse, alcohol, financial mishap, loss of job, quarreling couple, and cheating is like a devil raiding the family. It is hard to control a family that has already gone out of its odd uncontrollable means. When responsibility slips away from parents' hands, kids are seen loitering down the streets with any means of survival—selling drugs, dropping out of school, prostituting, and hanging out with bad companies in town. It is common in single irresponsible mothers' families as well as poor-managed families where couples don't give a fuck about kids or even about what is going to happen in a family relationship. The irresponsibility of the family always leads to uncontrollable manageability of the family and even family members' dispersals in different directions. Some of the things that impair family manageability are things like drug abuse, alcoholism, bad love, and poor financial budgeting, which always lead to uncontrollable issues.

6.2   Uncontrollable Children in Uncontrollable Family.

Kids, teenagers, children, and adult children are the family's long-term assets, and a couple should always be ready to care for and be responsible for the cause of the family's creation. Children move in an uncontrollable direction after parents go in different directions that aren't the legal and right way to be responsible for a family. Children join in the use of drugs, prostitution, and alcoholism. They join bad companies, live a miserable life, and even commit early crimes because children copy and exemplify their parents' actions. Kids start drinking at the age of ten or so because their parents introduced them to all the things beyond their age. Since parents have sex in front of kids and make love in the presence of children, that negative action of parents creates a haven for children to start having sex at whatever age with their peer group. Some of the things that the children do is have early sex, do drugs, drop out of school, join bad company, serve jail time, commit crimes, and even rebel against their parents.

6.3   Uncontrollable disease is the world a pandemic.

Epidemic disease, locust, and catastrophic illness can be out of control from the hands of God, government, or man. AIDS, herpes, asthma, cancer, and other tougher diseases have gone out of control from God's and man's hands, and natural diseases and disasters add another huge problem that kills human beings. Why should disease kill human beings in any way if God has blessed man naturally and made him immune to the world's creation effects? But it is okay because that maay man's population is reduced so there is enough food for the living ones. The tougher disease destroys human lives in a way that there is a feeling that no God is present to prevent the carophic disasters. There is no way that man can dodge effective death or natural death because God says so, and it would continue until the mighty creation of the world comes down here to rule the world himself. There will be no diseases in the living place after your death. We should sometimes try to avoid disease in every possible way.

6.4   Out of Control Community leads to an underdeveloped country.

A community that goes out of control is like a river that exceeds the water flow that season. Community leaders fall out on not managing a community's rights, and every family, member, or individual acts or moves in a different direction because the human mind's actions are controlled by law, regulation, and policy in a society or in the country. Illness in society occurs when a community falls into the dimension of sickness and havoc by losing its cultural lifestyle, values, and way of life. It is out of control when every family practices illegal life stuff and does harmful action that brings down the entire community of people. When a community gets a strong belief, and the concept of a mindset that is not relevant direction to the life of an individual solution, that wrong concept can eventually lead to disaster and havoc where every individual member of the family goes in different directions of the crimes or wrong action that is worse, nothing less than a disaster.

6.5   Out of Control Nation leads to uncontrollable world`s finance.

If a country can't control its budget, domestic production against international import, citizen's mindset, crime issues, and international affairs, and even control jobs and citizens' way of lives, it means that the nation is in hot water and there is an immediate need for better changes to correct socially havoc society. If a nation can create a healthy family, it would lead to a healthy society, and that could bring a happy nation into a controllable nation. An out-of-control nation is in crisis, at war with huge expenses, fighting national crimes, disasters, economic recession, or fighting back foreign suction. A country is always the best in doing good for its citizens and controlling its citizens' way of life as well as the country's economy and citizens' way of living. If there is civil war and other effective locust against a nation, there is always suddenly an overdraft to the nation account budgeting supports. New government is a solution to national havoc occur disaster.

6.6   Uncontrollable Generation leads to the country`s rebellion.

A generation is sick; it destroys, murders, and is swept away by social catastrophes when there is the presence of ignorance, illiteracy, poverty, disease, crimes, and havoc of hatred. A strong cornerstone generation emerges and dies as it was with communism slavery. Stone Age men disappeared as every other uncontrollable generation emerged in any century. The generation of terrorism, technology, and modernization is now currently stepping out of control, and the world is developing each new generation per century. Criminals' generation or civil war-affected generation is another victim generation of refuge, such as the generation of national disasters like tsunami and hurricane Katrina. Generations of epidemic incurable diseases of AIDS, herpes, cancer, and Ebola are desperately in need of help. Any generation's erosion and uprising depend on the world's way of life changes in dilemma-like phenomenon. Every generation is creatable and erodible by changes.

7.   Lawless Is a Mindless Society havoc.

7.1   Rapists

Human behaviors and feelings of sexual desire must be fulfilling according to society's policy, norms, regulations, and laws, and it will cause the cost of crime if the sex order is an issue in any society. The human mind is like water in the ocean, and it can do anything it feels like doing in the absence of law for guidance. Many societies live with rapists because people in that locality have gotten used to rape as a normal act, and that is not important at all. My *makuti* hut was nearest to a rapist's house, and every night all I heard was a young teenage girl crying the whole night. Her fifty-five-year-old husband would never stop raping her during every turn of his intercourse until daylight. Raping is believed to be a normal practice, just like killing is a fair deal in some societies. Many societies have norms to encourage protractors to be victimized, and victims don't feel any harm in that at all, while culprits feel proud of what crime they commit every day while raping. Rapists commit crimes of raping in the absence of laws, regulations, and law enforcement in place.

7.2   Murderers

The human nature of the hatred feeling has encouraged the

killing and murdering of each other like irrational animals in the jungle wild. Human beings of today are cannibalistic predators and become wild to kill murders and eat parts of their murdered humans. There are no tame humans in today's world as food scarcity, security, jobs, and basic human basic have been reduced to a minimum or to nothing; human being is growing from tame to wild animals that can kill and feed on other humans. Murderers or killers of another human are present in a society without laws or law enforcement force to track and diminish them or eradicate their negative acts toward lives of a society or nation. In the society I come from, murdering is somehow not a big deal, as many people die, and it may not mean anything as it may mean a big deal in American society. Murdering is a crime, and it has to be leveled with law and law enforcement corrections in any society or nation.

7.3   Cheaters

Cheating is an act of greediness, low self-dignity, low self-esteem, and hypocrisy of oneself. Cheating is sometimes a self-deception and another party's destruction. One can forge and report a false rape case to law enforcement, or one can have seven girlfriends at the same time, which is supposed to be considered a monogamy law violation in America. The worst act against human trust is cheating or devaluing oneself in a clear way by contradicting himself in what he says and what he does. Cheating is not an inborn character, but rather one that develops in the character of people who do not feel or face heavy loss as cheating consequences. Victims of cheating are lovers with broken hearts, business partners, parties to an agreement, peace dealers, or even right exchangers who could also fall into the cheating pitfall. Cheating should be punishable in a society or in a nation with a property law and law enforcement in place to track down cheaters.

7.4   Looting or Robbery in a country.

Any time there is no law and law enforcement in place, people in the locality turn from humans into animals who don't think rationally; instead, they act inhumanly and do what their hearts desire without the use of brain judgments. Looting and robbery is a desperate act of a person who knows there is no law or law enforcement present to rule out his knowingly committed crime or animal bad behavior that crops up in a human's mindless mind. As Hurricane Katrina hit New Orland, law enforcement operability was gone. Eventually, looting and robbery were a crime present at the time. The human mind is corrected and guided to do the legal and the right thing every day in the presence of the law and law enforcement, as well as to build up manners in society. The human thought of taking free stuff from any source by force in the absence of respondent force is irrational, and it is criminal freedom in heaven's locality where there is no enforcement of law in place to fight crime.

7.5   Adultery or Fornication is an act against moral society.

It was confusing me as our commander of USFK, Unit 15214, in Korea freed us to have the weekend off, and he commanded that adultery was punishable in the US Army Military Code of Justice. Our commander commanded, "Don't have sex with a partner other than a marriage partner, or else you will have violated the UCMJ code of conduct." I wonder why many soldiers have wives, and they make babies as if the continuation of the baby-booming era is forever. Now I have realized why army life is not civilian, or else why should adultery and fornication be punishable in the army and not in the state that I come from? It is the right way to correct a human person to stay in marriage or get married if she/he wants to have sexual intercourse in a legal or right way. If civilians got to have civilian values just like army values, I think American societies might be well off from certain society's social diseases like non-punishable adultery or free-going fornication. It is a society's health issue to make sure that sexual life is under control and is monitored for a proper change in a succeeding nation.

7.6   Molestation and Suicides are pillars of a failed community.

Molestation and a suicidal lawless mind can develop in a

person as long as society has emerged in a direction that doesn't care about people's sexual lives and there is too much freedom in America. If life is lacking the love substance, it is useless, and a useless feeling person can cause harm to him/herself and to society. And that is exactly what is killing many Americans in shooting crime cases. There has to be a way in a society where everyone must have a loved one in any way to create a happy society atmosphere through equality in love in society. There are a lot of equality opportunities in American society, but there is no love equality in American society, and that is why there are suicide shootings and killings everywhere. Having no love partners for life, single Americans have been causing child molestation in America. There is no difference between masturbation and molestation in American society, where an individual victim of America who lacks love can simply turn to have sex with him/her or find a child or a dog/cat to have sex with instead of a moral standard of humane behaviors.

7.7   Homosexual (Gay, Lesbian)

There is no love equality opportunity in America, and every year, the number of gays, lesbians, and single Americans is doubling three times, and one day, after millions of years, America will be only a land inhabited by gays and lesbians. A society that allows too much freedom and where women lead to their own advantage to choose which man to use, bring down, break hearts, destroy, or kill the spirit of love spirit is like a balloon in the air driven by wind in any direction it goes. I go to the gays and lesbians club not because I'm part of them but to empathize with them on their rights; the constitution of the United States has denied them dignity rights two times. Washington, DC, has failed miserably to introduce a law that will guide American love equality opportunity, failure to accept gay rights, and even failure to create a correct society free of evil sexual activities like acts of gay or lesbian causes since the first time or lower the cause of gay activities in America. Everyone in America will be gay, including the president or bishops.

7.8 Prostitutions and Bad love are evil of immorality.

Prostitution and bad love acts are considered a harmless crimes in America, although it is punishable, but it needs to be a society's love equal opportunity issue in America. Freedom is granted to teenagers, and the fact that parents release young teenagers as adults into a world of independent life is a major cause of prostitution and reckless love in America, and it can be stopped by law enforcement, forcing parents to limit teenagers' freedom and stop early release of eighteen-year-old adults in a complicated world of men and women. Prostitution is common in the poor middle class because of teenagers from bad families, loss of jobs, drug users, human sex trafficking, and single mothers who cannot provide food to their kids in a broken society that is facing consequences of irresponsible sexual acts without law enforcement. Washington needs a law to guide parents' involvement in their children's marriage and love affairs and in making a decision to support their adult children's love life affairs. Prostitution is a mindless society crisis issue.

7.9   Hatred, Discrimination, or Racism

Society is sick and becomes corrupted in the presence of uncontrollable hatred, discrimination, or racism. Now, in America, a known true hatred or discrimination has switched instead of disappearing, or it has become an institutional hatred or discrimination where its hidden code of practice is hard to crack, meaning by the law of discrimination and racism. Washington, DC, needs to introduce a law that will protect minors from the hidden code of institutionalized racism of hatred. How many times do I have to search for a job because I'm a black American, Muslim, of dark skin color, gay, Iraqi war disabled, and having a low education level and accented English? For the love of American stable society, there has to be a review of the Congress law review every year, and editing of the passed bills must be actively done in Congress because many laws enforce that a correct human American society can become another loop creating another disease in society of either a crime or social sickness that hinders the society's healthy atmosphere.

7.10   The Corruption, Illegal, or Lawless citizens in the poorest governance country.

Healthy family makes a healthy society, and a healthiest nation is born again. If every family is born free of drugs, corruption, and illegal stuffs, then our nation will avoid social illness, and a nation will be able to progress to a much more healthier standard than now. Regular citizens are corrupt and commit illegal mindless crimes simply because law enforcement is dodged at the time or there is no law at all. In the implementation of a tough law in America, there is corruption and illegal acts because Washington has never reviewed and tracked laws guiding the fast-growing technological American society in the world. Washington needs to run faster in governing law-making and enforcement in a faster-growing American society. There is a little open window of opportunity to corrupt; stealing or doing illegal acts is unforgivable for any individual American. A healthy American society is a matter of making and correcting a system using changeable laws by Capitol Hill.

8. Africa Is the Garden of Eden

8.1 Serpent in the Garden of Africa

Where is the serpent staying? Or don't we have a Garden of Eden anymore? You might suspect two places in the world today where the Garden of Eden might be, and they are the countries of Iraq and the continent of Africa. Wherever the Garden of Eden might be now, there is a serpent still in the Garden of Eden. Africa, as the current Garden of Eden, is full of many serpents, as that one serpent in the first Garden of Eden multiples, and Africa is a full Garden of Serpents. Whatever devil, magic, Satan, witch, voodoo, juju, black angels, and black ghosts one might be able to look for is present in Africa. Africa has got a blue-, red-, black-eyed devil residing there, and because Africa is now still a Garden of Eden, many more evils of devils acting like serpents are still being created to exist by God. Africa got all gods, magic, and many more devils, including a big twelve-horn dragon that has his home in Africa. Africa hosts the Islamic Allah, Christian God, traditional African gods, and many serpents that have distorted the African mind as God's creation is progressing in the Garden of Eden.

8.2 Adam and Eve Still Naked in Africa

How many naked pictures or human degrading video clips of naked humans have you seen so far on national TV like CNN, BBC, and Discovery channel, and many more media? They show pictures of human Africans walking naked without clothes on. Although there are naked humans in any other parts of the world, African nakedness may probably have caught much attention in the present world. Yes, in the Garden of Eden, where much of God's creation is still in progress, Adam and Eve are still naked in Africa. Naturally, Africans living in the jungle bushes are more closers to God than Africans who pray five times a day and live in modern cities. Every living jungle bush serves as a home for many villagers, and men and women live in acceptance of their nakedness, for they are patiently waiting for God the Creator to tell them when to cover their nakedness. Black people are patient with God in his creation and when his mighty kingdom will come to rule the black people's continent of Africa. The naked man and woman of Africa are true images of Adam and Eve living in the jungle bushes of African villages.

8.3   Animals and Plants in the Evergreen Planet of Africa

Africa is the main supplier of world zoo animals, and more animals of any species are still undercover in any jungle part of Africa. The conducive weather atmosphere is hosting living beings of any kind, ranging from big to unseen animals, in the thicker, dense rainfall forests of Africa. In the Garden of Eden, there are all species in a oommunity kingdom of all plants and animals. The dense forest of Africa is serving as a natural game park for all sorts of animals where they are an attraction to tourists. In the present Garden of Eden of Africa, living plants are evergreen, just like the imaginary old Garden of Eden, and this evergreen place is the home of living creatures where some species have still not been discovered in the garden, which is not modernized or civilized yet. African villagers are surviving on all wild fruit-bearing plants, and bush meat is found everywhere in any jungle, and that is what makes Bushmen have accepted to live comfortably in the Garden of Eden. Africa is the last Garden of Eden, where animals and plants exist to benefit the created man.

8.4   Naturally Blessed Garden of African`s Eden

The naturally blessed Africa is home for the created Adam and Eve, as Adam and Eve accepted to live in the jungle bushes without clothes and to daily eat and survive on wild garden fruits, leaves, and all sorts of bush meat. The diamond, gold, silver, oil, zinc, uranium, and iron ore are all minerals that Africa is blessed with as a true natural Garden of Eden. His creation shows that the sun shines every day and how he created Adam and Eve to enjoy the moon and starlight to see in the night instead of electricity. Rainfall has no timetable for African farmers, and also the source of water is naturally found in rivers, swamps, seas, oceans, and many holes that are dug underground. The blessed people of Africa are shining with different dialects, cultures, ways of life, and traditional differences.

The fertile land of Africa is blessed, as farmers call it the natural home of growth for any plants. Africa is mighty blessed with its natural landscapes, animals, plants, and her people.

8.5   God still in Creation in the Garden of Eden of Africa

The African continent is the present Garden of Eden, where God is progressively doing his mighty creation. There is no hurry in Africa, for there is nobody who is keeping a timetable of where would the last modern building stand before the last minute time ticks before the demolition of the earth that man has developed. The character of the black man is a question of God's creation, and the black man's land is under God's creation, as well as man's civilization in creation. God is patient in his creation, and Africans are also patient with God's creation. Lands of Africa are forming in shape as well and many Africans today are speaking many foreign languages instead of the eroded traditional African dialect. In the Garden of Eden, the serpent is tempting naked Africans to eat the fruit of knowledge so that Bushmen Adams and Eves of Africa will clothe their nakedness, and God will be upset so as to punish both white Adams and Eves as well as black Adams and Eves who will eat the fruit of wisdom to know what is wrong from what is right. God is progressively creating Africa in languages, cultures, and mind characters, developing infrastructures and people's skins.

9. The Devil's Eyes in East Africa
9.1   White-eyed God is the Creator of Eastern Africa

The white-eyed god of Eastern Africa is a lovely Allah God who created the land of Eastern Africa, its entire ethnic tribal people, and even its support of demarcation. God of the universe created Eastern Africa with a huge blessing of resourceful people, underground minerals, arable land, and culture, faith in Allah and God, and prior dignity and love of our Lord. The white-eyed god looks down from heaven upon Eastern Africa, and he loves his people, namely, Dingadinga, Dinka, Amhara, Triganya, Luo, Massai, Acholi, Chaaga, Kikuyu, Somali, Afar, Oromia, Turkana and all Eastern Africans such as Kenyan, Somalis, Sudanese, Ugandan, Tanzanian, Eritrean, Djibouti, and Ethiopian. God created us, and we must love ourselves as Eastern Africans regardless of our different cultures, skin colors, differing faiths, languages, politics, and lifestyle variety. White-eyed god loves Eastern Africa because he got nothing to take from Eastern Africans than what he wants to add.

9.2   The Blue-eyed Men of the Western Christianity and the Middle East Islamic.

The blue-eyed devil came to Eastern Africa a long time ago to find out where the hell every race of the world originated from and there Eastern Africa where every human in the world would trace his Stone Age creation back to East Africa. Every religion and kingdom in the world has touched down on Eastern Africa. Because Eastern Africa is blessed by a white-eyed god, its richness attracts blue-eyed devils to come and exploit Eastern Africa and rob its resources as well as its people. The blue-eyed devil controls Eastern African leaders' minds through his wealthy richness, and then Eastern Africans kill themselves like fishes at the cost of the blue-eyed devil. People who are rich in God-fearing cultures, lifestyles, love, and ancestry beliefs are now being exploited and robbed of their cultures, faith, and workforce, and the dignity of citizenship is being destroyed by a blue-eyed devil's work in Eastern Africa. Interference of the blue-eyed devil in Eastern African politics will never leave Eastern Africa as a safe haven for Eastern African citizens and foreigners.

9.3 Red-eyed Devil (Middle Eastern Men of Islam)

The red-eyed devil, too, is interfering and has been interfering with Eastern African internal affairs by enslaving Eastern African citizens. He steals resources, murders and grabs Eastern African land, and owns it under his stingy names. Red-eyed devil is more dangerous than blue-eyed devil; red-eyed devil is more racial, full of hatred, loves his damn religion, forces everyone else to accept his shitty religion, and loves to rule by damn autocratic power, which is full of dictatorship. Eastern Africans are messed up by this one red-eyed devil who entered Eastern Africa a long time ago, and now he is a danger to the lives of Eastern African citizens. Eastern indigenous African citizens have got their modern economic structure messed up; politics have altered, and people are confused by blue- and red-eyed devil's ideology of empty promises, and his wealth will never repair Eastern African's internal problems. Red-eyed and blue-eyed devils have created division in Eastern Africa with their damn religious faith, way of life, and political hypocrisies spread across Africa.

9.4   Black-eyed Devil (The Indigenous People of Africa)

White-eyed god created us with different colors, in regional lands, different languages, and a variety of characters; his love is also shining on us. As God created Eastern Africa, we created for ourselves different language accents, cultures, faiths, mindsets, and lifestyles; also, blue- and red-eyed devils created us land demarcations called countries, and we now fall apart from loving each other because of the blue- and red-eyed devils between us as Eastern Africans. Our poverty, illiteracy, backwardness, stupidity, uncivilization, tribalism, and many more negatives about us are being broadcasted in the air by the blue- and red-eyed devils in order to destroy us more. Black-eyed devil is sitting within us, and as Eastern Africans, we need to love ourselves and stop the hatred of color, religion, tribal issues, and different lifestyles, and reject red-

and blue-eyed devils' desire of wanting to destroy our ancestor cultures, religions, lifestyles, and exchanging our lifestyles for his. The black devil of Eastern Africa is nothing other than our tribal, religion, racism, and hatred issues.

9.5   Dark-eyed devil (The Real Serpent Devil in the Garden of Africa)

As Eastern Africans, we need to destroy every devil living in Eastern Africa; be it red-, blue-, black-, and dark-eyed devils, it must be destroyed. Eastern Africa is the central Garden of Eden, where the original serpent that deceived Adam and Eve still lives today. The same serpent of Adam and Eve has turned into a dark-eyed devil that is now destroying Eastern African citizens one by one. Blue- or red-eyed devil religions are not helping in this case; even Eastern African idols, magic, witches, and small ancestors' gods is not helping by destroying Eastern Africans' dark-eyed devil. Eastern Africans must stand up against the common dark-eyed devil, and eradication of this devil must be done with allies close to white-eyed god as we seek out our original Creator. We Eastern Africans live under one unity, love, culture, way of life, and true people of great faith and dignity. The serpent that is altering the African mind, creating hatred, quarrel, fighting, and conflict among Africans, must go, as well as Eastern Africans must destroy red-, blue-, black-, and dark-eyed devils in Eastern Africa.

10. Africans' Long Divisions
10.1   By Races, Tribes, Clans, and Societies, we created ourselves.

By the dimension measurement of God, he created the African continent and divided it into a variety of languages, tribes, regional lands, and colors of skin, and even our personal characters were created to suit the Creator's heart's desire. We created ourselves into having different enhanced language accents divided clans, families, tribal lines, and society groups. God didn't make us to have our differences cause the present havoc of human death of genocide, tribal killing, religion butchery, and murdering at the lives borderline of our racial issues. African tribes, races, cultures, languages, and societies are extended across Africa from East, West, Central, North, and even Southern Africa. We have the same accent in every African language, every tribe in every demarcated country of Africa, and our societies are extended out to include margin borders connected within the African motherland. By race, tribe, clan, community, or even society, Africans cannot be dichotomized by any devil as long division lasts in a minute of time.

10.2   By White Man's Dominance and Colonization Era, we changed the Creator narrative.

The long division of Africans came as the result of a white man stepping out of Africa shortly after being created in Africa and his return to Africa had caused long division in Africa. White man is the brother of a black man from the same skinned colorless mother, and the white brother has exploited Africa and controlled Africa for his benefit; eventually, this is where his Western idealism of imperialism will exist for a long division. Domination and supremacy of white man will keep tiding down Africa until Jesus returns to judge the living and dead white and black people out of domination and modern slavery. Westerner's power in the modern colonization era is keeping Africa divided so natural resources, people, products, power, and knowledge would flow to Western countries out of Africa. The long division of Africa can simply be solved by African leaders who can make use of the natural resources of African people and mineral resources, so begging from the West will stop there.

10.3   By Religious Faiths, African Gods, Witches, and Magicians; Humane erode the Creator's image of divinity

African long division is relying heavily on African poisons, faiths, African gods, witches, magicians, and the power of African serpents. Poisoning Africans by a religion which emerged outside Africa is a crime of human dichotomy, and this religion of political gains and hatred of racial shit will keep African citizens divided for a long time. Religion domination has created another modern colonization in Africa, and it's being used by the master of the religion as a means to push on with their countries' racial or tribal interested vision across Africa. Any Arab type born in Africa must be African and must serve in the interests of Africa rather than serve the Middle East. Africans must limit the use of their internal ancestors' gods, witches, and magicians against themselves in order to preserve traveling and the lives of Africans in unity without jeopardy of fear in the tribal use of witches and dangerous voodoo against Africans. Faith in God should not longer divide Africa if God's faith is purely used to exactly serve the purpose of the living God rather than a living person's interests from the Western or Middle Eastern world.

10.4   By Different system of Government, we developed atomic bombs.

How long African leaders, presidents, officials, and governments of Africa are going to keep dividing African citizens against each other? When would genocide, ethnic cleansing, land scotch rebellion, insurgencies, terrorism, government supporting tribal issues, racial and religion factions, and autocratic governments stop in Africa? Africans blame external devils, but not blaming internal devils is a failure cause of self-correction and improvement within Africa. Africa is full of too many shits, and these dangers are considered to be autocratic, anarchic, dictatorship, terrorist, less democratic, and socialist government types that keep dividing

African citizens against each, and no modern advancement in development is reached in the poorest continent. How long would African citizens keep blaming their government failures, and how long would the Western world keep blaming African governments for total failures in encouraging the long division of Africa by not applying the rule of the constitution, corruption, tribalism, and malicious diseases?

10.5 By Different Cultures, Lifestyles, and Norms, we created human hatred, racism and discrimination

Should racial cultures, lifestyles, and African traditional norms divide us too? Or where there is diversity, there is always too much conflict of danger unless there is a proper rule of law to govern the human mindset in the right path. Thousands of tribes across Africa with hundreds of cultures and a variety of lifestyles are now a typical problem to have African citizens live together in the comfort zone of sharing modern civilized values and coexisting together as one citizen of Africa. African local languages, accents, tribal norms, and local culture are furthering the long division of Africa. Traditional marriages, dances, mindsets, racial issues, and the variety of the ways of life are affecting Africa by not letting its citizens to live in peace together in corporate Africa. African governments must set a standards of living and coexistence of African citizens in corporate civilized Africa.

10.6   By Language or Dialect Diversity; humane is divided.

Did God the Creator mean to divide Africans by having them created with many different languages, dialects, and accents that spark up diversity conflict in creating the African long division? European colonists added a burden to the widely African long division by introducing their languages to Africa, and that added the burden of many languages to the already burdened division of African languages. If we can't understand ourselves as Africans under the variety of languages, dialects, and accents, then how can Africans adopt the unity of love and prosperity and grow together. This long division of Africa must be stopped by having African leaders come together and agree to have one adopted written languages used for the entirety of Africans citizens' communication. If we have languages of understanding, then we can have unity and love of our cultures. We can throw away colonists' languages and create our own African language to be written and used for the communication in the continent of Africa, and this language will centre our culture and way of life.

10.7   By Geographical Regions of Rivers and Seas, the creator is visible.

Africans have been divided since creation, and that is why our conflicts center around our long division, which will last after God himself gets down here to meet with African leaders and citizens to discuss solutions relating to African brotherhood killings. True indigenous Africans were invaded by invaders that now lead to conflicts of ethnicity, religions, languages, cultures, races, and citizens of political mindsets on hatred issues. By God's long division, Africa is a continental land divided by rivers, swamps, seas, geographical regional divisions, and vegetation of desert and green dense rain forest of Africa. With God having created different skin colors and physical structures of Africans, it may not serve the purpose in the long division of African citizens. Africans have the same characteristics of content, and we should love ourselves as white people love themselves without any tougher interracial contradiction. African leaders must stop the long division of African citizens by deploying the force of African citizens' development in corporate love of unity, peace, togetherness, and prosperity of Africans as one citizen of Africa guided by law.

11.   Rising Dummy Citizens by the corrupt Government.

11.1   The Ungodly Government Constitution is a genocide in its ethnic cleansing.

Undemocratic government that is not for the people, not from the people, not to the people, not by the people, and not godly to her people must have the task of creating a dummy citizen or a rising radical blue-eyed citizen. Since every government must derive its constitution from the values of either religious or original people's way of life, it might be certain that some government comes up by power, and not even the constitution drives values out of the Bible, the Koran, or from the people; eventually citizens grow up with the radical mindset because government's ungodly constitution is not teaching them anything of the right value. Ungodly constituted government has citizens growing rough, hostile, and rude without peaceful means of humility and kindness among fellow citizens. Ungodly constituted government indirectly teaches citizens to do ungodly things, and it also encourages ungodly citizens to mistreat world citizens in their acts as compared to citizens of terror. Those dictatorship, autocratic, and kingship governments may not teach citizens right.

11.2   Constitutional Rights for selective special Citizens with upper privilege.

Constitutional rights are amended and meant to create the right citizens as a country's head capital office knows the direction of fellow citizens. Right, to press and freedom of speech create dummy citizens who talk too much until they sometimes get into trouble by insulting what they do not support. Americans are considered talkative citizens in the world because of their press and freedom of speech, but the Chinese are the most quiet citizens in the world as each constitution created damned citizens in a mindset direction from the capital office. Constitutional laws affect how a citizen thinks and acts in daily life; any act that is not covered by the Constitution is a citizen's playing ground, like marriage, infidelity or adultery, which is unconstitutional in many Western countries. Constitutional rights make citizens walk on a trail of footsteps, following each other even to hell if that is where the road leads them. Constitutional law teaches and educates citizens in any way of life that may make them look dummies when compared with other country citizens.

11.3   The Preaching of Evils to the Society, Nation, or Community can deter a great superior nation.

Many African citizens will witness a murder and laugh about it without reporting the crime scene to the authorities. Citizens will be looking out to find where there is a mob, robbery, stealing, murdering, and other sort of crimes not covered by constitutional law or in a country without laws to prevent crime. If the government preaches evil deeds in its capital office while the citizens are the audience listening, it means the government is responsible for evil actions that the citizens will take against the targeted host country. The society of evil is the one that has gained the power of mind control of citizens who are of valueless deeds and practice known good character, which is a negative society or other societies, like the hatred of young youth who kill black Africans seems to be normal to society but abnormal in other societies. Nation is a buildup from a family to a community to a society and to a nation. Family is a small nation; a bad family's evil deeds create damned citizens.

11.4   Media Control Citizens in a Mental Mindset Cage

Locking information down is the best way for that government to create and prosper dummy citizens who will know nothing in any other part of the world except what information they are allowed to know. CNN, Fox 5, and any other news media in America have a key issue by Washington on what news teaches and educates Americans about. Dummy citizens will know only what they are allowed to know and not what they are supposed to know. Mental mindset cage is bad for redneck fellows as well as for jungle citizens who are locked down on BET, Discovery Channel, and other propaganda media that control the mindset of citizens, which makes the audience think like those TV scriptwriters or those movie producers. Governor Sarah Palin called Africa a country instead of a continent because she is a dummy citizen and a victim of information lockdown by Washington. A graduate American will ask me where Sudan is. But she might accept being dumb if a middle school student in India or Africa would name all fifty states of the United States.

11.5   Bills and Passed Laws Lead to Citizens' Dumping Ways of Mindset

Judging everything that humans do is dangerous to life, and not judging every human action is also more dangerous to life's happiness, but passing bills and amended laws creates growth in the unlawful natural way of life. Too many suicides or many gays in America are a signal that the passing of the bill of amendment to so much freedom by Washington is another violation of life's natural rule and the policy of natural creation that woman is not supposed to be too free or be too locked down either but should be loved in balance with man's happiness. There is too much religious freedom until no American is more typically religious; Bishops are gays or molest kids, and the more the society is extraordinarily liberal, the more evils are invited into the natural life of the society. Dummy citizens are gays, lesbians, molesters, and people with suicidal tendencies because the American way of life created them. The Child Support Bill of Rights is a good place to scapegoat culprits, but it is also raising dummy kids who lack a fatherhood image and later become a society headache. Every passed bill and amended law had two effects: bad and good sides.

11.6   Restriction on Crossing Racial Boundaries Creates Unmixable Bowl of Salads

Even after defecating, you still see your colorful stool going down in the toilet bowl after your yesterday's meal of a mixed bowl of salads. The American bowl of salads will never get mixed until we don't see any more white, black, or Indian segregated schools, churches, and neighborhoods or when we can see common intermarriages across boundaries closed by racism. The racism concept has given rise to foolish citizens in any institutionalized society where superiority is preached by elders to their young generation, and that creates overlooking of other racial hosts. Religion and cultures are also creating dummy citizens when they act more religious or more secular. How many young virgin girls can you count in America compared to that of the Middle East, and is being a virgin a dumb personal cultural idea or a government-supported law idea? Any important value we have in a society is a damp value to other societies, and that makes us look like dumb citizens in the eyes of our opposite society. God creates us in an unmixable way, and we cannot mix what God has separated.

12.   The Land of Tensions

12.1   Sexual Tension

The land of tension is a state of tension in mind in which men and women of creation interact and react against their sexual needs and desires. It is not what we want and how we want it as we cannot get it the way we want that brings the fight. Desire to be loved, hunting for love, and being more attractive in a scene that catches men's or women's eyes are the cause why gentlemen and ladies dress in kill-me-quick body display dressing. Dressed in a sexy dress with half the boobs visible and emphasizing the butt, in the manner of ever-ready intercourse dressing on the street is an attraction for sexual predators across many cities in America. Gays, lesbians, molesters, and sexual assault cases are a matter of law debate in the White House. Child support, divorces, love homicides, and broken families are all the tensions that arise from lawless sexual relationships, with too much freedom given to kisses, intercourse, and dating. STDs, broken hearts, fatherless kids, teenage pregnancy, school dropouts, prostitution, and many more are the results of sexual action in the American free way of life.

12.2   Racial Tension

Getting paid on the basis of how you look or getting hired because of your accent, as well as getting a raise or promotion depending on where you are all hurdles and offensive acts of institutionalized racism. Washington needs to pass a bill and make it a law to punish institutional racism. The American bowl of salads will never mix until Jesus returns to help mix it for America. Indians go to Indian schools, food stores, restaurants, and churches, while white Americans live in their neighborhood, schools, and churches and own their separated part of America without the main isolated black America. I think the Malcolm X ideology would work better for Americans to have division of states according to white states, black states, Indian states, Asian states, Spanish states, African states, and more states that would belong or be owned by a specific race. Dark against light skin, whites against blacks and Spanish against whites are just a few, as we cannot even differentiate anymore if racial tension is because of a racial war or a fight of skin and face. The other issues are male over female issues at work as well as Muslim, Christian, and pagan indirect discrimination acts.

12.3   Wage and Income Tension

A truck was loaded with Mexican crossing borders into the United States and the cheap labor industries in America, and this act has been fueling labor tension of jobs and profit making versus labor for making survival life. Middle class, medium class and the rich class in America are problematic causes of economic trauma. Every recession and national depict debt. Fighting to defend the position of your wage, wealth and richness are the tension of income that has rolled out a greedy legacy to many Americans. The indirect corruption must have a law to govern and track down institutionalized crime on the usage of employees for the benefit of individual greedy owners. If there are no job industries in America that offer low wages, Spanish border issues could come down, as well as tension between the neutralized Americans against the born Americans would be lower to prevail peace at workplaces. Stores like Wal-Mart that use associates to control wealth must get checked up for indirect corruption and usage or labor abuse in the business. Small businesses never grow up, and big businesses never lose their portions, and that tension is harsh.

12.4   Religious Tension

Muslim Americans have no homes to live in, nor can they freely walk around as expected after September 11. Many have lost jobs and find it hard to get jobs, and living is harder for them in a very religious and racial institutionalized American society. The hidden code of racial rejection during job search, denial of promotion, or being wrongful accused is common, and it is complicated to identify in most cases. Arab Americans can't even have dinner together with their black American friends on the Muslim Ramadan dinner break evening, just like the Jewish Americans who will never share the love of God with Christians. Many divided denominations of faith raise red-hot tension in every religion, just like the bloodshed between Sunnis and Shia Muslims. Catholic Christians, Protestants, Salvation Army, Baptism, and many more who are at faith war under different gods of many Bibles. Buddhists, Sikhs, Christians, Muslims, pagans, and witches are religious humans who will never have dinner together to share the love of one Creator and even to appreciate the Creator's powerful gifts.

12.5   Drug and Prostitution Tension

Federal government will make a lot of money after legalizing marijuana, cocaine, or any other inhalant drugs. Personal health is not a public health hazard in the case of non-transmitting disease. The drug war in the Gulf of Mexico and around the States' borders cannot be a problem if business drug dealers can pay the customs duty and other related charges. How are drugs related to sex, poverty, crimes, prostitution, and human trafficking? This tension is caused by the feeling of pleasure in humans who want to live life as if they are in heaven. Daily, the feeling of happiness, thrill, love, and joyful lifestyle, with the heart filled every minute with joyous happiness, cannot be found on earth; we should better wait till we die or else the tension of desirable joyous life versus the natural law of scarcity will kill you in a minute. Everything is here to give you a life in its fullness but differentiate earth from heaven and earth from hell by accepting the scarcity of what is available for you to live a full life. A triply enjoyable life where you have drug addiction, sex, and money indicates a troubled life.

12.6   Greed and War Tension

The greed of power and wealth to be famous and selfish love is the human ego of taking advantage of what God provides or the chance granted by your society or country. Greedy tension arises in a person after letting selfish love enter his heart. Whether one wants to be on top, lead till he/she dies and still in favorite power of decadency to his loved ones or else one will remain trash sleeping under the bridge until dies. Conflict in men is because of aggressiveness and is needed to succeed your fellow opposing men. Women are peaceful with other women or men of different races, but not with men. War is a result of control followed by manipulation and exploits what you defeat under control. Human greed causes war, and men are never satisfied and need more eventually, leading good men to gain control and advance their greediness in the world. The desire of needing pleasure and food causes man to launch an attack on his host; eventually, man gets into a fight to control power so he can get his pleasure across what he wants.

13   The Wasted Citizens

13.1   Judge Sentence to Aid Murder or Genocide of Citizens

If one American, Briton, or Australian dies because of either clear or unclear causes of death, there is nationwide grief, and an investigation is done by the FBI. Murdering and committing genocide against citizens is a priority duty of some governments in Third World countries. Citizens are considered culprits, wrongdoers, lawbreakers, traitors, and disobedient; as a result, the government wastes useless citizens by fire squads, the death penalty, electrocution, genocide, assassination, or mob killing. The government wastes its citizens by launching offensive civil war, uprisings, rebellions, or mass land scorching ethnic cleaning. A mass grave is an out-wood doom of escaping disability of amputee, displaces, refugees, exile, and persecution are mean open ways that the bad government wastes helpless citizens in their country of origin. Government control by one minority, one race, one religion, one ethnic group, or even by one family generation ruling without practicing the law of democratic ruling is associated with the huge number of wasted citizens' lives. The wasted citizens are innocent, helpless, powerless, and ignorant too.

13.3   Keep Them Down on Crime or Illiteracy so the superior can win

The wasted citizens are among the categories of the citizens whom the government denies, keeps down, controls, and denies an opportunity for education, learning, self-awareness, jobs, or even denies success in mental growth, just like African Americans who were denied their African origin cultures, motherland connection, self-awareness, education, and future advancement as a society of late slavery. If there is another powerful society on top of a weak society or there is the presence of an oppressive, hated, racial government in power over isolated citizens, the lower rank citizens or society are undermined the right to justice and equality. Since high-position opportunities are controlled by the oppressive government that is racial, hatred, or religious fundamental, half of the citizens of the country will be wasted as they would lack because of illiteracy, crimes, joblessness, homelessness, pessimism, and every generation will remain in the wastage period in that country.

13.4   Wasted Citizens' Power and Knowledge is the creation of the poorest country.

All men were created equal, and there should be no overlooking, mistreatment, or prejudice where lowly grown society or citizens who haven't been given an opportunity to prosper would be wasted in human havoc. The human mind is a very terrible thing to be wasted; millions of citizens' minds are simply wasted in many self-centred governments. A government that is controlled by rednecks or powers by fundamentals that don't exercise the power of democracy is likely to favor certain societies, communities, tribes, and races over other societies and citizens. The government divides its citizens by giving more advancement, prosperity, and growth to favor some citizens and institutionally denies other citizens the right to knowledge and power learned through mind-building. Justice and equal sharing of the country's resources for the benefit of every citizen's advancement and prosperity is key for the country to preserve and honor the power and knowledge of the citizens generally to reap the scientific level of the States' knowledge base type.

13.5   Citizens' Denegation of Life and Chances can create a lack of opportunities.

Since a bad government that emerges from power-controlled dominance by one ethnic group, race, religion, or high class divides its citizens and power side citizens, the result is always unequal, and injustice grows and advances in citizens of the same country. Citizens regard themselves being denied, abandoned and refused, and they fight as they neglected by their own government when the national issue of injustice and equality arises in resources, power, growth, and job sharing is a concern. Just like African Americans, the Spanish and the minority group of Latinas in the United States of America have been struggling for decades to have their minority leaders advance into the White House as Obama has broken through for black people worldwide, whereas the first Spanish president in America has a long way to travel to reach the White House. Citizens who are denied life and a chance for prosperity and advancement growth are left mentally unstable by the government.

13.6   Forcing Citizens out of the country for Immigration resettlement is giving a host country a successful labor force

The first and foremost unexhausted natural resource for any country is its citizens, who come in a variety of skin colors, faiths, races, tribes, languages, and cultures. In spite of the benefits that the citizens created as huge first revenues towards government earnings, some governments create catastrophic havoc in citizens' lives that would lead the citizens to be exiled and immigrated out of the country. African governments head the list in this crime of exile of citizens. The government is using the act of forcing to make its citizens to flee and go into exile out of the country by the action of genocide, murdering, civil war, epidemics, lack of jobs, lack of prosperity, opportunism, and education of high standard. The responsibility of the government is to create a comfortable heaven for its citizens for every need of individual citizens. It is an advantageous sharing as the government uses its citizens to pay taxes and other revenues while citizens, to make their lives easy earn back what they have paid the government in revenue. Citizens in exile are useless or are used by the country of exile.

13.7   Cultural Lifestyle in the name of the empire.

If the government becomes a faith-based religion in a country of multi-faiths, cultures, races, and even different societies of different beliefs, that government would cause citizens trouble or deny freedom of worship. Some governments would sit at the gateway to heaven so that government religious officials would select the country whose citizens are to be directed to heaven while the rest are pointed to hell. A government that judges its citizens on religious laws before God's judgments causes double punishable acts to its citizens, as God will judge and punish the very same citizens also. Many governments can deny their citizens freedom of culture, lifestyle, and religion and even deny their citizens the way of life. It is worse to have the government commit genocide against its citizens because of faith matters; religious choice is a specific personal matter, and the government rules the people on a general basis and not on specific individual citizen choices. It is okay to have a government drive its constitution out of the Bible or the Koran so long the country is dominated by one religion, race, culture, and lifestyle.

14.   Types of Dictators

14.1   Self-dictatorship

What is it in a person that causes self-quarrels, hatred, jealousy, rudeness, unhappiness, stress, anxiousness, covetousness, and self-contradiction? Human self-dictatorship is the cause of self-blaming, self-suicide, self-denial, selfishness, self-centeredness, self-hatred, and all personal self-contradicting issues. In whatever a person does, there is always a contradicting thought, and every decision making must be dictated in the human mind in between reasoning and before an action movies is initiated. Between the judgmental mind and the reasoning rational of the human person, there arises the thinking dictatorship in personal thinking, suggestion, opinion, reasoning, and advising capacity of mental operation ability. A human being dictates other human beings' ways of life, culture, religion, dressing style, and even skin color, and this is what makes a person with a dictating mind an idiot. A typical person who dictates his mind too much can become isolated, antisocial, and even become gay.

14.1   God Dictated its Creation

How many times would gays, lesbians, people with broken hearts, obsessed, disabled, blind, deaf, slain, dead, and even murdered complain to God about all these life's tragedies? God is a Creator, Father Almighty, superpower, and Omniscient of all his creatures, and he has right way to dictate any creature's way of life, including human being's way of thinking and acting. Every time severe weather comes with, natural disasters kill and sweep away human lives and ants, too, but who can say a word? It is only he in heaven who knows why there are incurable diseases like AIDS, herpes, wars, devils, racial hatred, and many worldly life complications. Should an atheist keep blaming nature that created itself, or should those who believe in His Majesty blame the Father of creation? Whatever cause of bad life gets in its best offers, it is a disadvantage, and human must act on it for the benefit to gain half-life instead, one may end up having both full and half-life happiness.

14.2   The Three Powers in Dictatorship of a mankind

If God is a supernatural power in his omniscient world, should a devil have the right to dictate either God's mighty deed or even his good work? The devil who owns man's work and takes credit for himself is a typical dictator of God's work and deeds. The devil dictates God's work and will because there a lower rank level of man. If there is no man below the devil, the devil wouldn't dictate and disobey God's vision. Man and devil, on the other hand, are typical friends or enemies competing on who should be beside God. The relationship between man and devil is of money, gifts, fear, and quarrels on who should be a good faithful son of God. Man's greediness and the making of life cause him to use the devil to gain wealth, and the devil acts like he owns everything in the world by giving man who adores him a portion of magic, witch sorcery, and cult power. The devil acquires little power from God over a man just as man who adores the devil acquires little power from the devil and acts powerful over a man who has got no God or devil power.

14.3   Government System of Dictatorship

A government that dictates its citizens' will, way of life, religious freedom, right to live, freedom of speech, and press is considered an anti-citizen's government. Good dictatorship faith governments are considered better than bad dictatorship deed governments. Good dictatorship faith government is one that establishes rule and a lawful constitution to rule a country by dictatorship for the future good, and the people change for the betterment of the next generation, which knows well for a change. A bad dictator government is one that oppresses, commits genocides and murders, is racial, and exiles its citizens over unnecessary changes that could benefit certain citizens in the country. The anti-computer group and anti-slavery group arose in America a long time ago to stop a change in the advancing technology, but the US government dictates the opinion rights of those citizens, and today, for our benefit, I am writing this book on my laptop. The government denied citizens' proposals in good faith.

14.4   Lifestyle System in Dictatorship

The original American way of life has been dictating every other immigrant's way of life as soon as they enter America. Every human being's environment has its own way of life, and at the same time, people who have their own lifestyle stay on it to protect and guard it against any aggression changes emerging from any generation, intruders, and factors that force the way of life changes in the society. America is protecting its way of life by having me here in the US Army as a guardian of freedom and the American way of life. Regular citizens are struggling and suffering as victims of the current American way of life. As a result, the American way of life is dictating half of American citizens' rights to pursue happiness; many gays, lesbians, homeless, criminals, molesters, murderers, rapists, and drunkards blame the way of life in America as the primary cause of all evils in any American society. If society is sitting on hatching rotten eggs, chickens will never emerge as young clean chickens will never come to live.

14.5   Culture and Society Dictatorship

A young Muslim woman was stoned to death because of an adultery case against her, and a young African girl was killed by her father to save the honor of a family after she caused shame to the family by having a boyfriend and trying to get married outside the tribe. A bishop who molested a ten-year-old altar boy and the gays' club in America are illnesses in the society caused by the society's cultures and way of life that dictate an individual's way of wanting to live. God has never created any culture or commanded a man to live in a recommended way of life because older dead generation of men came up with ideas of creating society, culture and the way of life. Every coming generation is affected by the already set society system of life, culture, and religion, whereas every generation has to create its own culture and way of life. The balance in a happy life lies between a man and a woman; a man should be happy, or else a woman will never be happy in that society or nation.

14.6   Dictating Religion System of a mankind

Those who have their lives taken away in the name of Allah or God may have to find other happiness in the next world they are going into, or else their happiness is terminated forever. Every religious way of life is dictating human being's earthly way of life, and those believers deny themselves earthly life in the same hope that heavenly life is going to be better than this earthly life. The worst hope is that we don't know if there is any heavenly life after death since there is no one dead who has come back to life and told living beings that there is a heavenly life better than this earthly life. Religious believers are considered brave as they always deny themselves earthly life but not those blessed by God like Muhammad, Elijah, Job, David, and Jesus, who died without leaving a wife and children in the world. Religious life dictates the human bodily feeling to have sex at any time and at any age regardless of law, status, shame, family honor, financial status, or even without considering whether God would like it or not to have sex outside marriage.

14.7   Human Dictatorship in Racism

Since human beings are claiming power over all God-created creatures and because there is no other creature anywhere in the world to compete with a man in intellectual power, man is misusing God-granted power over creatures. The way man is slaughtering, killing, and eating any living thing that is eatable is a crime against the matrix natural law. Because power is a primary cause of dictatorship, it is eventually God who is dictating man's way of life, and man is dictating animals' living states. That God has created the world; finally, he created man and gave him authority all over what he has created. The food matrix shows man depending heavily on animal meats, products, and by-products, and man-enslaved donkeys, horses, oxen, and dogs are doing man's work. Man also puts other animals in jailed houses and calls them pets, such as cats, dogs, rabbits, birds, and even some snakes. Thousands of more animals are sentenced to life imprisonment in zoos, national parks, and reserves or are even killed and eaten as bush meat. Man dictates his way of life over any created creature.

14.8   Rebellion Act of humanity

Rebel action is an accountability of aggressive response to oppressive mistreatment by an enemy partner. Wild or even tame animals overreact most of the time to send messages of equality and just treatment through their rebel attacks to let man know that there is unfair treatment between creatures. The only human being who has never or not yet taken up an army struggle against man's unfair treatment is a woman. Every culture or way of life in any society, tribe, religion, family, or community can either indirectly or direct benefit a female or a woman, and that advantage is what a calm woman enjoys whatever side of culture reflects them, or else a woman is an emotional creature just like a cow who cannot lead a rebel army struggle against the dominant man. A rebel act is a rebellion, for example, when a snake and python bite or when bees, wasps, or scorpions sting man. Rebels in every nation are humans who claim right and fair treatment and share inequality, as God is also involved in the fair happiness and living of all creatures.

15.   The Enemy within us.

15.1.   The Enemy Within Our Relationship

15.1.1. Bad Family Member

The enemy within any relationship can be either a member of family, a friend, or a partner in love. Conflict can never stop from getting into the relationship of relatives, and there are enemies such as a brother against brother, sister against sister, aunt turned against uncle, and so on. He who kills and murders his children, mother, daddy, sister, brother, and aunt is a family's worst enemy. Family conflict always grows within the family blood relationship, and relatives or family members can easily stop it before it is too late and someone dies or gets killed by another in that family. A family may have more than one blood-related enemy within a family or more depending on how the family copes with trouble, family problems and crises, as well as family conflict.

15.1.2 Bad Lover or Friend

The common death in the United States of America is of lovers, friends, and family members who are murdered or killed. The enemy in love or in friendship is worse than a stranger or an unknown enemy from outside. Chances of controlling and escaping harm from the enemy within love or friendship are limited to zero or less most of the time. Identify the enemy in love, friendship, or even in a family and apply the principle of total separation and vow to be strangers, even with a blood relative, in order to save lives. Boyfriend murdering his girlfriend, a wife killing her husband, a father murdering his children, or a friend killing his/her friend is not rare as it is very common, and these culprits are enemies within a relationship or in love. Identify a potential and serious enemy in love, friendship, or family and isolate them with the help of local law enforcement.

15.2   Enemy within a Country

15.2.1 Bad Citizen

How many Americans within America are daily diagnosed with the betrayal of being enemies within their own country? If a citizen gets his/her hope betrayed by not having his/her country fulfill some citizens' promises, citizens can rebel and become enemies within the country. Bad citizens are the ones rotting away in a country with bad contracting mental national issues. Because a citizen enemy within a country feels neglected, ignored, racially targeted, hated, or isolated, they can easily join a chosen part of terrorism or lead their own terror against people in the country.

15.2.2 Badass Spy

Within a group of people, there are spies, snitchers, investigators, Trojan horses, or even news collectors, but most people may not know there is an enemy within the group, a family, a community, a country, or even within an army. Some spies are made from good followers whose mistreatment by other people turns them into bad people, so they act as enemies within or collaborate with your enemy. Your husband and boyfriend/girlfriend can work as a spy in your relationship to ensure a secure and healthy relationship, and that very spy is the enemy within that has a determined target, and his spying mission is a time bomb, or it can stop when mission is proved or fulfilled.

15.2.3 Neutralized Foreigner

In any country where foreigners are neutralized citizens, war turns to come home, and a government fights outside the country and within the country to defend native citizens' right to liberty. In America, where foreigners flow in like flying locusts, which was stopped and nailed down by Bush Jr. after September 11, it is tough as the US government fights two terrorism wars, that within the country and the one outside the country. The worst enemy is the enemy within the United States, but the enemy within is the one that goes outside there and multiplies as they turn, shooting back at the country they live in firsthand for safety. Fighting the war within and defeating the enemy within doesn't need aggressiveness, toughness, or offensiveness. Otherwise, it gets worse with the violation of many constitutional rights; it is advisable to use peaceful means and other means of social change for eradication. There are too many enemies within America because of the freedom of the press.

15.3   The Enemy within the War Line

Besides a direct enemy at whom my weapon is pointed, there is another unknown enemy within us whom we may not be aware of, and that enemy is within our squad, platoon, coy, battalion, or even within our patrolling area. The frontline enemy is direct and easy to tackle, but the twisted enemy within needs the same skill and means as what he/she is using to conquer without damaging the reputation or violation of any law, policy, or rule of our engagement. It takes patience, caution, warning, or the right steps to prove, control, catch, and get rid of the enemy within a frontline. It is tougher as a soldier at Camp Humphreys; our phones are taped at any callout or calls in, Internet usage, movement within or out of the post, or at vacation time. I mean, everything you do as a soldier must be double-checked to ensure activity that the enemy within is free on the border near North Korea. Keeping an eye on the direct enemy across the block, as well as searching for the enemy within us, is a rule in fighting an undefeatable war, and we are knowledgeable about it.

15.4   The Enemy within the World

Was Jesus Christ the enemy within the world or a savior within the world, and what about Prophet Muhammad? Do humans forget that the worst enemy within the world is a human being? Otherwise, God would turn animals into his humans and human beings to be wild animals who can eat grasses and wild leaves. How destructive is a human being against each other and even against earth, which can create and command a man to take care of it. Are these developed countries with huge warhead atomic bombs destructive or are the developing countries the troublesome enemy within the world. Devil is or may not be the enemy within the world since man sells or leases the devil power for money to survive. The Creator is not an enemy either against his creations, but it might be the one that is created and given a brain to think. Every day, human population passes away, killed and murdered by another man's action which is hundred percent in the world.

15.5   The Enemy within a Communal Group

15.5.1 Racial and Faith within the Group

Every man has a judgmental mind, and it goes out of control sometimes, and it is hard to have one group do something irrational, and that group sooner or later faces the resistance force of the enemy within. Even brothers argue and differ on what is irrational or rational thought, and they become enemies of each other. White or

Arab slave masters, who were enslaving black people, argued and differed among themselves on what racism was causing in the blood of black people; eventually, that has left an old black man today to remain sitting in the back of the bus even though a black man is a pilot in the United States. Even in the faith group, the enemy is the Protestant Church, Shia Muslims or Jews who persecuted Jesus Christ. There is always one individual who does not abide by a tribe or society's rule of law.

15.5.2 *The Political Party*

The more humans grow intelligent and smart, the worse the enemy within he/she becomes; otherwise, all politicians are the worst enemies in any game. Grilling or drilling politicians is the act of playing a dirty game, and that game ends after one of the enemies within is dead. Criticism, agitation, and drilling are a few but dangerous means that quickly reveal the political party's enemy within or outside the party. It is very easy for politicians to identify the enemy within when it comes to politics, and it is very easy for politicians to kill or destroy the enemy within politics. Birds of the same feathers do not fly together when it comes to politics. Unless a politician wants to share their skills, political parties are nothing but a bunch of greedy, power-centric people calling themselves as leaders over paupers called citizens in a socialized nation.

15.6   The Enemy within the Decision

How many times would you convince your loved one, kid, enemy, or even persuade a disagreeing party to accept what are all the side benefits? The enemy in decision-making is tougher when it comes to a peace signing deal, negotiations, bargaining, trading discounts, or a love deal sealed between lovers of interests. It is hard to convince who wants to grab away a huge party of the shares and the woman who thinks she is the topmost beautiful woman in the world in place of the first created woman, Eve. It is a dirty game played by greedy politicians who will have great shares or negotiate the business profit price in a fair way without giving rise to an enemy within the final decision-making. It is tougher to defeat the enemy in the final decision-making when he is the only one who gets what you want, and your persuasion to get it at a fair price is nothing to the greedy enemy in the final decision-making. You either leave it or take it at an unfair price because it is the rule of a society's norms and culture. Group living is unfair in any society.

15.7   Leading Enemy into divided and conquer

When you have got no other power left and are so weak and so exhausted of energy or so defeated you let the direct enemy pass through your territory. It is surrender, and you give in for the victorious enemy to exploit, take, and play around his/her win after the defector becomes the defeated. The leading enemy is the enemy who gets all the power and no one can compromise them, and they have any right in whatever they want to do, and they can do it without any objective. Looking at North Korea from my patrolling territory, is North Korea a leading enemy in the world, or are we in the US Army the most leading enemy in the world as many countries think? In the power of economy, warheads, technology, people, and intellectuals, we believe that the leading enemy is identified through its demand and power control as everything that the world dreams to have is here at home; just sit back and let them come to you. The leading enemy is tough to defeat and very hard to undermine for a short period of time but can be defeated in a long time.

15.8   The Outside Enemy

In my family, the enemy outside my fence might be a stranger, an intruder, or a faraway enemy. You worry too much about the outside known enemy rather than the enemy within, but the worst enemy is the enemy within. As I try to sleep between the wall border of North Korea and South Korea, no sleep comes into my eyes because the outside enemy is just too close to my nose, but I am worried too much if there is an enemy in my platoon armed with M240 Bravo. It could maybe a bad citizen enemy within or a relative battle buddy enemy within. The outside enemy is always a target, and we know where our artillery barrels are pointing or what to do when a fireguard shoots at the enemy in a raid. It is harder to predict what to do at the scene when the enemy within starts his/her rampant shooting in the mall, shop, garrison, school, or even while praying for life in the church. The enemy outside is better at a target, otherwise, for preparation advantages, the enemy within suddenly kills. The outside enemy is easily spotted and could be visible in tactics.

16. The Gaming Time
16.1   The Politician's Dirty Game Time

Politicians are the world's greediest people, filling their stomachs with anything that they can grab in the form of what people pay or citizens' expenses. It is not a lie but the truth. Fill your mouth with words to preach about people's problems with a few ways to fix them, and people will consent with you and place you in Oval or Triangle office. Citizens are using their hard-earned taxes to pay the president and other party politicians so that the playing game politician would work for people. Politicians' greediness drives them to work for the public, and their playing game is earning them pocket money for survival. A greedy heart always looks at the benefits side of the problem solution, and that is why too many problems between people cannot be solved by politicians. The greedy games daily played by politicians are eradicable by the scene truth solution in the real problem in an ideal world. Even when a politician is dying, he will still plan and try to leave a seed of greediness behind to benefit the next generation after his death and that always fuels conflicts with what we could control as black people against what other races can control as people. The game of politics is dirty and greedy, but at the same time, it is life resourceful and famous names honors in vain after death.

16.2   The Game of Man Versus Life game

How do you play a life game to be resourceful and survive from being a jobless person to a homeowner or from a street life to being a millionaire? A man rising from the ashes or from a middle-class struggling family to become a top millionaire is a life game-winner. Passing headache exams, tests, quizzes, or homework is part of playing the life game where the struggler will be the executive of tomorrow if he wins the life gaming time. This life's game of struggle has changed many natural things that have lost their original and true natural meaning, like a man and woman's love of reconciliation, which is now to buy, love, or sell it to a guy or woman who has got enough money to support the cause of the family love. A living person grabs anything on his way rolling downhill of life, and anything man grabs for a living is at its own disadvantage. The nature of the job each does determines how hard or easy she/he plays the game of struggle against life. You are paid on how hard you struggle playing your stake of time against life. Man's game against life is deathly and destroys the nature of the original life that God has created.

16.3   People of Faith in the Game of All Time

God loves and forgives those humans who judge too much rather than those who blaspheme his name. If you are a living religious faith person who is surviving on a food drive from any living thing's body, then you are wrong. The religious person still fears people and the evils of bad deeds that make faithful people non-religious. Life game time in modern religion is taking a generational age of wealth, power, resources, and materialism controls against each other mankind in another race for the sake of the same God. After your prayers, you pick up your knife to lure, kill, rob and loot your next-door brother, sister or stranger who is also a son of the living God. Pastors, bishops, priests, and preachers are game players for their wealthy survival between God, man, and evil. Those who sell witchcraft, magic, gods, and sorcery look for a return of goods and money for survival. The same God of one universe is a divided divine for all religions, and the religious conflict is not about God; rather, it is man's own greediness game to acquire wealth and fame against other races and sections of people.

16.4 Game of Acquiring Wealth Versus Game of Losing Inheritance

What good can a rich man do to help poor peasants get rich too, or what other good thing can a developed country do to help an underdeveloped country get developed besides making a peasant poorer and the rich keeping himself rich for generations with exploitation benefits of the poor? Human beings are living a life by playing a game of acquiring wealth for survival's sake, from selling drugs to selling magic and witchcraft to playing a game in order to live a natural life. Helpless peasants are controlled so that one can exploit their underdeveloped resources, for there is one God who plays a game better than humans by creating people within their resources. Denying oneself sleep and working hard to death to fulfill the dream of wealth gains is a tactical game in human life to gain the whole world, in the process, maybe losing his soul. If you can break in through somebody else's door or the bank or kill the owner to rob, then you are good at earning a living by acquiring wealth, which everybody knows about.

16.5   Survivors in the Life Game

Living life by chance is good luck for an idle man to receive life as gifts from the natural father of creation, who said to the man not to worry about tomorrow. He told man to just sit there and wait for food to drop from the heaven's open sky and that he would get a life to survive. Survivors of a massacre or genocide have more chances to live than a pastor of the church who pockets congregation money in order to pay his/her bill. It is a matter of saving life by saving face; humans are full of shit when it comes to living a resourceful life on someone else's life's expenses at the cost of his blood. You defend what you are eating with the first strong guiding hand while letting the other hand grab more resources from the weak peasant. If you have a fat stomach, it means you might be stressed out as you overeat yourself, your stomach bank serving as a people grabber. It is the game time when you can run from being a millionaire to a peasant or from rich to poor and from poor to rich, depending on good game players.

16.6   The Lovers' Game Time of all the time

Love is not natural anymore, as lovers pay huge amounts of money to get love from each other. It gets to the point of acquiring wealth by selling your daughter or son to a rich man or family so that you can be rich as a parents. Women in the West are taking advantage of being a woman over man who pays a lot of money to show their care in return for a woman's love. Paying dowry or family tributes is a huge demand as a natural love in the game time of the Third World countries. It is now full of too many switching points, where gays switch to be lesbians or, a straight person trying to be gay or a retired lesbian finally finding a dream love to be straight. The love game is bitter when it takes away lives, and it is not reimbursed when it breaks lovers' hearts as well, as it cannot be repaid in full when love steals all your wealth or no money is left in your pocket. It is very ironic as God has created every good thing for man's survival, but man is dying in spite of all survival needs.

16.7   War Competition by a game

The most dangerous creature that God has ever created is human being. He made locks to lock his door and made him a machine gun out of the knowledge that God gave him. Wild animals don't communicate; also, they have many life issues like humans, but wild or tame animals have a better relationship than human beings. We communicate and have an analytical brain, but humans still fight a horrible war like animals that have no brains. Every war is a competition on which of the combatants is ready to win war and inherit freedom and control. When there is little to eat still, humans' person multiply and survive. There is a war, and a competitive war is a competitive race to see who is going to eat first or by reducing the population so that food will be enough for all. What does human power have to do with what you are going to eat today and tomorrow, as well as what your next generation's kids will eat? It is a control of greediness and hunger that leads humans to mistreat each other, so that it leads to war for securing food to eat.

16.8   Learning Race within game of racism or tribalism

Learning is a process of acquiring knowledge in order to control power, whereby greedy power mongers can now eat enough of freedom. What about every country that gets developed, civilized, educated, industrialized, westernized, and become rich? Would there still be a war or conflict of greediness or power control? Learners race in a class, school, and level to rise to the top in order to gain honor and academic advancement, and the destiny of the learning race is to control wealth and control power so that man or woman will have access to wants and needs to ease his/her life. It is a matter of acquiring food to eat while you are awaiting your death. If human person is willing and to put too much breathing in living life first rather than eating to live, there is always a racial problem in power control and greediness in everything we can engulf just for the sake of living by eating on the earth while waiting for death day. Learning how to race against each other on who will live a better life is a source of many diseases where knowledgeable men can simply use and mistreat less knowledgeable humans.

17. Uprooted People
17.1   Refugees

What else can uproot ordinary citizens if not civil war, natural disaster, epidemic of national disease or locality famine, drought, and genocidal human catastrophe? I'm a product—a refugee—of a civil war disaster and a person who has faced many uprooting disasters just like any other tsunami victim in the world. Refugees are products of uprooting catastrophic causes of nationwide disaster. I was a refugee person who had no place to live other than in the open, under trees, or inside dark bushes, making nest houses like birds or holes like ground moles. There is no food, water, shelter, security, or life in any nature for refugees; you can ask victims of Hurricane Katrina in New Orland who were in a four-day exile refuge. Refugees are the most uprooted people from their original lifestyle, original culture, vernacular language, original religion, and even from their political mindset as well as from their loved environmental ecosystem. A refugee is a person who loses everything life may contain before a new life kicks in a survivor's lifestyle.

17.2   Displaced people

War, disaster, or disease move away humans from their original place of living; as a result, they lose everything that belongs to their own in an original lifestyles as also fleeing urgently is always the result and a mean to dodge an erupted disaster that crops up in a comfortable living environment. I was displaced from my parents when I was seven years old, and up till now, when I'm twenty-five years old, I have never seen my relatives and family since 1987. A displaced person is a casualty of the most intense disaster either be it a war or a natural disaster like Katrina. You don't own the same house and never live in the same place as your life and living place are displaced with you, and then you have to start life from scratch and afresh in the surroundings where you got displaced. I came to America as a refugee war displaced person with nothing other than my hands and head, but now I'm serving in the US Army and plan to do a lot in this world only if God gives me power and lets me do whatever changes I might implement so that society may change for the better.

17.3   The Criminals

Criminals are the most uprooted people in any corner of the world, and because they always don't have a life foundation from whichever family, community, society, or nation they come from now, they remain reckless humans who want to pursue life's success in different odd ways. Criminals are the most cannibal humans, bloodthirsty and greedy lazy idiots, as well as failures in making life in the true legal way. If there is no law, there is a crime, and there are criminals, and that nation or society must come down to its knees. Criminals are people uprooted from the love of their family, society, community, or nation or have lost the attachment of love with everybody in the world. Life can kill or severely wound and leave you disabled for a lifetime. They are uprooted from personal wallets, earnings, emotional love, original home, lifestyle, family, culture, religion, and political mindset, and criminals are even criminals are uprooted from government welfare too.

17.4   The Jobless persons

Having a job in the modern world is a fundamental means of making life, and losing a job and is then not able to find another job for a long time is a family or personal life disaster. Joblessness is mostly associated with the loss of a house, family, friends, loved ones, robbery, stealing, drug use, trauma, stress, prostitution, and life struggle. A jobless person is a person displaced from his/her working environment where she/he earns his/her pay, pays monthly bills, schedules pay, has coworkers and benefits of insurance, retirement plan, and many other good things associated with having a job. Many jobless persons may lose hope and life's self-determination, and that can be associated with losing hope to make another life after getting another job. Many jobless people who can't find another job are the sources of drug dealing business or are crime sources; they have always become a burden to crisis centers. Joblessness is a societal sickness that causes an idle mind in every living person who will commit crime by doing anything associated with life-making or trying to provide for his or her family.

17.5   The Sentenced or convicted

The jobless groups of people in the same cycle are now criminals, and the government will treat them like people of their own caused and made to become criminals. After a man finds himself in a screwed life full of hardship, there is no positivity that comes into mind other than doing illegal stuff or anything to make a living. In fact, there should be no judge in this world or anybody who can judge anybody else's way of committing a crime or doing things. Being sentenced by a judge for the crime committed always increases criminals' activities after being released. Every person sentenced for his/her guilty crime always argues with an inner point of defence and who is to be blamed for the crime committed, and that is what modern judges need to understand. There always has to be an external source to be blamed for any committed crime rather than the culprit themselves. Sentencing a culprit is good for correcting and making an excellent society, but at the same time society must be responsible for its individual crime causes and who is to be blamed too.

17.6   The Slaves

If the society or a family is strengthened to live in order of dignity with the full resource of support, there would be no ill issues like slavery. There are still slavery cases in Africa today, and those slavery cases must be eradicated by having a government-supported society eradicate its financial crises or control its persons on external causes that make regular citizens fall into crimes or do nothing that would cause an idle mind to do crime. Slaves are uprooted people who have no original homes, cultures, beliefs, religions, lifestyles of their forefathers, languages, and taboos and cannot even cope with the new life environment. Children of African Americans or Africans will suffer and continuously suffer because of their original forefathers' slavery mistakes. The child who emerges from a slavery background will never get honor for his diligent work either in white or Arab society, but will still bring about the force of a change, which can be done as Obama did.

17.7   The Lost Men and women of the western world

Lost men reflect the lost boys of Sudan, and that means the loss of the original family values, mothers breastfeeding their children, a generation playing with friends, and kids' whole lives. Lost men are men who have lost their original lifestyles, accented languages, dialects, families, tribes, and communities, or have even lost the society lifestyle, just like me right here in between South and North Korea, who has got no immediate connection with my family, friends, lifestyles as I used to live on the States' side. Lost men have got grief for their families and love and hope for their original homes, as many of them have lost lives in the war frontline action. Men who die natural deaths are the most who have lost the world but still have the advantage of gaining another world that we don't see as we call it heaven for the blessed ones. Lost men are one like me, who cannot get married or mingle in any society because of their unfit appearance and physically deformed look, accented language, and differing culture, religion, and lifestyle.

17.8   The Lost men and women of Identity, culture, religion and language

The most uprooted person will definitely lose his/her identity of the original look, appearance, culture, and accented language or dialect. People who completely face disaster because of identity loss will lose their parental or ancestors' names, dialect accents, lineage connection, love, and values, and that is why Caribbean black African people are associated with Africans in Africa more than African Americans are with Africans. Loss of identity is a human personal identifying disaster as it destroys personal self-association with whom or where she/he belongs in the world society. Loss of personal identity doesn't occur after one or two generations, but after many generations who fall into the same mistake of losing the society's original value or lost connection with the original cultural sources. Uprooted people who lose self-identity are always immigrants, asylum seekers, refugees, criminals, and exile and war captives. Self-identity is a responsibility of a healthy society.

17.9   The Lost Family, or Clan.

Losing family identity is associated with those who have lost their jobs, been killed at war frontline, been a drug dealer, jailed for a crime for life, irresponsible love as well as death resulting in family separation. I lost my family twenty-some years before, when I was seven years old, and that marked an association with the homeless guys, runaway kids, or adopted children who had already lost connection with those who had given them birth or parental connections. Those who lost connection with their families due to war separation, parental separation, jailed time serving, death, or even distant work are basically a voluntarily hole for trauma factors, as well, as they have lost hope for a better life, pushing in struggle. Crime is always the result of too much stress, trauma, and a hopeless lifestyle. Loss of family must be stopped by a personal ego wanting separation or cannot be stopped under natural death. I'm a victim of family loss separation, but I will never do crime or lose hope for life struggle as I'm pursuing and striving for excellence while doing legal things to better half of my life.

18. Western Erosion
18.1   The Western Culture Erosion

What is Western culture erosion around the world if not their English dominance with either a British or an American English accent? Otherwise, the ravaged Africa is a piece poisonous continent where all Western or Middle Eastern cultures crimp in and cripple citizens of Africa to speak in the colonial language of Creek and chick. Western food, cultures of dressing, and clothing styles have entered the world far away from the Western world. Black Africans in the Western world are role models in leading the way and showing others far away, Black people in any part of the world, to dress up, rap up, gang up, and nigger up like Black Americans in the Western world. Western culture erosion is the power evolution of the Western culture to dominate the world society on how women dress up to kill men quickly with freedom in exercising free choice of sexual life. Culture of creating an independent family as well as freedom in marriage of age mates and no sex with over- or under-aged is taking effect in every culture. Modern sexuality is dependent on the freedom of choice.

18.2   The Western Education Erosion

Every other world is coping with examples from the way, leading the Western world system of education and incorporating Western education standards into the Third World's education culture. Domination of the English language and it's coping with accents is a top learning system of erosion where every country in the world is seeking ways to improve the standard of communication in English. Spanish, French, Arabic, Italian, German, and other Western languages are the basis for learning, and these languages have created room for the erosion of other worldly languages and systems of learning. Online, distance correspondence, and home education is a Western system of education that is eroding other systems of learning in other parts of the world. The system of a Western education model, curriculum, classes, learning facility, and structures of school buildings is getting dominance and taking control in the world. Categories of learning, studies, and subjects of learning and materials used for teaching aids are more of the leading world-class examples in the switching education mode.

18.3   Selling Democracy by Erosion of Other Systems

Selling the system of excellent governance in the world of autocracy, anarchy, socialism, communism, liberalism, dictatorship, and other fake democracies is the long-lived mission agenda of the United States and the United Kingdom. Whether the other world wants it or not, if a country doesn't come to democracy, democracy will come to you. Democracy can come to you in terms of bullets and shelling; also, you resist its power of control or else peace erosion of democracy is the best way to inherit good governance.

Every country in the world is trying to adopt democracy as the best system of government, and the driving force of this policy in world affairs is creating erosion of the other systems of government in any part of the world to quieten its function. Democracy is eroding more systems of governments in the world as long as the United States and the United Kingdom keep their power updated for more than fifty rounds of generations in the world cycle of the democracy struggle.

18.4   The Western Hamburger Erosion

Now, there are Burger King, McDonald's, Kentucky Fried Chicken, and other Western fast-food restaurants in any corner of the world or in a country that deserves food recipes to be quickly eroded away by Western culture's cooking styles. It is very common to see this kind of food erosion taking place in developing countries, which still have the old traditional method of cooking and the old recipe that is used for modern cooking and integrated cooking style. Easy distribution of Western world products is the best way to speed up infestation to spread Western democracy to countries that are rigid in accepting democracy. The taste of hamburgers is the same as an excellent governance democracy, and every country that allows hamburgers to enter its territory is always tempted to adopt the democratic system, too. Hamburger erosion is the best way to convince radical world governments to inherit democracy rather than a radical invasive war.

18.5   The Western Traditional Love and Lifestyle Erosion

Western world is infesting other parts of the world with its people's freedom to property, to press, to speech, and to love. Every women's rights organization out there may probably trace its root support back to the United States or the United Kingdom. Human life's happiness is the core cause of people's struggle, and seeing Americans in this happy mode must tempt and convince other citizens of the world to wish for the same democracy. How many guys and lesbians are unhappy, many with social diseases in the United States and United Kingdom compared to that of social diseases out there? Only if American women swear allegiance to the truth and treat American men honestly, who gave them freedom of happiness and equality for equally created man and woman, there is going to be fewer social problems in America compared to its Middle Eastern counterpart. Western lifestyle is growing faster in modern, free, developing fourth-world countries, and that is lifestyle erosion from the West.

18.6   The Traveling Western Religion and Language Erosion

Democracy infestation of the Western world can quickly spread out around the world if missionaries resume strong activities of spreading the Christ mission in the third, fourth, and even fifth worlds. Bringing Jesus Lord to people who don't know him is also bringing democracy to those who don't have it. Democracy is a happy way of people living, and it doesn't just start from the top of the government house coming down to the main street, but it starts from individual, family, and community levels and it rises up to the national level. Democracy is a lifestyle way of life that slowly processes itself, and it can never be enforced for a quick change in other culture-dominant societies. Traveling Americans who have a hobby of traveling must carry on with their democracy, and wherever they go, there must be a seed of democracy left there to grow. It takes a friendly way to cultivate the seed of democracy, and that seed can healthily be monitored to grow under the continued friendship of love, connection, and the trust level of giving and taking hands.

18.7   The Western Condom Technology is Eroding traditional love making

Everyone in the world is now loitering around with a box of condoms in his/her pocket, ready to fuck immediately, not appreciating the power of democracy that gives people safe sex. Technology is spreading democracy around the world, only if Washington opens its products to the world business beyond Western world borders. Having Washington open its technology market business exchange to third, fourth, fifth, or every developing country in the world, the quicker the democracy spreads, the quicker these countries can inherit the power of development to host power that might become anti-American later. A massive technological production is an icon power of the Western world, and that secret must be maintained by every next American generation to control and continuously rule in supremacy. The power of supremacy is centered on the nuclei of technology, and every country lacking democracy is lacking that power of supremacy.

19. The Burden Carriers
19.1   Children are Burdened by Parents

If parents don't have a family plan to control the birth of children, they would eventually run into a huge responsibility that is considered a burden. Parents are burden carriers when they have harder sex to push sperm inside, and mothers bear suffering for nine months and then later labor like hell to bring about the delivery of the newborn baby. Children burden their parents as parents are responsible for feeding, clothing, schooling, disciplining, and raising them for eighteen years in America. By the law, America has reduced that child's parental burden by letting parents have the right to kick out their older children after eighteen years of age. The burden bearers for eighteen years are victims who are placed on child support with kids they would never see, discipline, or recognize in their lifetime. Taking care of kids, children, and older youths is a burden to the parents, and this is much worse in other countries where a thirty-seven-year-old daughter or son still sits in his parental home, dependent on the family for food. Children are burdened on their parents as needs and wants are provided, and that encourages many Third World countries to ask for dowry for payback.

19.2   Women are Burdened by Men and Children

Women are the most victims of the burden men pose on

them, as well as children, who can also become a mother's huge burden of responsibility for care. Even in America, men and women were created equally, and the law treats them equally; women are still burden bearers for men and children. Women still do domestic work after getting off from work, and men do little kitchen cleaning; also, for feeding, taking care of, and loving children, rely heavily on women compared to American men who can't even feed kids and show love to their children whereas a mother is automatically committed naturally to take care of children. In the Muslim world or other cultures, a woman is considered and treated as half a person by a man, and this characteristic way man that treat women has led to suffering and putting a huge burden on women who have no voice to be heard in a male-dominated society. Man is burdening woman financially and emotionally.

19.3   Men are Carrier of Burdens from Bad Women

Men are burden carriers for women, and this is remarkable as it includes the cost of gifts, presents, wedding rings, flowers, and surprises, as well as taking her shopping. Since God created a sensible human-like woman and handed over the role to man to care for the delicate woman, man has huge expenses to incur to take care of this delicate human person of a woman. Woman is a financial responsibility, and that is why a poor man will not get a woman and dies without marrying. Woman was created for man for fun and companionship, and that reason alone has burdened man in today's financial crises. Exclusive mention should be made about the payment of dowry, tributes, and huge funds for marriage and wedding payment by a man to just have a woman. Man bears the burden of a woman who behaves like a child and is too emotional, cheats, and is conceding, and even a woman is too bossy, posing a burden on her man. A woman may burden a man financially, emotionally, physically, and spiritually by consistently undermining him in various facets of life while reaping significant benefits for herself.

19.4   Humans are Burdens by the God and Devil deeds

Our daily tears and troubles because God's mercy to fall from heaven on to us, and that is because mankind is a huge burden to God in his creation. The most troublesome and dangerous creature in the world is man. Every care, love, providence, and fulfillment is a work of God to satisfy man in his life and have all needs from God. Natural disasters, diseases, death, and sudden occurrences are life-threatening factors in man's life, and man considers these uncontrollable factors to be God's or evil burdens. The devil brings death, suffering, and poverty to man, and this is a very dangerous life factor where man experiences the devil's evil works. How many times do I need to pray, adore, and worship God as the danger to life exceeds the level of waiting while my god has no immediate answer or quick solution for life's problems? Devil, Satan, and magical witches are also facing burdens from man who burn, destroy, and betray the devil's dirty work to God.

19.5   Animals are burdening by the mankind's creation

Animals are painless feeling objects. Man would slide his knife in, cut the throats open, and use his mouth to suck fresh blood out for his survival. Regardless of that, animals like cows, goats, sheep, beef, pigs, chickens, and wild bush meat are living things just like man too. Animals' rights and living things activists have witnessed the man food matrix and heavy burden of creating animals to have them butchered themselves or killed, slaughtered, and discriminated for their benefit's sake. Since animals don't speak and don't act like men, man is taking advantage of mute animals to use them for his workload: pets, food, and other domestic uses. Animals' rebellion is rising, and angry animals fight, kill, and prey on men in the jungle of bushes of Africa or in any zoo in the world. It is unbelievable how chicks, cows, or pigs run away from man's sharp knife while being slaughtered, but man doesn't understand how these animals feel, and the burden is on animals as God created man in charge to take care of the animals as well as everything that is living.

19.6 Unwanted Peoples are Burdens by bad government or society

Overweight, fatty people, ugly human people, people of dark skin color, poor people, and a sinful generation are hated by other human people who think God created them well to show the beauty of creation and live life in a beautiful and handsome world. An unwanted person is a burden bearer for who creates him/her and those who reject him/her away from the family, community, and society, as well as sentenced to death by the nation. An unwanted person is affected by incurable diseases and is a crime-infested, sinful person and even a person on whom witches fall. It is very discriminating, rude, and inhuman to deny, chase away, and hate people who don't look, sound, act, and are different from us. An unwanted person is treated exactly like an animal or is more mistreated than an animal when we sentence him to the death penalty for murdering another person for the reason of unwanted social issues. Unwanted humans are victims of God's creation, human hatred being the culprit. It's a moral wrong to hate and chase away homeless, criminals, and prostitutes away from us.

19.7 Life's Burden Carriers are damped citizens by bad systems in the way of life.

Child soldiers, fat ladies, disabled amputees, blind, deaf, mentally retarded, and even prostitutes on the street are all victims of life's causes, and it is legally and morally wrong to hate and murder those humans who are struggling against life threats. Thieves, rapists, lesbians, gays, single, and even the nature of humans, both male and female, are all victims of the creation and humans' ego that is uncontrolled in the sense of human hatred. Life is a burden to mankind, and its consequences are so severe, cutting deep inside human bodies and hurting the living souls of the victims created to suffer in order to live. Life is a burden to a man who is not dead but is a living, moving grave, and inside the grave, there is also a man who is tired of lying there for a hundred years. Life is a burden for a man who worries, is stressed out, depressed, and traumatizes over thinking about food, clothes, homes, and even needs of love from either humans or God. Life makes man suffer too much when man needs all his created wants and he cannot find them, although all of man's beneficial life wants are just in the world. Love is the only key to happiness, and man needs to live a life full of love.

20. Name Erosion
20.1   African Names Are Eroded by White Supremacy

Name erosion is taking place in every culture's washed-away society, and I mean many Third World countries or countries where religion hasn't emerged or has no history of discovering Jesus or Muhammad. Every African has got three names plus the surname and the father's name. Every African's first name is always the erosion name, like James, Jacob, John, or Jean. These are always forefront names followed by complicated African family names. In many years to come, Africans will keep their original cultural family names but will use other Western or Middle Eastern names. Every African child can now bear one family name, and it is going to disappear very soon or else white men's names will probably be used instead. African names interchange between tribes, regions, countries, and many clans. This is erosion of African names. Intermarriage is another cause of the exchange of African names, and it erodes away family names as well as tribal names.

20.2   The Christian Name erosion

How many times would Christian names erode people and replace people's names in the world? Jesus Christ himself didn't inherit any Christian names before him, and now every Christian is taking Christian names, which are even considered white people's names. If you can get Jesus without a Christian name, it is like a sin to those who love God as his names, like Mary, Jacob, Daniel, and many more names, are used to erode away other tribal, religious, country, and family names. Christianity is the topic of erosion where many Third World countries are losing names to Western Christianity missionaries and to the church. Christian names are always first names, and the second names are family names in many Africans' naming way of erosion. Many Westerners claim Christian names as their names rather than religious names at all. Christianity is eroding worldly names in competition with Islamic name erosion changes.

20.3   The Muslim Name Erosion

Islam is competing with Christianity in worldly names' erosion; every Christian must have a Christian names at the Baptist or birth time, as well as every Muslim must have names with a Muslim name at the baptizing or at the birth time in a Muslim family. In Islam, African names' erosion, just like every Middle Eastern, have already lost the original names other than Islamic names. Islamic naming is eroding every other name in a Muslim neighborhood, or the expansion of Islamic names means more loss of names in any conversion. Islamic names' erosion has no mercy on ethnic, tribal, family, racial, and even white people's names of Christianity are erased away by the Muslim naming system. Even Christians converted to Islam are bearing two names as Christian–

Muslim names like Muhammad Elijah, Ali Abraham, or Jacob Ahmed. Many Africans still mix their tribe, family, and ethnic names with Muslim names, and that will still go away after the last generation. Islam is competitive with Christianity in eroding the entire world's name changes.

20.4   The Western Names Erosion

There are two Western naming systems: white people's cultural names and Western Christian names, and people in the Third World who want to be of the Western world get confused about which names to take or cannot differentiate between Christian names or white people's names. White people's names are eroding indigenous marginalized people's names in most parts of the Third World. Names like Jack, Carroll, Jeanne, Robert are very common in the world of modern civilization as this causes name erosion in the modern world of those who associate themselves with white people from the West. Christian names are also Western names, and these names are named or taken as first names to show a sense of civilization in the backward world. Africans would name their children with city or civilized modern names before sending them to school. It is not the time when white slaves' master will force their slaves to bear their names and that all black Americans should have white names.

20.5   The Traditional Names erosion inside the Game of ages

Competitive name erosion between Christianity, Islamic, Western, and traditional names is now an epic of historic name erosion in the new century. Tribal, ethnic, racial, religious, family name or surname is a remarkable identifier of the person to indicate where she/he comes from. Many tribes or families must keep their names in spite of being baptized as they either become Muslim or Christian, and these individuals still carry on their dominant family names into the new faith. Most Africans reserve their middle or last names as their family names, but the first or second names are basically Christian, Muslim, or Western world names. In most Third World countries or conservative communities, family or ancestor names are kept alive for generations, or some other families love to keep their family names in the rotation naming cycle to keep them alive and safe from name erosion in the next coming future family generations.

20.6   The Modern Civilized Names Erosion

Civilization or modernity has a factor in name erosion, as it is also competitive with other name erosion like religious, cultural, traditional, and Western name erosion. Before naming your newborn, you might take a look at the naming lists depending on whether you need Christian, Muslim, Western, traditional, or civilized names. Out of every five people in China or Korea, one person is Kim, and this is very common in every culture or tribe or racial name, like other names loved by only black Americans rather than white people. Civilized names are picked up regardless of their religious, ethnic, racial or cultural background and meaning, or because they sound easy or sweet, one can choose. Most modern names have no meaning or could be made up name by putting letters together. Unlike most traditional names which are so full of meaning that hence so traditional, religious or family names are harder to get eroded away easily as compared to other names.

CHAPTER 3

ALL ASSISTANTSHIPS FOR THE LOST BOYS AND GIRLS FROM 19886 – NOW

GREAT APPRECIATION TO ALL HELPING HANDS ORGANIZATIONS, CHARITIES, AND GOVERNMENTAL STATES FOR HELPING LOST BOYS AND LOST GIRLS (FORMER RED ARMY OF SOUTH SUDAN).

The South Sudan former Red Army (the current Lost boys and girls of South Sudan) are so grateful and thankful for the great assistance, help, and support received from governmental services, Non-governmental services, donors, first responders, SPLA/M and UNHCR roles in providing food, water, education, medication, housings, transportations, guidance, nursing feedings, protections, sheltering and many other things offers for general welfares and health for red army and lost boys and girls particularly. I am gratefully giving thanks to the endless listings of these highlighted as follows.

1. The SPLA and SPLM (Sudan People Liberation Army and The Sudan People Liberation Movement; current ruling party of the South Sudan sovereignty state)

2.   The Ethiopian government under Mengistu Haile Mariam (1983-1991) greatly supported the Red Army (village boys as refugees for sheltering, food, and medical provisions.

3.   The UNHCR, for the provision of food, medicine, shelter, housing, water, clothing, and many other non-food items from 1985 until now operating in Panyido and Kakuma refugee camps.

4.   Radar Barner

5.   UNESCO

6.   The **International Committee of the Red Cross (ICRC)**

7.   UNICEF

8.   kENYA government

9.   Sudan GOVERNMENT

10.   UGANDAN GOVERNMENT

11.   SOUTH African GOVERNMENT

12.   Lutheran World Food (LWF)

13.   WOVisionOD PROGRAM (WFP)

14.   GERMAN TZ

15.   International Rescue committee

16.   World Vision

17.   Lutheran ministry of GEORGIA

18.   Catholic Relief Care CRS)

19.   Friends of Sudan

20.   Sudan council of churches

21.   Episcopal Church of South Sudan

22.   Sevenths day Adventist

23.   NPA

24.   SISTER LOUISE scholarship

25.   NIS and JVA

26.   US GOVERNMENT

27.   US DEPARTMENT OF IMMIGRATION

28.   AUSTRALIAN GOVERNMENT

29.   CANADIAN GOVERNMENT

30.   Australian department of immigration

31.   Japanese refugee network

32.   Don Bosco

33.   Arap foundation for education

34.   Lost Boys Foundation of Atlanta, Georgia, Mary William)

   a.   Lost Boys Foundations and Association in all fifty States in the United States

35.   Lost boys and girls volunteers across the United States of America

36.   All churches across America who help lost boys/girls of South Sudan (1999-UNTIL NOW)

37.	All foster care families in the United States who care for underage lost boys and girls

38.	SOUTH SUDAN INDEPENDENT MOVEMENT (SSIM UNDER RIEK MACHAR, 1991)

39.	SPLA IG and IO

40.	DOCTOR WITHOUT BORDERS

41.	MEDICINE SAN FORTIER

42.	WORLD HEALTH ORGANIZATION (WHO)

43.	WORLD WATER PROJECT

44.	INTERNATIONAL ORGANIZATION FOR IMMIGRATION (IOM)

45.	ALL WORLD DONORS WHO DONATES FOR RED ARMY AND LOST BOYS AND GIRLS

46.	International Rescue Committee

47.	Lutheran Immigration and Refugee Service

48.	Doctors Without Borders

49.	Save the Children OF SUDAN

50.	International Refugee Assistance Project Alight

51.	Jesuit Refugee Service (JRS)

52.   Organization for Refuge, Asylum, & Migration

Kakuma is a town in northwestern Turkana County, Kenya. It is the site of a UNHCR refugee camp established in 1992.[1] The population of Kakuma town was 60,000 in 2014, having grown from around 8,000 in 1990. In 1991, the camp was established to host unaccompanied minors who had fled the war in Sudan and from camps in Ethiopia. It was estimated that there were 12,000 "lost boys and girls" who had fled here via Egypt in 1990/91.[2]

Kakuma is situated in the second poorest region in Kenya, and as a result, of this poverty, there are ongoing tensions between the refugees and the local community that have occasionally resulted in violence. Compared to the wider region, the Kakuma camp has better health facilities and a higher percentage of children in full-time education, which resulted in a general notion that the refugees were better off than the locals. The host community is composed largely of nomadic pastoralists who stick to their traditions and do not cooperate with refugees. Camps are becoming a normal part of the regional socio-economic landscape and a part of livelihood options available in the region. Kakuma is one of two large refugee camps in Kenya; the second and biggest one is Dadaab.

Malnutrition, communicable disease outbreaks, and malaria are all ongoing problems, while donor support has faltered due to conflicts in other parts of the world.[3] Many people in Kakuma are long-term refugees, living in hopelessness and desperation. The situation is particularly bad for young people.[4] Many of the refugees hope to leave Kakuma for third-country resettlement in another country. For example, the "Lost Boys of Sudan" were a special group who were resettled from the camp to the United States.

Climate

Semi-arid climate with average temperatures reaching 40 °C and only drop to the low 30s at night: dry and windswept, dust storms. Kakuma is wedged between two dry riverbeds, and the occasional rain can lead to flooding.

The only plants that survive are thorny bushes and a few flat-topped trees. As agriculture is almost impossible, this results in fierce competition among different local groups for ownership of cattle. Refugees are not allowed to keep animals due to the potential for conflict between the refugees and the local Turkana people. This camp was made because of the Lost boys, even though they were not all boys.

Kakuma Refugees`Camp structure and organization

The complex comprises four parts (Kakuma I-IV) and is managed by the Kenyan government and the Kenyan Department of Refugee Affairs in conjunction with the UNHCR. As of December 2020, the site hosts around 200,000 people, mostly refugees from the civil war in South Sudan.[5]

Staff members are housed outside the camp in three large compounds with various amenities, including a swimming pool, bars, shops, recreational centres, and exercise rooms for weights, yoga, and aerobics. The WFP and UNHCR have fully air-conditioned, self-contained rooms, and all compounds have electricity and water.

The 5 pm curfew at the camp means no help available for refugees after 5 pm., Don Bosco has a special role in the camp because they are the only workers who can help refugees in emergency situations at night.

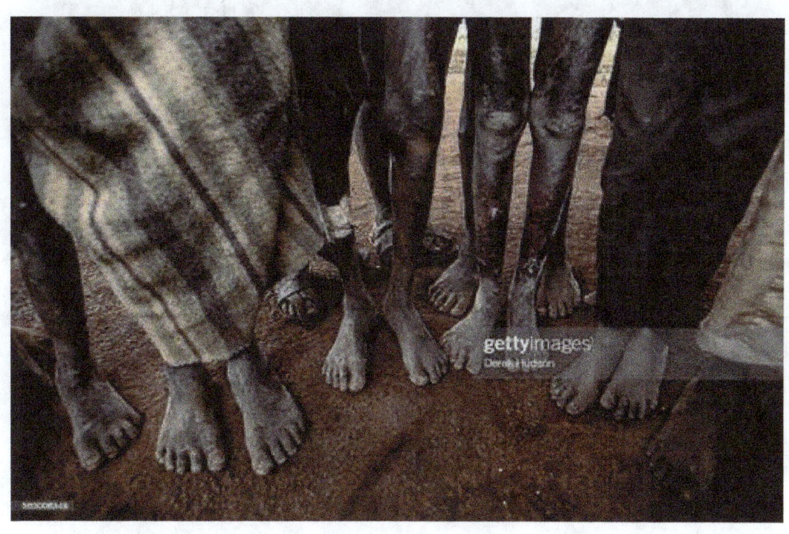

REFERENCES AND FOOTNOTES

Source: United Nations Children's Fund (UNICEF) Date: 06 Jan 2004

C H I L D S O L D I E R S G L O B A L R E P O R T 2 0 0 4

C H I L D S O L D I E R S G L O B A L R E P O R T 2 0 0 8

Coalition to Stop the Use of Child Soldiers

Nicolas Clemesac

Regional Advocacy Officer

South Sudan Post, Issue No 11 November and January 2007

JRS Grands Lacs

Bujumbura, February 2007

http://www.essex.ac.uk/armedcon/story_id/000215.html

http://www.unicef.org/infobycountry/sudan_50760.html

http://www.unhcr.org/refworld/country/456d621e2/DZA.html

http://genocide.change.org/blog/view/daily_darfur_child_soldiers_2008_displacements_and_tensions_in_kordofan

http://www.globalsecurity.org/military/world/war/sudan-civil-war2.htm

THE ODYSSEY OF SOUTH SUDAN RED ARMY

Khartoum, Dec 22 (Reuters

Al-Ayam Xinhua, News agency

http://www.unsudanig.org/docs/Sudan%20Humanitarian%20Over view%20Vol2%20Iss6%20June06.pdf

https://www.google.com/search?q=child+soldiers+of+south+sudan &espv=2&biw=1366&bih=659&site=webhp&tbm=isch&tbo=u&s ource=univ&sa=X&ved=0ahUKEwi_j-34jtvMAhWISSYKHXRpDBsQ7AkIRw&dpr=1

http://news.bbc.co.uk/2/hi/8173079.stm

http://www.un.org/cyberschoolbus/briefing/soldiers/index.htm

About The Author

The author is one of the four thousand South Sudanese lost boys and girls resettled in the United States and Australia between 1999- 2005. After my village was burned down in Yirol (Burdit vicinity) district in 1985 -87. I t separated from my family as SPLA soldiers attacked the town of Yirol early in the morning of 1986, and General Marial Chanoug Yol, the commander of the SPLA, led us to flee early as children of ages from 6-25 years in the jungle trek fleeing to Western Ethiopia.

Due to a hostile civil war between SPLA/M revolutionaries and the Sudan military regime, which killed two million people, I the author had no choice as many thousands of other children than to trek barefooted from various villages crossed war troubled South Sudan to Western Ethiopia, where mainstream of the SPLA/M trained it soldiers. Many children were forcibly conscripted into SPLA/M forces and he became a child rebel in the uprising against the Khartoum government from 1987 to 1992. I was among 10,000 child soldiers and refugees in organized refugee camps to stay in Panyido, Sarapam, Itang, Dimma and Bilpam (1987-1991). I trekked with the Red Army of Panyido refugee camp during the downfall of the Ethiopian government in 1991 to Pachalla and crossed to Kenya through the border town of Lokichioggio with 16,000 Red Army's 1992 and with other red armies disarmed by

UNICEF for children and sent to school in Kenya at the same time from Polataka. We were stationed in the Kakuma refugee camp as unaccompanied minors in 17 groups of minors by UNHCR for 10 years before 4000 thousands of unaccompanied minors got resettled to the United States of America and Australia (1999-2005).

I joined the United States Army in 2010 after completion of my bachelor's degree in Computer science (2008). Military trained in Fort Leonardwood, MO, and did Advance Instruction Training in Fort Lee, Virginia (2010). Stationed in South Korea under command 194th Support Bridge in South Korea and brought back to the mainland under command, serving in the US Army 36th Combat Engineers Brigade station in Fort Hood, Texas. Served under command 36th infantry of Texas National Guards at Camp Mabry Austin and Weslaco, Texas, as a commissioned 2nd Lieutenant officer after completion of Reserved Officers Training Courses at the University of Texas at Austin, Texas. The author is a bachelor's degree holder in computer science from Herzing University (2004-2008), an MA in intelligence operations from American Military University (2011-2012), MS in Computer Science at the University of Texas, Austin (2013-2015); MPA at Arizona States University (2015-2017). The author earned many IT certifications in various fields. Born in South Sudan and resettled to the United States (2001) as a resident of Atlanta, Georgia, where he became a US citizen, went to school, and enlisted into US Army forces.